THE KISS OF
THE SNOW QUEEN

"Locked In." Drawing by Hans Christian Andersen, n.d.

THE KISS OF
THE SNOW QUEEN

HANS CHRISTIAN ANDERSEN
AND MAN'S REDEMPTION
BY WOMAN

Wolfgang Lederer

University of California Press
Berkeley · Los Angeles · London

University of California Press
Berkeley and Los Angeles, California

University of California Press, Ltd.
Oxford, England

First Paperback Printing 1990

Library of Congress Cataloging-in-Publication Data

Lederer, Wolfgang.
  The kiss of the Snow Queen.

  Includes index.
    1. Andersen, H. C. (Hans Christian), 1805–1875.
Snedronningen.   2. Andersen, H. C. (Hans Christian),
1805-1875—Biography—Psychology.   3. Authors,
Danish—19th century—Biography.   4. Psychoanalysis and
folklore.   I. Title.
PT8117.S63L4   1986   839.8'136   86-7125
ISBN 0-520-07190-5 (alk. paper)

Printed in the United States of America
1   2   3   4   5   6   7   8   9

Contents

Illustrations

The original artworks and photographs belong to the Hans Christian Andersen Museum, Odense, Denmark, and are reproduced by permission of the museum.

Frontispiece. "Locked In." Drawing by Hans Christian Andersen, n.d.

FOLLOWING PAGE 90

Self-portrait of Hans Christian Andersen, n.d.

Jonas Collin. Painting by J. V. Gertner, 1840.

Simon Meisling. Anonymous painting, n.d.

Riborg Voigt. Daguerreotype, ca. 1845.

Hans Christian Andersen. Painting by C. A. Jensen, 1836.

Jenny Lind. Lithograph after a painting by E. Magnus, 1846.

Edvard and Henriette Collin. Painting by W. Marstrand, 1842.

Grand Duke Carl Alexander of Sachsen-Weimar-Eisenach. Lithograph, n.d.

Hans Christian Andersen. Photograph by C. Weller, 1865.

Hans Christian Andersen in his room at Nyhaven. Photograph by C. Weller, 1874.

Preface

About a hundred miles north of San Francisco, in the valley of the Russian River, lies the Mendocino State Hospital for the Mentally Ill. It is now closed, but while it functioned it was, as such places go, one of the most agreeable, competent, and innovative in the whole country. For about sixteen years I would drive up there once a month to preside at a case conference.

I looked forward to those excursions. Not only was the drive a lovely one, with vast orchards in bloom in the spring, vineyards heavy with grapes in the fall, and an occasional dusting of snow on distant mountains in the wintertime, but the group of psychiatric residents with whom I was to meet presented a unique challenge. For reasons not clear to me, they came, in part, not directly from medical school and internship; a good many of them had been general practitioners or surgeons or public health officials for years and were now switching to psychiatry in middle life. One or two of them had been ministers before they went to medical school. These people brought their particular background and experience to our discussions and did not hesitate to express conflicting and original points of view. Perhaps because of this, even the younger residents tended to show more initiative than is commonly the case.

One day one of these younger residents came up with a new suggestion: instead of discussing cases in our usual manner, why not try to analyze a work of fiction, a fairy tale perhaps, as if it were a psychiatric case? The proposal was quickly accepted by everyone; so, on my next visit we sat around a tape recorder and listened to a reading, by the resident's wife, of Hans Christian Andersen's *The Snow Queen.*

As I remember it, we were in midsummer: looking out the window I could see the sun glaring down on parched, yellow hills and on the scattered live oaks that somehow thrive in that heat. Inside, the air conditioning was on and, at first, disturbed us with its periodic blowing and rattling. But we forgot it as we listened to the voice of an invisible woman, and to a story that took us into snow, Nordic night, and a time long before noise and technology.

It was a story, we thought, for children. But we were quickly drawn into it—the younger ones and the no-longer-so-young ones alike. We interrupted the tape whenever anyone had something to say. We pondered and theorized and argued; the time went so fast that by common agreement we spent another several hours on it the next month.

Since then the Snow Queen has haunted me.

Even at the first go-round, at the Mendocino Hospital, we found more than ever we expected. The tale is full of symbols, relationships, and veiled meanings; looking into it is like looking into one of those dark, marshy ponds of which Andersen is so fond. The eye understands little at first but in time discerns more and more, and we perceive: in that deceptive stillness struggles of life and death are being waged.

I was drawn to look as deeply as I could: this is the essence of fascination. It was not enough to come back to *The Snow Queen* over and over again; I had to know Andersen and his other works. What would have informed me most—his diaries—remained inaccessible. I do not know Danish, and they have never been translated. The same is true for most of his letters and for the majority of the articles published about the man and his work in the yearly *Anderseniana*. Of these, I could have knowledge only through summaries and reviews written by experts or, when it seemed particularly important, through the able services of a professional translator.[1] I could, of course, study the biographies of Andersen written in English and, first and foremost, two of his autobiographies in English translation.[2] Of the 4500 or so articles about Andersen that have been published all over the world, I could consult those I could find and that were written in languages I understand. Taken all together, this gave a rich enough yield—like an archeological dig in a particularly productive mound: uncovering many items that supplement or illustrate what is already known and some perhaps that, shedding a new light, bring a new understanding.

A great excitement is generated by such discoveries, an excitement not always easily communicable. The "find" that so elates the finder may seem insignificant to others. But I share this fond belief with fellow "diggers": that what I found is beautiful not to me only; that it may also please others, and inform them, and—who knows—make a difference in their view of man. It is in this sense that the present study is offered.

Acknowledgments

The author wishes to express his gratitude to Professors Alan Dundes (Department of Anthropology, University of California, Berkeley) and Herbert Fingarette (Center for Advanced Studies, Stanford University) for their invaluable suggestions; to Peter Tjaller for his painstaking translations; to Florence Myer for her meticulous editing and preparation of the manuscript; to James H. Clark, Director of the University of California Press, without whose devoted efforts this book never would have seen the light of day; and to Ala, who never lost faith.

PART ONE

THE SNOW QUEEN

1

Introduction

> Now then! We will begin. When the story is done you
> shall know a great deal more than you know now.

So reads the rather unusual opening of Andersen's *The Snow Queen*.[1] We are immediately invited to see the author in a crowd of listeners—a crowd of children, of course. They know him well as the old storyteller, the kindly giant with the high forehead and the long nose, whose bumbling movements are so likely to upset things on the table. The children have finished their supper in the nursery and now, just before bedtime and to their utter delight, here comes "Uncle" Hans Christian, and he is willing to tell them a tale. Though they want to listen, they probably find it hard to calm down; therefore, Hans Christian promises them something so they will more readily sit still: "you shall know a great deal more than you know now."

But wait: is this really what children want? Surely they are curious, but what they crave is not so much knowledge as it is entertainment. They want adventure, mystery, miracles of all sorts—ghosts that fly through the air, plants and animals that talk, and for the hero and the heroine, great feats of endurance and derring-do. But knowledge? Does not Andersen, the great storyteller, know better than to offer them knowledge?

Indeed he does. The children will get all the mysteries, miracles, and acts of courage they could ask for; in fact, he casts such a spell that he hardly needs to call the youngsters to attention. Why, then, the emphatic announcement and promise: "you shall know a great deal more than you know now"?

The answer lies not in the story itself, but in brief remarks by Andersen that have been recorded for us. Thus he once said: "I get an idea for grownups and then tell my tale to the little ones, while remembering that Mother and Father will be listening and must have something to think about." Or again: "Children understand only the trappings."[2] Contrary to general belief, it would therefore seem that he told his stories mainly for adults; and as he grew older, this was increasingly true.

And so it is not at all farfetched to assume that the initial promise of greater knowledge was directed, not at the children, who were all ears anyway, but at the adults, who may well have been tempted not to listen; or if they listened, not to apply their thinking to what they heard. Is not a fairy tale beneath the dignity of an adult? Could it possibly deserve more than benign condescension?[3]

Since Andersen serves notice that he is about to teach us something, the present effort is not out of line if it intends to examine *The Snow Queen* bit by bit to see what Andersen may have wished us to learn. We may even be excused if we go further, not only looking for what *he* knew and his listeners *did not* yet explicitly know, but also inquiring whether he did not say even more than he knew he said, or knew he knew. For those readers who delight primarily in personalities, let us add that most of what Andersen wrote was autobiographical. "Most of what I have written," he said, "is a reflection of myself. Every character is from life. I know and have known them all."[4] And for readers more interested in great truths and ideas, let us claim (as Robert Graves has done)[5] that the poets and the ancient, intuitive language of poetry are our best access and revelation, not of facts but of truths, of those general verities by which we live—or by which we should be living. And that Andersen is a great poet—who can doubt it?

And so, let us proceed to *The Snow Queen*, A Tale in Seven Stories, and to . . .

The First Story

Which Has to Do with a Mirror and Its Fragments

It would seem that "a terribly bad hobgoblin, a goblin of the wickedest sort and, in fact, the devil himself" had manufactured a mirror in the reflection of which everything good and beautiful dwindled to nothing at all, while everything worthless and ugly became most conspicuous and even uglier than ever. The best people became hideous and "if a good, pious thought passed through anyone's mind, it showed in the mirror as a carnal grin."[1] The Devil laughed aloud and thought his invention very funny.

His delighted pupils carried it about until "there was not a person alive nor a land on earth that had not been distorted." "Then they wanted to fly up to heaven itself, to scoff at the angels and our Lord. The higher they flew with the mirror, the wider it grinned. They could hardly manage to hold it. Higher they flew. . . . Then the grinning mirror trembled with such violence that it slipped from their hands and fell to earth, where it shattered into hundreds of millions of billions of bits." Now it caused even more trouble, for if a fragment smaller than a grain of sand got in someone's eye, it would distort everything he saw and make him see only the bad side of things. If someone got a splinter into his heart, his heart would turn into a lump of ice. These fine bits of glass are still flying through the air, "and now you shall hear what happened."

But before we hear what happened, let us pause and see what we may already have been told. (We shall pause constantly in our narrative, for which we apologize. The eager reader had perhaps best go to the appendix and read the whole story as Andersen wrote it before continuing with the present halting examination.)

We note, to begin with, a certain fusion, or perhaps confusion: "He was a bad goblin . . . in fact, he was the devil himself."[2] But there are no goblins in Christianity, and no devil in Northern heathen religion. Andersen, of course, was well aware of this; yet in his fairy tales—just as is regularly the case in genuine, or "folk" tales (*Volks-Märchen*)—Christian and pre-Christian elements are constantly mixed and interwoven. The narrator appears to be piously Christian, but the "heathen" characters and practices put us on notice that the matters here dealt with far transcend any single dogmatic frame, and that we are to hear of general verities valid at any time and for any faith.

Then there is the distorting mirror that splinters into bits. And before it splinters itself, it splinters the whole world: for to make everything appear ugly and evil and wrong—to criticize everything—is to sow dissent and strife. The mirror, in effect, says no to all of God's creation; it is, like Goethe's Mephistopheles, *der Geist der stets verneint* (the spirit who forever negates). The mirror is not just an invention or an attribute of the Devil, it is the Devil himself, just as all throughout heathen mythology the attributes of the gods are also representations and avatars of these same gods. (Dionysos is not only adorned with grapevines, he *is* the grapevine; the great goddesses not only carry vessels of various kinds, they *are* vessels—of abundance, fertility, illness, or whatever.)[3]

The concept of splintering has an ancient and important role in religious thinking. In many theological systems that consider the godhead one and perfect, the multiplicity of things and phenomena in our so patently imperfect world is considered a defect, an error of God, a blemish to be removed. Hinduism does away with it by considering all creation *maya*, an illusion of the senses that the seeker for salvation must strive to overcome.[4] The Gnostics exonerated God by assuming that the world was not His creation at all but the work of a wicked demiurge who, in defiance of the Unknowable God, had created the multiplicity of separate phenomena that we know as the world and which therefore is altogether evil and destined, some day, to vanish.[5] The Kabbalah, similarly, considers the created world essentially a mistaken extrusion of the Unknowable God (*En Soph*) and calls upon right-thinking men (*zaddikim*) to help God put the world back together.[6] And as to Christian teachings, let me quote these passages from the work of an eminent theologian: "The Devil is he who divides, who cuts all communication and reduces man to ultimate solitude. . . . The Devil answers Jesus: 'My name is legion, for we are many.' The transition from singular to plural reveals the action of Evil in the world, the innocent being created by God breaks up, atomizes into isolated fragments, and this constitutes Hell."[7]

We shall hear more about Hell in our story, but at this point let us recall another term and concept applicable to splintering as the work of the Devil and of those who follow him, and that term is: Sin. Sinning, the opposite of atonement (at-one-ment), is everything that splinters mankind or splinters a man within himself and thus increases his distance from God. Splintering is sinning is the opposite of loving—love being the force that unites, that bridges and overcomes antagonisms and separateness.

So we know that our story will have to do with sinning. Splintering, or criticism, will play an important role. But we have also been given hints as to other sins, or other aspects of sin.

The devils are carrying the mirror to heaven; they wish to apply it to God himself. In so doing, they are striving too high (the German term *sie überheben sich* has the double meaning of "they are carrying more than they are able" and "they are arrogant, impertinent"). The devils are guilty of excessive pride and ambition, of *hubris*. Hubris is arrogance toward God, the original offense of Satan who, being next to God, considered himself God's equal.[8] Because of this arrogance, Satan—Lucifer—was thrown from the heavens, so it is not surprising that in his attempt to regain the empyrean in the avatar of the distorting mirror he "trembles increasingly" and finally shatters, to fall back to earth.

The particular association of hubris and shattering—this time by way of punishment—is familiar to us from the story of the tower of Babel. The attempt to be "as gods, knowing good and evil" (Gen. 3:5) had caused mankind's expulsion from Eden in the first place. Now they said:

> Go to, let us build us . . . a tower, whose top may reach unto heaven. . . . And the Lord said, Behold, the people is one, and they have all one language; and this they begin to do: and now nothing will be restrained from them, which they have imagined to do. Go to, let us go down, and there confound their language, that they may not understand one another's speech. So the Lord scattered them abroad from thence upon the face of the earth: and they left off to build the city.
>
> (Gen. 11:4–8)

Therefore mankind was splintered (like the mirror) and alienated from itself. Men tried to know and to do too much, to rise too high, and to be too much like the gods. Twice, therefore, in the Old Testament, hubris has the content of an excessive thirst for knowledge—or a thirst for forbidden knowledge—and we shall see that this too is germane to our story.

Forbidden knowledge may be of two kinds, pertaining either to the sacred, or to the sexual, or in some instances to both. The forbidden knowledge obtained by Adam and Eve when they ate the apple from the Tree of Knowledge seems to have related to sex, since they had no awareness of it before but managed to procreate after. And in our story, too, sex seems to be involved, since the mirror has the ability to convert "a good, pious thought" into "a carnal grin"—the sort of grin that becomes appropriate when a hidden sexual activity or an unsuspected sexual opportunity becomes known.

So we have been alerted by the first story what the following ones will be about: we can expect to be told of impiety, impertinence, and grievous sin—though just exactly what sin or sins we shall encounter remains uncertain. And now it is high time to go on to . . .

3

The Second Story

A Little Boy

> In the big city it was so crowded with houses and people that
> few found room for even a small garden and most people
> had to be content with a flowerpot, but two poor children
> who lived there managed to have a garden that was a little
> bigger than a flowerpot. These children were not brother and
> sister, but they loved each other just as much as if they had
> been. Their parents lived close to each other in the garrets of
> two adjoining houses. Where the roofs met and where the
> rain gutter ran between the two houses, their two small win-
> dows faced each other. . . . In these windows, the parents
> had a large box where they planted vegetables for their use,
> and a little rose bush too. . . . Then it occurred to them to put
> these boxes across the gutter, where they . . . looked exactly
> like two walls of flowers . . . the rose bushes threw long
> sprays . . . toward each other . . . and the children were
> often allowed to take their little stools out on the roof under
> the roses, where they had a wonderful time playing together.
> Winter, of course, put an end to this pleasure. The windows
> often frosted over completely. But they would heat copper
> pennies on the stove and press these hot coins against the
> frosted glass. Then they had the finest of peepholes, and
> behind them appeared a bright, friendly eye, one at each
> window. . . . His name was Kay and hers was Gerda.

We are thus presented with a charming, idyllic childhood
setting. If we were to criticize anything (having a tiny devil's
splinter in our own eye), we would say that it is a little too
quaint or a little contrived. How did Andersen ever think it
up?

Well, he did not think it up at all. He had just such an
arrangement of flower boxes when he was a little boy[1]
(though he always played there alone), and we are tipped

off to the probability that he is about to tell us a very personal story about his own childhood. Just how personal—that we cannot judge unless we know something of the facts of his youth. Because such knowledge should make the story that much more interesting, let us briefly relate what may be pertinent.

The "lovely story, happy and full of incident" that, according to Andersen, is the story of his life (*TS*) began on 2 April 1805 in the Danish provincial capital of Odense "called after the pagan god, Odin, who, as tradition states, lived here." His father was a shoemaker, "scarcely twenty-two years old, a man of a richly gifted and truly poetic mind. His wife, a few years older than himself, was ignorant of life and of the world, but possessed a heart full of love." That she was "a few years older" than her husband is rather an understatement and conveys a certain embarrassment on the part of the author. Some of his biographers make her fifteen years older, and give their ages at Hans Christian's birth as twenty-three and thirty-eight[2] or twenty-five and forty,[3] respectively. Bredsdorff, probably the best informed, states that the father was born in 1782, the mother in 1775, so that she would have been seven years his senior.[4]

They were quite poor. His father "had himself made his shoemaking bench, and the bedstead with which he began housekeeping; this bedstead he had made out of the wooden frame which had borne, only a short time before, the coffin of the deceased Count Trampe, as he lay in state, and the remnants of the black cloth on the woodwork kept the fact still in remembrance. Instead of a noble corpse, surrounded by crepe and wax-lights, here lay . . . a living and weeping child,—that was myself, Hans Christian Andersen" (*FT*, 1).

Again, he seems to be eager to slide over a circumstance hinted at but surely deeply hurtful to him. If his father had "begun housekeeping" with a bedstead that "only a short time before had borne a coffin"—so short a time that the black cloth still was attached to it—then father had started housekeeping, and presumably had been wedded only a short time before Hans Christian's birth. This is the more likely as the child's mother had, six years before, given birth to an illegitimate daughter. This girl had been put out to nurse, and so Hans Christian may not have known of his half-sister as a child;[5] all the more did her existence haunt him as a man. He never mentions her in his autobiography.

He also does not mention that his mother was herself illegitimate, one of three illegitimate half-sisters borne by her mother to three different men; he does, however, pay tribute to the hardships of her childhood, when she "had been driven out by her parents to beg, and once when she was not able to do it, she sat for a whole day under a bridge and wept" (*TS*, 4). Clearly, she became the model for *The Little Match Girl* and similar figures in Andersen's writings.

His father, too, had suffered deprivations. Andersen tells us—and presumably was told—that his father's parents had been well-to-do farmers, but their cattle died and their farmhouse burned down; lastly—and by implication because of it—the grandfather had lost his reason. The grandmother had to move the family to Odense, where she found employment tending the gardens of the local lunatic asylum, Greyfriars Hospital. This "quiet and most amiable old woman, with mild blue eyes and a fine figure" would tell the boy how her own grandmother had been a rich noble lady in the city of Cassel who had run away from parents and home and married a "comedy-player," "for all of which her posterity had now to do penance." But all of this history, including the story of the farm, appears to have been a fairy tale of her own invention[6]—though to my knowledge Andersen never said and perhaps never knew this to be so. Apparently his grandfather had been, like his father, a cobbler. His father hated his menial work, was not very good at it, and always regretted his lack of a formal education. He made up for it by reading a great deal on his own, and by reading to Hans Christian from books of plays and tales of adventure; and only at such moments did he seem really cheerful. At other times he was withdrawn, associated seldom with his equals, and spent much time sitting silently, deep in thought.

Andersen seems to have to try hard to say good things about his mother. Surely she kept the home as neat and presentable as their circumstances permitted[7] and took good care of her family, first as a housewife and later as a washer-woman. But she was steeped in religion and superstition, and she suffered from an anxious temperament. She was as incapable of understanding her son and joining him in his flights of fancy as the duck who hatched the Ugly Duckling.

His favorite companions by far were his father and his grandmother. His father, in addition to reading plays, eventually started him on the manufacture of puppets and stages where these plays could be enacted. For years Hans Christian would spend most of his time sewing costumes for his theater-dolls and writing plays for them. It was also his father who introduced him to poetry and who, by his occasional free-thinking and "blasphemous" utterances, provided, to mother's great discomfiture, glimpses of a wider and less terrible world than hers.

Not that there was a shortage of frightening events: "One of my first recollections, although very slight in itself, had for me a good deal of importance, from the power by which the fancy of a child impressed it upon my soul; it was a family festival . . . in that very . . . house which I had always looked on with fear and trembling . . . the Odense house of correction." The jailers, acquainted with his parents, had invited them to a family dinner:

> The house of correction was for me a great store-house of stories about robbers and thieves; often I had stood, but always at a safe distance, and listened to the singing of the men within and of the women spinning at their wheels. I went with my parents to the jailers; the heavy iron-bolted gate was opened and again locked with the key from the rattling bunch; we mounted a steep staircase—we ate and drank, and two of the prisoners waited at the table; they could not induce me to taste of anything, the sweetest things I pushed away; my mother told them I was sick and I was laid on a bed . . . I know that I was afraid, and was kept on the stretch all the time; and yet I was in a pleasant humor, making up stories of how I had entered a castle full of robbers.
>
> (FT, 4)

Andersen was so young at that time that his parents had to carry him all the way home; but regardless of whether his memory of the events is altogether accurate, the mixture of terror and humorous fantasy is very much "Andersen" and stayed with him all his life.

When he was three years old, French and Spanish troops came through Odense on their way to Sweden.

> I remember very well those dark-brown men bustling in the streets, and the cannon that were fired in the market place . . . the castle of Kolding was burnt . . . the school-houses were changed into guard-rooms. . . . A Spanish soldier one day took me in his arms and pressed against my lips a silvery image, which he carried on his breast. I remember that my mother became angry because, she said, it was something Catholic, but I was pleased with the image, and the foreign soldier danced with me, kissed me, and shed tears. . . . I saw one of his comrades carried to execution for having killed a Frenchman.
>
> (FT, 5)

In his sixth year the great comet of 1811 appeared, which his mother told him would destroy the earth. With the village women he stood and looked at "the frightful and mighty fire-ball with its large, shining tail," and he

> listened to all the superstitious stories and fully believed them. My father joined us, but he was not of the others' opinion at all, and gave them a correct and sound explanation; then my mother sighed, the women shook their heads, my father laughed and went away. I caught the idea that my father was not of our faith, and that threw me into a great fright . . . I expected every moment that the comet would rush down, and the day of judgement come.
>
> (FT, 6)

Somewhat later again, he supposedly faced up to another threat in this manner:

> Sometimes, during the harvest, my mother went into the field to glean. I accompanied her. . . . One day we went to a place the bailiff of which was well known for being a man of a rude and savage disposition. We saw him coming with a huge whip in his hand, and my mother and all the others ran

away. I had wooden shoes on my bare feet, and in my haste I lost these, and then the thorns pricked me so that I could not run, and thus I was left behind and alone. The man came up and lifted his whip to strike me, when I looked him in the face and involuntarily exclaimed: "How dare you strike me, when God can see it?" The strong, stern man looked at me, and at once became mild; he patted me on my cheeks, asked me my name, and gave me money.

(*FT*, 10)

As the Italians say, "Si non è vero, è ben trovato." It may not be true, but it makes a good story. It also illustrates for the first time Andersen's very special and very personal relationship to Divine Providence. This, too, stayed with him all his life.

But of all the grown-ups around Hans Christian, it was his grandmother who treated him as her "joy and delight," who came to see him daily, and in whose company he delighted. The old woman had an unending supply of folktales that she loved to tell. From the asylum gardens she brought him flowers that he was permitted to arrange and put in water. Though they were meant for the whole family, he considered them his very own. And every once in a while she took the boy with her to the asylum, where there were more flowers to play with—"a circumstance upon which I set great importance"—and "better food to eat than I could expect at home"—an admission that reflects heavily upon either their poverty or his mother's cooking.

He encountered many of the "harmless" patients in the garden, but at times he was also permitted to go inside where the "raving mad" were kept in cells:

On one occasion when the attendants were out of the way, I lay down upon the floor, and peeped through the crack of the door into one of these cells. I saw within a lady almost naked, lying on her straw bed; her hair hung down over her shoulders, and she sang with a very beautiful voice. All at once she sprang up, and threw herself against the door where I lay; the little valve through which she received her food burst open; she stared down upon me, and stretched out her long arm toward me. I screamed for terror—I felt the tips of her fingers touching my clothes—I was half dead when the attendant came; and even in later years that sight[8] and that feeling remained within my soul.

(FT, 7)

He had somewhat better luck in the adjacent poorhouse, where he found the old women an attentive audience to lectures he delivered on such topics as human anatomy and similar matters of ignorance and fancy. The crones were filled with astonishment at his eloquence and found him "a remarkably wise child that would not live long."

They rewarded him by telling him tales in return, and thus "a world as rich as that of the thousand and one nights was revealed to me." However, these stories together with his glimpses of the insane patients operated so powerfully upon his imagination that when it grew dark he scarcely dared go out of the house. "I was therefore permitted," he recalls, "generally at sunset, to lay me down in my parents' bed with its long flowered curtains . . . and here . . . lay I in a waking dream, as if the actual world did not concern me" *(FT, 8)*.

The matter of insanity presented a very personal threat. His "weak-minded" grandfather, who almost never talked to him, and who employed himself by whittling strange beasts out of wood and giving them away to the country children, was a well-known "character" in town. One day Hans Christian heard the street boys shouting after his grandfather; he hid himself in terror behind a flight of steps "for I knew I was of his flesh and blood" *(FT, 8)*.

Hans Christian seems to have been hiding from "the actual world" much of the time:

I was a very quiet child, never went out into the street to play with other children; I only liked the company of girls. I still remember a beautiful little girl[9] of about eight who kissed me and told me she wanted to marry me; this pleased me, and I allowed her to kiss me though I never kissed her, and I allowed no one else apart from her to kiss me. I felt a strange dislike for grown-up girls, or for girls of more than twelve; they really made me shudder; in fact I used the expression

about anything which I did not like touching that it was very
"girlish."[10]

But even with younger girls he had bad experiences. He
tried to impress one of them, whom he did like, by telling
her that he owned a castle. He said that he was "a changed
child of high birth" and that the angels of God came down
and spoke to him. But the girl looked queerly at him and
said to a bystander: "He is a fool like his grandpa." He
"shivered at the words" (*FT*, 9).

It is not clear whether he attended school regularly or for
long. At one time he was sent to a school that "consisted
mostly of girls. . . . The mistress dared not beat me, as my
mother had made it a condition of my going that I should not
be touched. One day having got a hit of the rod I rose immediately, took my book, and without further ceremony went
home to my mother, asked that I might go to another school,
and that was granted me" (*FT*, 9). This episode must have
confirmed to him that he was both "special" and fragile, with
none of the robustness of a "real boy"—an awareness from
which he suffered all his life. As to the flower boxes up on the
roof, there too he played alone and never with a girl or any
other child. He would imagine plays, or stare into the sun-
illumined leaves of his favorite gooseberry bush. "I was a
singularly dreamy child," he writes, "and so constantly went
about with my eyes shut, as at last to give the impression of
having weak sight"—a strange boy indeed!

As Hans Christian entered his seventh year, his father became increasingly restless. He pondered works of history and
scripture. But when he tried to discuss them with his wife,
she would not understand him, and therefore he grew more
and more silent. To the horror of his family he would say
things like: "Christ was a man like us, but an extraordinary
man," or "There is no other devil than that which we have in
our own hearts," so that, when one morning he awoke to
find three scratches on his arm, his son was entirely of the
opinion of the mother and of the neighbors that the Devil had
been to visit him in the night to prove to him that he really

existed. (That the Devil plays his role in the story of the Snow Queen we have already noted; whether Hans Christian ever settled in his own mind the question of the Devil's actual or merely allegorical existence, I do not know.)

His father's inner ferment now culminated in action: he volunteered to join the armies of his hero, Napoleon.[11] The morning his detachment marched off Hans Christian lay sick abed with the measles; his beloved grandmother came into the room and, thinking no doubt he would soon be an orphan, told him it would be best for him if he died. It was perhaps on this occasion that the boy along with high fever suffered convulsions. His mother called in, not a doctor, but a "wise woman," who measured his frail arms and legs with a bit of woolen yarn and prescribed an amulet compounded of graveyard earth and the heart of a mole.[12] The remedy must have been considered highly efficacious, for the patient recovered.

His father returned about two years later, when the boy was nine.[13] We do not hear how much, or whether, he had been missed. We do know that "the voluntary soldier returned to his work-stool. Everything fell into its old course. I played again with my dolls, acted comedies, and always in 'German' . . . a sort of gibberish which I made up." The "again" would suggest that perhaps such activities were frowned upon in father's absence. Indeed the more practical mother could see only one use in her son's play with dolls: the sewing involved in the manufacture of doll costumes could prepare the boy to become a tailor. For the rest, she considered literature and dramatics superfluous and foolish, if not sinful, and, fearing that such excitements might drive her son mad,[14] may well have suppressed these activities while father was away trying to live out his notions of glory.

He came back crestfallen. His regiment had advanced no farther than Holstein. Peace had been concluded before he had heard a shot fired in anger, and he had suffered mainly from various illnesses. He returned broken in body and soul, visible evidence, according to the mother, of the folly of leaving home.

He lasted two more years. One morning he awoke in a state of delirium, fancying he had received orders from Napoleon to take command of the army. The mother promptly sent Hans Christian to the "wise woman"—the witch—who lived on a heath near the town. Once again the old hag measured the boy's arm with a woolen thread,

> made extraordinary signs, and at last laid a green twig upon my breast. It was, she said, a piece of the same kind of tree upon which our Savior was crucified. "Go now," she said, "by the river towards home. If your father will die this time, then you will meet his ghost." My anxiety and distress can be imagined—I, who was so full of superstition, and whose imagination was so easily excited. "And thou has not met anything, hast thou?" inquired my mother when I got home. I assured her, with beating heart, that I had not. My father died the third day after that.[15] His corpse lay on the bed; I therefore slept with my mother.
>
> (*TS*, 17–18)

The mother now had to "go out washing." And so the boy, at age eleven, was left alone at home to play with his little theater, his doll clothes, and his books. He was tall for his age, his hair was "long, bright, and almost yellow," and he must already have been possessed of the appealing charm that served him so well all his life. The widow of a clergyman who lived nearby took an interest in the strange lad and opened her door to him. "Hers was the first house belonging to the educated class into which I was kindly received"—the first of a great many.

The widow encouraged his interest in poetry and drama, and soon he was writing plays he insistently declaimed to anyone who would listen. This pleased him no end, but it seems to have distressed his mother. In order that he might not be "at loose ends," she decided one day to send him to work in a cloth manufactory, "not for the sake of the money, but that she might know where I was, and what I was doing." (Considering that she earned their livelihood by washing other people's laundry in the often icy river,[16] it is not clear why she should have had to play down the importance of the money. But the "poor, ragged lads" who worked in the manufactory were considered unfit company for her boy, and shameful associations. Both she and his grandmother clung to a certain fiction of gentility, which must, in spite of all "practical" admonitions, have strengthened the boy in his growing belief that he was made for better things.)

The workers in the factory were "merry fellows," who made "many a coarse joke." He learned there that "to the innocent ears of a child the impure remains very unintelligible. It took no hold upon my heart." But his stay there was brief:

> I was possessed at that time of a remarkably beautiful and high soprano voice, and I knew it; because when I sang in my parents' little garden, the people in the street stood and listened, and the fine folks in the garden of the states-councillor, which adjoined ours, listened at the fence. When, therefore, the people at the manufactory asked me whether I could sing, I immediately began, and all the looms stood still: all the journeymen listened to me. I had to sing again and again, whilst the other boys had my work given to them to do. . . . One day, however, when I was in my best singing vein, and everybody spoke of the extraordinary brilliancy of my voice, one of the journeymen said that I was a girl, and not a boy. He seized hold of me. I cried and screamed. The other journeymen thought it very amusing, and held me fast by my arms and legs. I screamed aloud, and was as much ashamed as a girl; and then, darting from them, rushed home to my mother, who immediately promised me that I should never go there again.
>
> (*TS*, 23)

Another attempt to put him to work—this time in a tobacco factory—also failed, perhaps for similar reasons. Officially he was removed because, according to his mother, the tobacco might be affecting his health.[17] He was next sent to a charity school where—it is not clear for how long—he was taught religion and the three R's; he resisted this influence so effectively that, in the end, he "could scarcely spell a word correctly." He may have made himself as unpopular with his classmates as with the working boys in the factory. At any rate, one day a group of lads—"a wild crowd of them"—pursued him in the street, shouting after him: "There runs the play-writer!" He hid himself in a corner, wept, and prayed to God (*FT*, 21).

But he stuck to his resolve. He wanted to become a playwright or an actor, and he lost no opportunity to endear himself with anyone likely to support his purpose.

When he was thirteen, his mother decided that he must be confirmed. "The candidates for Confirmation could either enter their names with the provost or the chaplain. The children of the so-called superior families and the scholars of the grammar school went to the first, and the children of the poor to the second." Hans Christian was clearly a slum child, but he announced himself a candidate to the provost anyway. "I would hope that it was not lone vanity that impelled me. I had a sort of fear of the poor boys, who had laughed at me, and I always felt . . . an inward drawing towards the scholars of the grammar school, whom I regarded as far better than other boys. When I saw them playing in the church yard, I would stand outside the railings and wish that I were but among the fortunate ones." The provost accepted him, though "putting him in the lowest place." The other boys, however, would not associate with him, and "I had daily the feeling of having thrust myself in where people thought that I did not belong" (*FT*, 21–22). This was another problem that he wrestled with all his life.

He must not have been an easy pupil, for he had his own thoughts about everything—including divine matters. One day, while helping to pick hops in the country, he heard an old man saying "that God knew everything, both what had happened, and what would happen." And the boy thought: "Yes, God has now determined that I should live and get to be so many years old; but, if I now were to jump into the water and drown myself, then it would not be as He wished; and all at once I was firmly and resolutely determined to drown myself. I ran to where the water was deepest, and then a new thought passed through my soul. 'It is the devil who wishes to have power over me!' I uttered a loud cry and, running away from the place as if I were pursued, fell weeping into my mother's arms" (*FT*, 17–18). He was to be "tempted" to suicide rather easily all his life when things did not go well with him.[18]

That same year his mother remarried. The stepfather— once again a shoemaker and once again a man much younger than herself—paid no attention to Hans Christian's education nor, apparently, to Hans Christian. The family moved to a somewhat better house right by the river. And here, standing on a stone in the water, the boy would exercise his beautiful voice. He hoped to attract the attention of the Emperor of China who, it was said, lived beneath the river, and if not that, then at least the interest of some of the wealthy people who did live nearby and who had high connections. In this he was successful. He was beginning to be talked about, invited, and praised; occasionally he managed to be given some walk-on parts in the local theater, once even got to speak a couple of lines. One day a Colonel Høegh-Guldberg, who had business at the local residence-palace, took the boy along for an audience with the then crown prince of Denmark, Christian Frederik. It was a heady event, but the results were disappointing: the prince refused to support Hans Christian's ambition to go on the stage, and suggested that he learn a trade.

With the certainty peculiar to genius, Andersen persevered. At fourteen, having saved the fabulous sum of "thirteen rix dollars banco—about thirty shillings,"[19] he prayed and besought his mother—who once again wanted him to become apprenticed to a tailor—to let him set off to Copenhagen in pursuit of his fortune.

> "What wilt thou do there?" asked my mother. "I will become famous," returned I. . . . "People have at first an immense deal of adversity to go through, and then they will be famous." It was a wholly unintelligible impulse that guided me. I wept, I prayed, and at last my mother consented, after having first sent for a so-called wise woman out of the hospital, that she might read my future by the coffee grounds and

cards. "Your son will become a great man," said the old woman, "and in honour of him, Odense will one day be illuminated." My mother wept when she heard that, and I obtained permission to travel.

(*FT*, 22–23)

And so he prevailed. His mother packed his clothes, and arrangements were made for the post carriage to pick him up outside the city gates—as an illegal passenger who bribed the coachman but paid no fare. There his mother and his grandmother stood and wept as he departed; he was never to see the old woman again. She, who had been more influential on him than anyone, died the following year: "I do not even know her grave: she sleeps in the poor-house burial ground." But Hans Christian traveled into adventure: "The postilion blew his horn: it was a sunny afternoon, and the sunshine soon entered into my gay, child-like mind. I delighted in every novel object which met my eye, and I was journeying toward the goal of my soul's desire. When, however, I arrived at Nyborg on the Great Belt, and was borne in the ship away from my native island, I then truly felt how alone and forlorn I was. . . . I thought I was far away in the wide world" (*FT*, 24).

He was, after all, only fourteen. . . .

We know that he reached Copenhagen, and that he managed to survive there. So let this much of his life story—of the fairy tale of his life—be enough for the moment.[20] Let us, finally, get down to the story of the Snow Queen. And so we return to . . .

4

The Second Story (Once Again)
A Little Boy and a Little Girl

Kay and Gerda, you recall, the two children who lived in
adjoining houses, could visit each other easily enough in
summer by stepping out into their joint roof garden, but to
visit together in the wintertime they had to go all the way
downstairs in one house, and all the way upstairs in the
other. One day the snow was whirling outside:

> "See the white bees swarming," the old grandmother
> said.
> "Do they have a queen bee, too?" the little boy asked, for
> he knew that real bees have one.
> "Yes, indeed they do," the grandmother said. "She flies
> in the thick of the swarm. . . . Many a wintry night she flies
> through the streets and peers in through the windows. Then
> they freeze over in a strange fashion, as if they were covered
> with flowers." . . .
> "Can the Snow Queen come in here?" the little girl asked.
> "Well, let her come!" cried the boy. "I would put her on
> the hot stove and melt her." But Grandmother stroked his
> head, and told them other stories.

Let us note in passing: the grandmother (it is always the
old grandmother, as even a middle-aged grandmother would
appear old to a child) is the only member of the two families, other than the two children, whom we ever meet; and
at that we do not know whose grandmother she was—Kay's
or Gerda's! As to the parents, once they had placed the
flower boxes across the gutters, apparently their work was
done—we never hear of them again. This is a remarkable
fact, and we shall have to come back to it later. And further,
it is clear that the Snow Queen presents some sort of

danger. Gerda is anxious lest she come in, but Kay brags that he is not afraid. "Let her come!" he says. He will kill her, he will put her on the stove and melt her. The grand-mother, wise and soothing, changes the topic.

But that evening . . .

> When little Kay was at home and half ready for bed, he climbed on the chair by the window and looked out through the little peephole. A few snowflakes were falling, and the largest flake of all alighted on the edge of one of the flower boxes. This flake grew bigger and bigger, until at last it turned into a woman, who was dressed in the finest white gauze . . . she was beautiful and she was graceful, but she was ice—shining, glittering ice. She was alive, for all that, and her eyes sparkled like two bright stars, but in them there was neither rest nor peace. She nodded toward the window and beckoned with her hand. The little boy was frightened and . . . jumped down from the chair.

The Snow Queen beckons to him: clearly, she is trying to seduce him in some manner and to some end known only to her. In a sense, she has chosen him, and he knows it. But as yet he is frightened and does not follow. He is not yet ready.

Indeed the very next day springtime comes, and the sum-mer that follows is more beautiful than any that went be-fore. Once again the children play in their little roof garden, and "the roses bloomed their splendid best." Gerda teaches Kay a hymn "in which there was a line about roses that reminded her of her own flowers":

> Where roses bloom so sweetly in the vale
> There shall you find the Christ Child, without fail.

It was a glorious summer.

But one day, as Kay and Gerda were looking at a picture book, Kay cried:

> "Oh! something hurt my heart. And now I've got some-thing in my eye." The little girl put her arm around his neck, and he blinked his eye. No, she couldn't see anything in it. "I think it's gone," he said. But it was not gone. It was one of

those splinters of glass from the magic mirror. . . . Poor Kay! A fragment had pierced his heart as well, and soon it would turn into a lump of ice. The pain had stopped, but the glass was still there.

"Why should you be crying?" he asked. "It makes you look so ugly. There's nothing the matter with me." And suddenly he took it into his head to say: "Ugh! that rose is all worm-eaten. And look, this one is crooked. And these roses, they are just as ugly as they can be."—and he broke them off.

Gerda cried, and when Kay saw that she was upset, he broke some more roses and left her. After that, when she brought out her books, he said they were fit only for babes in the cradle. Whenever grandmother told stories, he always broke in with a "but—." He also made fun of her, and imitated her and other people so cleverly that everybody laughed.[1]

Next winter, when the snow was flying about, he brought a large magnifying glass to look at the snowflakes on his blue coat, and he admired them saying: "They are much more interesting than real flowers, they are absolutely perfect. There isn't a flaw in them." And one day he came to Gerda only to shout: "I've been given permission to play in the big square where the other boys are!" and away he ran.

In the square some of the more adventuresome boys would tie their little sleds behind farmers' carts to be pulled along for sport. That day a big white sleigh drives up, the driver cloaked in a white fur coat and a white, shaggy cap. Kay hooks his sled on to it, and down the street they go, faster and faster. . . .

Out through the town gate they go. The driver nods to Kay, as to an old acquaintance, but Kay is frightened. He wants to untie his sled, but he cannot; he shouts, but no one hears him. As the snow whirls around him and they fly along, he tries to say his prayers—but all he can remember is his multiplication tables. Finally, the sleigh stops, the driver stands up and is "a woman, tall and slender and blinding white . . . the Snow Queen herself."

He is cold; she kisses him on the forehead. "He felt as if he were dying, but only for a moment. The he felt quite comfortable, and no longer noticed the cold." The Snow Queen kisses him once more, and he forgets little Gerda and the grandmother. "You won't get any more kisses now," says the Snow Queen, "or else I should kiss you to death." Kay looks at her; in his eyes she is beautiful, she is perfect. He tells her that he can do mental arithmetic even with fractions, and that he knows the size and population of all the countries: "She kept smiling, and he began to be afraid that he did not know as much as he thought he did." And off they go, flying over the black clouds and the glittering snow below, into the long winter night. . . .

Well now, we must interrupt again and ask two questions: First, why do the splinters of the Devil's mirror affect Kay in just the way they do? Second, who, exactly, is the Snow Queen?

As to the first: If we omit, for a moment, the metaphysics of the situation and concentrate on the observable changes in Kay—on the phenomenology of the situation—then the metamorphosis becomes suddenly quite familiar (one is tempted to say terribly familiar) to all of us, or at least to anyone who has had occasion to watch a boy grow up, or who once was a boy. Let us summarize what happens.

On the one hand, Kay becomes intolerant of sentimentality and "childish" stories; he has a sudden horror of misty-eyed, idealizing romanticism and piety. Instead he develops a highly obnoxious attitude of cynical contempt. On the other hand, like any good naturalist, he now observes not only the rose but also the worm; and he studies snowflakes no longer like a poet, for their sparkling beauty, but like a crystallographer with a magnifying glass, for the perfection of their structure. Henceforth out of sympathy with the company of (earthly) women—both young and old—he goes off to play dangerous games in the company of other boys. And by the time the Snow Queen carries him away, he has put off religion (he cannot remember his prayers). He bases his pride and his appeal for the favors of the Snow Queen on his mathematical skill (he can do mental arithmetic even with fractions) and his knowledge of facts (he knows the size and population of all the countries). In the process he begins to realize that he does not truly know very much. Though this is not explicitly stated, we can assume that he now is hungry for more facts, for more knowledge of the scientific kind.

He behaves, in short, like the typical adolescent.[2]

At puberty, when a boy is assailed by instinctual-sexual urges, he usually finds to his distress that he is confronted with two tasks for which society—our Western society, at least—provides no guiding ritual or path: To become the man he now begins to feel he should become, he must first of all peel himself out from the world of women in which, so far, he has grown up; and he must try to find some activities, generally recognized to be male, that would help him to consolidate his identity as a man.

The first task, differentiation from girls and women, is quite generally accomplished by physical avoidance and by rudeness in manner and appearance. The previously well-mannered, charming, and affectionate boy becomes "difficult": the family see less and less of him, and he avoids in particular all sentimental occasions. When confronted, he may exhibit a callous, aggressive arrogance, which he, evidently, considers very masculine.

The second task, that of finding a positive male identity, does indeed frequently have to do with the "games bigger boys play": with sports, dangerous modes of transportation such as motorcycles and hot-rods, and with delinquency. Or it may lead into the unsentimental, nonsticky world of mathematics, mechanics, physics, and philosophy—in short, to science and its applications. As Anna Freud has pointed out, such intellectualizing is one of the defense mechanisms available to the ego, and it is among the chief mechanisms used during adolescence.[3]

The effect of the splinters, therefore, appears to be that they bring about the onset of a perfectly normal, if disagreeable, adolescent phase. To that extent they can hardly be considered detrimental. But we do recall that the splinters are to represent sinfulness; in what manner adolescent withdrawal into intellectuality may be a sin is not at all clear. We shall have to come back to it later when we shall "know more than we know now."

But what of the Snow Queen herself?

There, luckily, we can draw on three converging sources: Andersen's fiction, his autobiography, and the mythology in which he was raised.

When Andersen was fifty-six years old—some sixteen years after he had written *The Snow Queen*—he published a tale called *The Ice Maiden*. It is a longish work, far from his best; it tells of an evil, vengeful supernatural being who lives in the glaciers and icy lakes of Switzerland. He calls her "the slayer, the crusher," because it is her pleasure to crush men and women—and children in particular—in the crevasses of her glaciers, to drown them in the glacier-lakes, or to bury them under avalanches. The story concerns a young man who, as a little boy, had been carried by his mother across a mountain pass. The hazardous journey leads over a glacier; mother and child slip and fall into a crevasse. Although companions eventually pull them out, the mother is dead and only the child can be revived. The Ice Maiden is furious: "a beautiful boy was snatched from me—one *whom I had kissed, but not yet kissed to death!* . . . He is mine! I will fetch him!"[4] Henceforth the Ice Maiden pursues him stubbornly, waits and bides her time, and finally manages to trick him into a lake and drown him—*on the eve of his wedding!*

I do not know whether Andersen actually heard such a legend while in Switzerland, or whether such a legend exists there. But we do know that the Ice Maiden first made her appearance in Andersen's life much earlier, when he was about ten or eleven years old. At that time, he tells us, his sick father had once stood by him at the frosted window of their room, and had pointed to "a figure as that of a maiden with outstretched arms. 'She is come to fetch me,' he said, in jest." Both the boy and his mother remembered this when he lay dead; that night, when a cricket chirped the whole night through, " 'He is dead,' said my mother, addressing it; 'thou needest not call him. The ice maiden has fetched him' " (*TS*, 17–18). The image must have impressed the boy deeply, since he gave it poetic expression forty-five years later.

The Ice Maiden, of course, is Death;[5] and that she is identical with the Snow Queen is suggested by the common elements of the frosted window at which they appear, by their frigid nature, and by the kisses of death they bestow.[6]

But we can add another element that may well have joined in to prepare the minds of Hans Christian and his father for such a mythological formulation of Death. In Norse mythology a goddess called Hel rules over Niflheim, or Niflhel, a cold and misty place whither go those dead who have died not in battle but by illness or old age. Niflheim is the Land of the Dead and Hel is the Queen of Death. *Hel* and *hell* are, of course, the same word; thus Niflheim, ruled by Hel, is Hell—the cold, Nordic equivalent of the hot Mediterranean Hell of the Church Fathers. (The Nordic counterpart to heaven is Valhalla, whither go only heroes fallen in battle. Alas, this is the fate Hans Christian's father sought, but it was denied him. Had he died a hero, a Valkyrie would have come to fetch him; since he died a sick man—no better than a child or a woman—therefore, according to his own remark, the Ice Maiden had to be his destined guide to Hell.)

The German word for Hell is *Hölle*, which is etymologically closely related. Drop the umlaut, and you get *Holle*—the name of a buxom woman who as "Frau Holle" inhabits German fairy tale. There she lives in the wintry colds and sleeps in a featherbed. And when, like any good German *Hausfrau*, she goes to the window of her house to shake out her eiderdown comforter, much of the downy stuffing escapes and falls gently down to earth as snow. So Frau Holle too is a Snow Queen, and she covers the earth with that snowy comforter so often compared, in the poetry of Northern lands, to a winding sheet, or shroud; to the white cloth that covers the dead. Thus Frau Holle, too, is not just a Queen of Snow; she is also Hölle and Hel—she is also Death.

I do not know whether the folktale of Frau Holle was available to Andersen, though in some form it probably was.[7] It is not a necessary part of our thesis. Andersen himself, after all, tells us that the Snow Queen (like the Ice Maiden) is Death: for she must not kiss Kay three times, lest he die. And only Death's kisses are the kisses of death.

Indeed, when she kissed Kay for the first time, he "felt as if he were dying, but only for a moment. Then he felt quite comfortable, and no longer noticed the cold." In other words, he does die, but he does not die altogether—only his human feelings die. On the second kiss his memories of Gerda and of Grandmother die, his feelings for them and his emotions die altogether, and nothing is left but "cold reason."

The death Kay dies is not a total death. It is more like a hibernation; it is the defensive-protective hibernation of the emotions during adolescence. At this stage of life—after the onset of physical-sexual maturity and drive, but before the readiness several years later to cope with the emotional involvements and the practical responsibilities that sexuality entails—a moratorium is generally needed. During this stage a boy's sensuality (at least as far as it involves others) and his overall relatedness to others and to girls in particular are likely to go into hibernation. But what further may be involved we shall see later on.

And meanwhile, what about poor little Gerda, scorned and alone?

5

The Third Story

The Flower Garden of the Woman Skilled in Magic

Gerda misses him, and she cries bitterly all through the long, long winter. Nobody can give her news of Kay. People say he must be dead, he must have drowned in the river not far from town. In the spring she complains to the sunshine:

> "Kay is dead and gone," little Gerda said.
> "I don't believe it," said the sunshine.
> "He's dead and gone," she said to the swallows.
> "We don't believe it," they sang. Finally, Gerda began to disbelieve it too.

And so, one morning she comes to a most peculiar resolve:

> "I'll put on my new red shoes, the ones Kay has never seen, and I'll go down by the river to ask about him."

What is peculiar, of course, are the red—probably lacquered—shoes. It is strange, too, that she would consider them the proper footwear for a walk to the river. But what she does with them is "curiouser" still:

> It was very early in the morning. She kissed her old grandmother, who was still asleep, put on her red shoes, and all by herself she hurried out through the town gate and down to the river. She asked it:
> "Is it true that you have taken my own playmate? I'll give you my red shoes if you will bring him back to me." It seemed to her that the waves nodded very strangely. So she took off the red shoes that were her dearest possession, and threw them into the river.

The shoes fall near the shore, and the waves wash them right back. In order to throw them in farther, she clambers into a boat lying among the reeds. The boat, it turns out, is not tied up, and as she walks to the far end of it and throws in her shoes once again, it breaks loose from the bank and starts to drift downstream. Gerda cries with fright, but there is no one to hear her except the sparrows. They fly along with her, twittering "We are here, we are here," as if to comfort her. Eventually she calms down. The red shoes float along behind for a while but cannot catch up with the boat. The landscape to both sides is lovely; there are cattle and sheep, "but not one single person did Gerda see. 'Perhaps the river will take me to little Kay,' she thought, and that made her feel more cheerful."

So we let her drift—"hour after hour"—and ask meanwhile: What *is* the significance of the red shoes? Again Andersen himself will help us out. The very same year he wrote *The Snow Queen*—he was then forty years old—he also wrote a story called *The Red Shoes*. Many readers will be familiar with it through the brilliant British film interpretation of the 1950s. The original story is slightly different and more gruesome than the film:

There was once a very nice, pretty little girl named Karen; she was so poor she had to go barefoot all summer. So "Old Mother Shoemaker," who lived in her village, made her a pair of shoes out of old scraps of red cloth. The first time the little girl wore them was at her mother's burial: "Of course, they were not right for mourning, but they were all she had." Just then a large old carriage came by, with a large old lady inside it. She took pity upon the little girl and adopted her. The girl "was sure that this happened because she wore red shoes, but the old lady said the shoes were hideous, and ordered them burned." Karen was given proper clothes and an education, and as she grew up, the mirror told her: "You are more than pretty. You are beautiful."

One day the queen and princess come through town, and the princess appears at the window of the castle, dressed all in white: "She didn't wear a train, and she didn't wear a gold crown, but she did wear a pair of splendid red morocco shoes." Karen thinks, "There's nothing in the world like a pair of red shoes!"

When Karen is old enough to be confirmed, the old lady takes her to buy a new dress and new shoes. In the cobbler's shop there is a pair of shoes made of red leather, just like those of the princess. "They must be patent leather to shine so," says the old lady; she buys them for the girl, but because she does not see well, she has no idea they are red! "If she had known that, she would never have let Karen wear them to confirmation." But this is just what Karen does.

As she walks up the aisle to the altar of the church, all eyes are on her red shoes, and she herself can think of nothing but her red shoes and the stir they create. The old lady is told that the shoes are red, admonishes Karen that it is "naughty" to wear them to church, and instructs her to wear black shoes henceforth. The very next Sunday Karen wears her red shoes to communion. At the church door an old soldier admires them, saying: "Oh, what beautiful shoes for dancing!" And, addressing the shoes: "Never come off when you dance!" At the altar the girl thinks only of her red shoes and forgets the Lord's prayer. After church she tries a few dancing steps, "and once she began, her feet kept on dancing. It was as if the shoes controlled her." She must dance on until someone takes off her shoes.

Shortly thereafter the old lady is taken ill, but Karen, instead of nursing her, accepts an invitation to a ball. Again, she wears her red shoes; and again, once she starts dancing, she cannot stop. This time, the shoes take over completely and won't come off:

> When she tried to turn to the right, the shoes turned to the left. When she wanted to dance up the ballroom, her shoes danced down. They danced down the stairs, into the street, and out through the gate of the town. Dance she did, and dance she must, straight into the dark woods. . . . She was terribly frightened, and tried to take off her shoes. She tore off her stockings, but the shoes had grown fast to her feet. And dance she did, for dance she must, over fields and valleys, in the rain and in the sun, by day and night.

Once she tries to dance into a church, but an angel with shining sword warns her off, cursing her: "Dance in your red shoes until you are pale and cold, and your flesh shrivels down to the skeleton." She dances on, her screams for mercy unanswered. One day she dances past the funeral of the old lady. She now knows herself to be "all alone in the world, and cursed by the angel of God."

She dances "across the wastelands" until she comes to the house where the executioner lives. She begs him to take his axe and to strike off her feet together with the red shoes. He complies, and the shoes dance away with her feet in them. The executioner makes her a pair of crutches and teaches her a hymn of repentance. She hobbles to church, but the red shoes dance in front of the door and frighten her off. Deeply repentant, she engages herself as a servant girl in a pastor's home. For years she serves faithfully, and on Sundays she listens to the organ only from afar. Finally, in response to her prayer, the angel of the Lord reappears and conducts her to church. Clearly she has been forgiven, but "she was so filled with the light of it, and with joy and with peace, that her heart broke. Her soul travelled along the shaft of sunlight to heaven, where no one questioned her about the red shoes."

It must now be perfectly clear that the red shoes, since one must not wear them to solemn and holy occasions such as funerals, confirmations, and holy communion— these shoes which are not admissible in church at all and which are therefore *unholy*—that they represent some sort of sin. As to which sin is meant, there are several clear indications.

The first time Karen, in defiance of custom, wears her red shoes to church is for her confirmation. This Christian ritual is timed for the onset of "the age of reason," somewhere between seven and fourteen years of age, and usually between twelve and fourteen; it symbolizes the informed and active consent of the young person to a Christian, moral way of life—in contrast to baptism in infancy which is merely a passive and involuntary admission into the Christian community. But the age of reason is also the age of puberty, and of menarche. The unholy, un-Christian path that opens up at that age is the path of sexual indulgence and license. Andersen makes a fine psychological point (and this may be one instance where he knew more than he knew he knew, and said more than he thought he said) when he gives Karen a first, crude pair of red (but not yet shiny) shoes in childhood. There is indeed a first spurt of sexuality around the age of five, and just as in the story it is usually suppressed by adult intervention. (The first pair of red shoes is burned! A still more delicate point is hinted at when we hear that Karen thinks the old lady adopted her *because* of her red shoes—a matter regarding which the old lady quickly disillusions her.) The second spurt of sexuality does indeed come around the time of menarche, and now its indulgence is a matter of moral choice. Karen *chooses* to give in to it. She becomes vain ("not just pretty, but beautiful"), and she is conscious of her sexual attractiveness. Soon her wanton desires override all other concerns, for she goes to the ball rather than tending the sick old woman.

But why must the shoes be red, rather than some other color? Red is and has always been the color symbolic of sexuality[1] or, in a more general sense, of all that is forbidden at most times or to most people, and permitted only under exceptional license. Thus red is the color of kings, whose person was sacred and forbidden to their subjects, and who for long periods in history were alone permitted to wear the imperial purple. But red is also the color of the red-light district, indicating that the forbidden is there licensed. It is the color of the stoplight, which we cannot drive through without sinning. And red is the color of blood and, in the context of adolescence, specifically menstrual blood. Hence Karen dons her shiny red shoes at menarche, just as Gerda suddenly has a pair of red shoes at that very same age (and just as the Sleeping Beauty pricks herself with a spindle, draws a drop of blood on her thirteenth birthday, and promptly falls asleep—a matter to which we shall have to come back).[2]

But why will the shoes not come off?

They won't come off because initially voluntary behavior becomes a part of our selves. Heinrich Zimmer, in his marvelous collection of essays published as *The King and the Corpse*, tells the story of "Abu Kassem's Slippers."[3] Abu Kassem is a rich miser whose worn-out ragged slippers have become the talk of the town: will he never afford himself new ones? For years he won't dream of it, but then one day in the public bath a joker manages to exchange Kassem's slippers for those of the Cadi of Bagdad. Kassem is in deep trouble: he is suspected of stealing and has to pay a big bribe. Upon receiving his old slippers back again, he is finally sick of them and throws them out the window. They fall into the Tigris, are fished out by poor fishermen, and returned to him. He continues in various ways to try and rid himself of them—burying them in his garden, sinking them in a pond, burning them—but every time they come back to him, and always he suffers dearly for the attempt. The slippers are part of him. They *are* his miserliness, which was originally a matter of his choosing, a deliberate and willed mode of conduct, but which became a part of his self-created ego and can no longer be put off. They are a choice that has become a habit and finally a compulsion—just as Karen's slippers, first freely chosen, grow to her feet, and eventually *compel* her to dance.

The slippers are "the shoes we fill"—the role we play in life. They are "the shoes we are to wear if they fit us." In the story of Cinderella the slipper of glass (symbolizing purity) fits only *her*. (Remember that her wicked step-sisters, in the unexpurgated version of the story, have to cut off some of their toes to squeeze their feet into the slipper, so that the pigeons coo: "Cucurrucoo, cucurrucoo, there's blood in the shoe, there's blood in the shoe!" The bleeding is a sign of impurity, but this time no doubt referable to the bleeding that goes with defloration. The wicked sisters are no longer virgins, whereas Cinderella is untouched—in her glass slipper there is nothing to hide. The pigeons, incidentally, are the proper arbiters: they are the love birds—the emblems of Venus—and we shall encounter them again.)

To rid ourselves of our slippers, or our shoes, once we have worn them a long time is almost impossible. Only a heroic act can accomplish it,[4] a shattering act of conversion is required; so Karen has the executioner cut off her legs to get rid of the red shoes. In other words, she forswears sexuality completely. (She cannot even consider marriage, because she has no right to the church. Every time she tries to approach the church, the red slippers dance before the door; they have now become memories she cannot shed.) She chooses a life of sexual abstinence and service. Such conversions from sinner to saint are by no means rare in the histories of religions: as if to say that once you are a sinner—once the red shoes have become part of you—there is no more return to ordinary humanity. The only possible alternative is sainthood.

Returning to Gerda and *her* red shoes, we can now see that the matter is more grave by far than first met the eye. She says of her red shoes that Kay has never seen them. In other words, her menarche or, taking the redness in a more metaphoric sense, her awakening to sexuality has happened since he left. We can now understand why she would want to take them with her, to put them on for her journey in search of Kay. She thinks: "Clearly, this, if anything will get him back, will lure him back from wherever it is he has withdrawn to." In her awakened sexuality she has indeed something to show him that will make his eyes pop. But when she comes to the river, she changes her mind.

The river—well, it is what The River always is, what Old Man River is: it is The River of Life, and it begins outside of the walled city that is childhood. Gerda has left the security of her walled hometown and has gone forth into the wide, wide world. She is to entrust herself to this river, and she is to be swept away by it. She must decide: is it right and proper to venture into the stream of life wearing the red shoes—considering the attention they will arouse—and is it right and proper to use them to attract Kay?

Gerda makes the crucial—and Christian—decision to remain pure. Like Karen, she had worn the red shoes "out through the gate of the town." But now, in the world, she hopes to find favor with Life, and to find Kay, precisely *because* she is renouncing sexuality and choosing the path of virtue. Nor is this decision an easy one: not only are the red shoes "her dearest possession," but when she casts them into the stream, *they come back* (like Abu Kassem's slippers!). We now understand what a breath-holding, what a hairbreadth matter it is whether she will become a wanton or whether she will have the strength of character to remain "pure"—to rid herself of a sexuality that has already threatened to become a habit. But lo—our heroine wins through. She casts the shoes once more into the stream, thus launching herself into the River of Life with no other protection or attribute than her naïveté and her faith in herself and in God. These are much the same attributes that once had to suffice when Hans Christian, at about the same age, launched himself, upon leaving the gate of walled Odense, across the waters of the Big Belt from Nyborg to Korsoer, to reach the big wide world of Copenhagen.

So Gerda drifts down the river, increasingly enchanted and unafraid; the red shoes vanish *but so do all people!* And this peculiar circumstance leads us on to the next adventure.

6

The Third Story (Once Again!)
The Flower Garden of the Woman Skilled in Magic

At long last Gerda does attract the attention of an "old, old woman," and this old woman wades into the stream to catch hold of the drifting boat with her crooked stick and to pull it to shore. But we know right away that this can be no ordinary human being.

The old woman, on whose big sun hat are painted the most glorious flowers, asks Gerda who she is and how she got here. "And when Gerda had told her everything and asked if she hadn't seen little Kay, the woman said *he had not yet come by, but that he might be along any day now*" (emphasis mine). (And we wonder right away: how can she be so sure? In so remote a place, why should he "be along any day now"?)

At any rate, the old woman consoles Gerda, takes her into her house, and offers her the most delicious cherries. While Gerda is eating, the old woman combs her hair with a golden comb, and in the process *Gerda gradually forgets all about Kay!* Then the woman "went out into her garden and pointed her crooked stick at all the rose bushes. In the full bloom of their beauty, all of them sank down into the black earth, without leaving a single trace behind. The old woman was afraid that if Gerda saw them they would remind her so strongly of her own roses, and of little Kay, that she would run away again." Then Gerda is led into the flower garden in which "every known flower of every season [is] in full bloom." Here she plays happily "for many a day." She has the feeling that there is a flower missing, but she doesn't quite know which one.

39

However, "one day she sat looking at the old woman's hat, and the prettiest of all flowers painted on it was a rose. . . . 'Why aren't there any roses here?' said Gerda." She goes into the garden to look for roses, finds none, and sits down to cry. Her tears fall on the ground where a rose-bush used to be. As they moisten the earth, the bush springs up again, as full of blossoms as when it disappeared. Gerda now remembers her own roses—and Kay. She is dismayed how much time she has wasted, and she asks the roses: "Don't you know where Kay is? Do you think that he is dead and gone?" And the roses reply: "He isn't dead. *We have been down in the earth where the dead people are, but Kay is not there*" (emphasis mine).

At this point we must once again interrupt and ask, Who is this old woman in her flower garden?

Well, to begin with, since she manages to have all flowers on earth in bloom in her garden all at the same time, she must certainly have a magical way with vegetation. She must, in fact, be a goddess of vegetation, somewhat like Ceres, or Flora. Or again, considering that the only place where all the flowers on earth are in bloom is the earth herself, we may as well call her Mother Earth, she who makes everything grow that grows out of the black earth, she who receives everything back that decays and becomes black earth once again. No wonder, then, that she can make the flowers grow and vanish at her will!

But she is more than that. Upon returning in response to Gerda's tears, the roses say that they have been in the realm of the dead. And since it was the old woman who sent them there—sent them there intact, so that they can reemerge intact—we suspect that she must be ruling down there too. Like all the great Earth Goddesses, she must number among her functions also that of the Goddess of Death.

In fact, she tipped us off to that effect as soon as Gerda asked after Kay. The old woman said: "*He has not yet come by, but he might be along any day now*" (emphasis mine). She was saying that he is not dead yet, but that of course he will be some day, and then he will be here with me. And indeed the only "place" we all eventually visit, no matter how far removed and out of the way it may seem, is the realm of death.

And further: death, like any deep sleep, is the realm of oblivion. Gerda does not drink of the waters of Lethe; she merely eats the cherries of the old woman who combs her hair with a golden comb. As she does so, she forgets what alone really matters to her—her love for Kay.

Yes, there can be no question: the Old Woman Skilled in Magic, whose daytime realm is as full of organic flowers as the realm of the Snow Queen is full of crystalline flowers, she is the goddess of organic death, just as the Snow Queen is the goddess of crystalline death.[1]

And this raises the further question: what is Gerda doing there? Like Kay, she resides in the realm of death, but she is not altogether dead. The similarity of their conditions can be further defined in that each of them is specifically dead to human relationships, to emotional interactions—as attested to in the case of Gerda by that fact that, once she has shed her red shoes, she no longer notices any people.

What is she then if she is not dead and yet not alive to the existence of others?

She is, in the realm of the flower-goddess, herself a flower. We know this because in this phase of her life—and at no other—she can talk to flowers, and they can talk to her. We know this because ever since her flaxen hair was combed with the golden comb she has forgotten everybody else and can think only of herself. As we shall see immediately, this is true of all the other flowers.

For in her renewed search for Kay, Gerda now asks one flower after the other whether they have seen him and can help her find him. Each flower, without any regard to the specific content of her question, merely answers by giving *its own story*. In fact, the flowers simply have no other story to tell but their own.[2]

What are these stories and what, if anything, do they have in common?

The tiger lily dreams of a Hindu woman about to be

burned on her husband's funeral pyre, while her lover looks on—"he whose fiery glances have pierced her heart more deeply than these flames that soon will burn her body to ashes." The trumpet flower tells of a beautiful maiden peering from the balustrade of an ancient castle in expectation of her love: "'Will he never come?'" she sighs. The snowdrops tell of a swing hung between two trees. On it, two pretty girls with frocks as white as snow are swinging; behind them on the swing stands their brother, holding on to the ropes and blowing soap bubbles: "A swinging board pictured in a bubble before it broke—that is my story." "It may be a very pretty story," says Gerda, "but you told it very sadly."

The hyacinths tell of three sisters, "quite transparent and very fair." They danced in the moonlight beside a calm lake: "The air was sweet, and the sisters disappeared into the forest. The fragrance of the air grew sweeter. Three coffins, in which lie the three sisters, glide out of the forest and across the lake. The fireflies hover about them like little flickering lights. Are the dancing sisters sleeping or are they dead? The fragrance of the flowers says they are dead, and the evening bell tolls for their funeral." The buttercups tell of an old grandmother and her granddaughter, "a poor but very pretty maid-servant, just home for a visit," sitting quietly in the first spring sunshine.

> What did the narcissus say?
> "I can see myself! I can see myself! Oh, how sweet is my own fragrance! Up in the narrow garret there is a little dancer, half dressed. First she stands on one leg. Then she stands on both, and kicks her heels at the whole world. . . . She pours water from the teapot over . . . her bodice. Cleanliness is such a virtue! Her white dress hangs from a hook. It too has been washed. . . ."
> "I'm not interested," said Gerda. "What a thing to tell me about!"

Indeed these stories are not interesting. They are overly romantic and sticky; they are kitsch. Some extol and exaggerate the "purity" and the "pure joys" of childhood—the color white is very much in evidence. Others talk of love in an overly sweet, unrealistic manner. They are full of weltschmerz and totally lacking in fulfillment. The narcissus is, appropriately, altogether narcissistic. All this seems like dime-store fiction or true confessions stuff for pulp magazines; we would be tempted to say it is unworthy of Andersen.

But we would be wrong. These are exactly the kinds of dreams and stories best suited to the needs and fears of adolescent girls who are so often bewildered by their own budding sexuality and afraid of the world. Unready to risk any real encounters, they seek refuge in risk-free dreams of romance. It is, after all, for them and for women who never transcend this stage that "true romances" are written.[3]

The flower, then, symbolizes self-involvement. And the flower stage ("les jeunes filles en fleur"), the stage of development that follows upon the awakening of puberty, constitutes a moratorium for the girl. In this regard it is quite analogous to the intellectuality moratorium of the boy.[4] And so it makes perfectly good sense that Gerda, having kicked off the red shoes (sexuality), should now overreact—as many girls do after their first brush with sex—and should withdraw to the safety of self-absorbed, narcissistic isolation.[5]

There is a certain danger that she might stay there. Being dead to her own sexual-procreative capabilities (these flowers never stop flowering and therefore never set seed, never bear fruit), she is also oblivious of time. She is as if asleep—quite as the Sleeping Beauty who, after she pricked her finger and bled for the first time, fell into a sleep that was to last a hundred years—until the right prince should come and wake her. But Gerda, luckily, already has a "prince." Once reminded of him, she "wakens" from her "sleep" and once again experiences a yearning for Kay. She finds self-absorption no longer interesting or satisfying. Being the resolute girl she is, she runs out of the garden and into the world of reality.

It is a bitter world. She had left home in the spring, but now summer has passed and it is "late in the fall." "Gracious, how long I have dallied!" she exclaims, "I can rest no longer." And indeed, from now on she will be restlessly driven, as our instincts and our needs do drive us. Reality is grim: everything is cold and bleak. Being barefoot, she is soon so tired and footsore! "Oh, how dreary and gray the wide world looked. . . . Only the blackthorn still bore fruit, and its fruit was so sour that it set your teeth on edge."

Poor Gerda. But she is to be helped, and in an unexpected way.

7

The Prince and the Princess

The next time Gerda is forced to rest, a crow comes hopping across the snow in front of her. Feeling kindly inclined toward the little girl, the crow asks her what she is doing in the great, wide world all alone. Gerda tells him her story and asks if he hasn't seen Kay. The crow nods gravely and caws: "Maybe I have, maybe I have!" Gerda, of course, is excited and wants to know more; the crow explains that he may have seen little Kay, but if it really was he, then he is now living with a princess and has surely forgotten Gerda. This calls for further explanations, and the crow wonders whether he cannot continue in crow talk, because he has difficulty with Gerda's language.

"I don't know [crow] language," said Gerda. "My grandmother knows it, just as well as she knows baby talk, and I do wish I had learned it."

The crow, as best he can, now tells the following story:

In the kingdom where they now are, there is a princess who is uncommonly clever—so clever she has read all the newspapers in the world and forgotten them again. One day she was sitting on her throne and humming a tune with the refrain: "Why, oh why, shouldn't I get married?" "That's an idea," she said, and she made up her mind to marry as soon as she could find the sort of husband who could give a good answer when anyone spoke to him, instead of just standing around looking impressive, "for that is so tiresome." So she had it announced in the newspapers that any presentable young man might go to the palace and talk to her. The one who spoke best, and who seemed most at home in the palace, would be chosen by the princess as her husband. Men flocked to the palace. Out in the street they were all glib talkers, but after they entered the palace where the guards were stationed in their silver-braided uniforms, and after they climbed the staircase lined with footmen in gold-embroidered livery, they arrived in the brilliantly lighted reception halls without a word to say. And when they stood in front of the princess on her throne, the best they could do was to echo the last words of her remarks, and she didn't care to hear them repeated.

On the third day a little person strode boldly up to the palace. His eyes sparkled and he had handsome long hair, but his clothes were poor. ("Oh, that was Kay," says Gerda. "Now I've found him!") On the staircase he was not taken aback by the footmen, but said to them: "It must be very tiresome to stand on the stairs. I'd rather go inside." His boots creaked dreadfully, but he did not care, and he walked straight to the princess, who was sitting on a pearl as big as a spinning wheel. To her he spoke as well as can be. He said he was not there to court the princess but to hear her wisdom. "This he liked, and she liked him."

Gerda is now sure that this was Kay, and she asks to be taken to him. That is not so simple, and the crow flies off to consult with his lady-love, who is tame and has the run of the palace. Upon his return, he announces that a way has been found. They can secretly go up the back stairs that lead to the princess's bedroom! Off they go to the palace, but before we follow them we should interrupt again and ask: What is the significance of the crow, and who is the princess?

The importance of the crow is that he can talk—he can talk to Gerda both in crow language and in her own. If Gerda were as wise as her old grandmother, she too could do what the old woman can do—namely, speak crow language and baby language. She would, in other words, be able to understand both nonverbal and preverbal language, the language of nature and natural processes, the language of instincts and drives, and therefore, perhaps, even the language of her own instincts. Animals had talked to her before, or had tried to. When she set out in her red shoes to find Kay, the swallows were reassuring her that he was not dead; and when she drifted down the stream, the sparrows tried to console her. During her narcissistic moratorium, when she was a self-satisfied, uninvolved flower, only flowers talked to her. But now she is once again in touch with her animal instincts and drives, and they, of course, once again put her on the trail of Kay.

Her grandmother would have understood the crow. Quite generally, in myth, religion, and fairy tale, such understanding, such wise attunement to the forces of nature, to animals and instincts and life processes of all sorts is attributed to women and constitutes their particular wisdom. Only rarely can a grown man speak to animals; if he does, he must possess an extraordinary degree of naïve, childlike purity and saintliness—as did St. Francis of Assisi—or a hard-won, magical intimacy with nature such as that of Castañeda's Don Juan, who can talk not only to animals but also to plants and to the very elements themselves.[1] But ordinarily such oneness with nature is, in men, thought to be lost in the process of growing up and becoming civilized—quite as the hero, Enkidu, in the Gilgamesh epic, loses communication with the wild animals as soon as the sacred prostitute has initiated him into the society of man.[2]

That the particular animal now talking to Gerda should be a crow (and it could as well be a raven, for these two animals are frequently interchangeable)[3] is not only fitting in terms of the wintry scene, but it may also constitute one of those frequent eruptions of pre-Christian lore in Andersen's superficially so Christian writings. His hometown, Odense, he tells us, was called after the heathen god, Odin, the Nordic god not only of war but also of wisdom and shamanistic magic. Odin's animals were two ravens called Thought and Memory, and like all companion animals, they are impersonations of the god himself and of all his cunning.[4] Little Gerda, having just remembered Kay and seeking ways of rejoining him, now encounters two ravens (or crows). If Andersen does not specifically tell us that their names are Memory and Thought, we could surely not think up names for them more fitting to the occasion. And lastly, that the instincts should find pre-Christian advocates would stand to reason.

So the crows are to lead Gerda to the princess and, perhaps, to Kay. And who is the princess?

She is just one impersonation, or avatar, of a figure or type exceedingly common in myth and fairy tale (and in everyday life) a type we shall call: the riddle princess.[5] By that term we designate a virgin who will not surrender her virginity except to an exceptional man, one who can prove himself a "real man" by virtue of passing some special, difficult, and usually dangerous test.

Portia, in *The Merchant of Venice*, is such a riddle princess: her suitors have to guess the right one of three caskets; in so doing they, like the suitors of the princess in our story, seem to run merely the risk of rejection—though Freud, in his essay "The Theme of the Choice of Caskets," found more ominous undertones.[6] Brunhilde, the Valkyrie, was another: she would wed only a man who could defeat her in combat—and one who could not was likely to be crushed to death by the maiden. Likewise, Sleeping Beauty was a far from innocuous lure: men who, for her sake, tried to penetrate the thicket of briars were impaled on the thorns and died miserably—until after a hundred years the right prince came along, the brambles parted of their own accord to give him easy passage, and he roused her with a kiss.[7] Andersen himself created, or recreated, the figure of a bloody riddle princess in his story *The Travelling Companion*.[8] She demanded that her suitors three times correctly guess her thoughts; if they did not, she would either hang them or chop off their heads. In her garden skeletons hung from every tree and rattled in the breeze; all the flowers were tied to human bones and human skulls grinned up from every flower pot. "What a charming garden for a princess!"[9] Other riddle princesses include the countless maidens who are guarded by a dragon, so that the hero who would save (and wed) them must risk life and limb to slay the beast. What does it all mean?

Over and over again this is the predicament of the virgin who wants to emerge from the flower stage and to become a woman: she needs a man strong enough, courageous enough to overcome her own ferocious resistance and to help her conquer her fear of her own sexuality.

In mythology the dragon may have a variety of meanings; the dragon guarding the maiden may, for instance, signify the wicked father who refuses to relinquish his hold over his daughter. But the dragon may also denote her own fierceness or shrewishness which, as in Shakespeare's play, badly needs taming.[10]

In fact the demands of the riddle princess are well justified in both biological and psychological terms: a man fit to become a husband and father should be strong and clever; he should have proven himself against other men, against nature, and against his own fears and terrors before a maiden may securely entrust herself and her eventual children to him. And if she is to trust him to be strong, he must at the very least be stronger than she, and must have proven it.

The princess in Andersen's story sets a mild test indeed: her suitor must merely be able to talk to her without being overawed. She does not, like the Sphinx, kill the man who fails; she merely exposes him to the ridicule of failure—but that alone would be enough to discourage many a man.

It does not discourage the young lad in his creaky boots. Once again the shoes are indicative of character: both the boy and his shoes are tough and strong and unafraid to creak—to arouse ridicule—anywhere. Hans Christian once wore such boots; they were his first pair of boots and he wore them for his confirmation. He wrote of them: "My delight was extremely great; my only fear was that not everybody would see them. . . . The boots creaked, and that inwardly pleased me . . . my whole devotion was disturbed . . . it caused me a horrible pang of conscience that my thoughts should be as much with my new boots as with God" (*TS*, 30). There are obvious echoes here of *The Red Shoes*, and indeed the "creaky boots" could be the boy's equivalent to the girl's red shoes, could be symbolic of *his* emergence into assertive sexuality. They did not manage to symbolize quite that much for Hans Christian; his considerable assertiveness never became sexual. But as to the boy in our story—how did he fare?

He walked straight to the princess "who was sitting on a pearl as big as a spinning wheel." She was thus sitting on a priceless jewel. Having already seen that accessories (such as shoes or ravens) symbolize character and personality, we have no difficulty interpreting the pearl here both *in parte* and *pro toto:* it is her own "jewel" the princess is sitting on, and again: she herself is the jewel, the priceless pearl the young man wishes to win.

But does he win her? Does he marry the princess as, according to the conditions she proclaimed and in line with all precedent, he would have every right to? Let us go with Gerda and find out:

That evening the two crows take Gerda up the little back staircase that leads to the bedroom. Gerda's heart beats with fear and longing—"it was just as if she were about to do something wrong." She also becomes anxious about "someone on the stairs behind us." Clearly, she feels tense and guilty about intruding upon an intimate scene, the prince and the princess in bed, and she is afraid of getting caught. But what is behind her and rushes past her up the walls are only dreams come to visit the royal couple, and they are hardly of an erotic nature: "from their shadows on the wall they seemed to be horses with spindly legs and waving manes. And there were shadows of huntsmen, ladies and gentleman, on horseback." And the crow explains: "They come to take the thoughts of their royal masters off to the chase."

When they enter the bedroom, the chaste nature of the "arrangement" is confirmed. (Just what the "arrangement" is, Andersen never makes explicit: no marriage is mentioned, and the prince is still referred to by that title—he has not become king as, upon marriage with the princess and in traditional fairy tale style, he would naturally become.) "In the middle of the room two beds hung from a massive stem of gold. Each of them looked like a lily. One bed was white,

and there lay the princess. The other was red, and there
Gerda hoped to find little Kay." She calls him, he awakens
and—it is not Kay at all, only a young man resembling him.
The princess also awakens and asks what is happening.
Gerda tells her story. She is kindly received and the prince,
for the remainder of the night, gives up his bed so that she
may sleep in it. The next day Gerda is dressed in silk and
velvet from head to heels and invited to stay at the palace
indefinitely.

The separate beds, shaped like lilies, and the fact that
the bed of the princess was—still—white indicate that she
is still a virgin. Is she then one of the "virgins" in the old,
matriarchal sense—that is, a woman who remains sover-
eign over all men, who "gives herself" never more than
sexually, who never commits herself and never "belongs"
to anyone, and whose husband remains, at best, a consort?[11] Or, more likely, is she—despite the boy's assertively
creaking boots and sexual interest (as symbolized by his
red bed)—herself still and in every sense *virgo intacta* and
the marriage unconsummated?

However that may be, the invitation to Gerda to stay at
the palace is equivalent to the previous invitation that she
stay in the Garden of the Old Woman Skilled in Magic. It is
an invitation to remain under the sign and the spell that
rules there. Having passed through the flower phase, having awakened from the sleep of the Sleeping Beauty, Gerda
is now encouraged to let herself be arrested at the next
phase, that of the riddle princess who yearns for but fears
womanhood and who therefore sets impossible tasks and
obstacles for the men who woo her. This too constitutes a
delay and a hesitation—a moratorium in which many a
maiden has remained well beyond the fading of her charms,
and beyond all hope.

But Gerda declines to stay. She merely asks for assistance
in finding Kay. And so the generous princely couple give
her a pair of boots and a muff and a brand new carriage of
pure gold. They wish her Godspeed, and off she goes again
in quest of her Kay.

8

The Little Robber Girl

Gerda is immediately waylaid. Robbers are dazzled by her splendid coach and seize it. Oddly, it appears that they are led by an Old Robber Woman! She is a real hag, with a bristly beard and long eyebrows that hang down over her eyes. She appraises Gerda: "She looks like a fat little lamb. What a dainty dish she will be!" As she said this, she drew out her knife, a dreadful, flashing thing. "Ouch!" the old woman howled. At just that moment her own little daughter had bitten her ear. This little girl, whom she carried on her back, was a wild and reckless creature. "She shall play with me," said the Little Robber Girl. "She must give me her muff and that pretty dress she wears, and sleep with me in my bed."

So Gerda is saved by the "little daughter" of the "old woman" (are we never to hear of *young* mothers or of *grown-up* daughters?), and they ride back to the robbers' lair in the golden carriage. The robber girl, stronger and much broader in the shoulders than Gerda, has tanned skin and coal-black eyes "almost sad in their expression." She puts her arm around Gerda and says, "They shan't kill you unless I get angry with you." Gerda tells her story, and the robber girl, apparently moved, responds, "Even if I should get angry with you they shan't kill you, because I'll do it myself!" Then she dries Gerda's tears and sticks her own hands into Gerda's soft, warm muff.

The carriage stops at last in the robbers' castle:

> The walls of it were cracked from bottom to top. Crows and ravens flew out of every loop hole, and bulldogs, huge enough to devour a man, jumped high in the air. But they did not bark, for that was forbidden.

In the middle of the smoky old hall a big fire was burning. . . . Soup was boiling in a big caldron, and hares and
rabbits were roasting on the spit.
   "Tonight you shall sleep with me and all my little animals," the robber girl said . . . they went over to a corner
that was strewn with rags and straw. On sticks and perches
around the bedding roosted nearly a hundred pigeons. . . .
"They are all mine," said the little robber girl. She seized the
one that was nearest to her, held it by the legs and shook it
until it flapped its wings. "Kiss it," she cried, and thrust the
bird in Gerda's face.

She then introduces her tethered reindeer:

"And here is my old sweetheart, Bae. . . . We have to keep a
sharp eye on him, or he would run away. . . . Every single
night I tickle his neck with my knife blade, for he is afraid of
that." . . . she pulled out a long knife, and rubbed it against
the reindeer's neck. After the poor animal had kicked up its
heels, the robber girl laughed and pulled Gerda down into
the bed with her.
   "Are you going to keep that knife in bed with you?"
Gerda asked, and looked a bit frightened.
   "I always sleep with my knife," the little robber girl said.
"You never can tell what may happen."

In spite of her fierceness the Little Robber Girl is good to
Gerda and listens to her story. After the robber girl has
fallen asleep—clasping one arm around Gerda's neck and
snoring loudly—Gerda cannot close her eyes, for she does
not know whether she is to live or die. "The robbers sat
around their fire, singing and drinking, and the old woman
was turning somersaults. It was a terrible sight for a little
girl to see."
   But just then two wild wood pigeons from high up the
wall talk to Gerda and tell her they have seen Kay flying
along in the sleigh of the Snow Queen, probably bound for
Lapland. The reindeer confirms that this is where the Queen
has her summer tent. Gerda gasps with excitement, but the
Little Robber Girl grumbles at her, "Lie still or I'll stick my
knife in your stomach."
   In the morning Gerda tells the Little Robber Girl all that

the wood pigeons have said. The robber girl is thoughtful and sympathetic: "Leave it to me!"

The first problem is to escape the old woman:

> "Listen!" the robber girl said to Gerda. "As you see, all the men are away. Mother is still here, and here she'll stay, but before the morning is over she will drink out of that big bottle, and then she usually dozes off for a nap. As soon as this happens, I will do you a good turn." She jumped out of bed, rushed over and threw her arms around her mother's neck, pulled at her beard bristles, and said: "Good morning, my dear nanny-goat."

As soon as the mother is asleep, the Little Robber Girl instructs the reindeer to carry Gerda to Lapland, where, after all, he is at home. She decides to keep Gerda's muff but returns her fur boots and gives her a pair of mother's mittens and some food. Gerda starts to cry with happiness, but the Little Robber Girl has no use for tears: "I don't care to see you blubbering," she says. Gerda is tied to the reindeer's back, the robber girl cuts the tether, and the reindeer bounds away "over stumps and stones, straight through the great forest, over swamps and across the plains, as fast as he could run." They see streaks of light in the heavens and the reindeer informs Gerda: "These are my old Northern Lights—see how they flash!" And on he runs, faster than ever, by night and day, until they arrive in Lapland.

And again we must ask, what is this all about?

The Old Robber Woman is, of course, a regular old witch. She eats little children, just like the witch in Hansel and Gretel, and just like all the other ugly old witches in all mythologies and at all times.[1] The cults of the great Mother Goddesses always included child sacrifice; and the goddesses of suppressed religions became witches just as the gods became demons and evil spirits of wild places. The child killed and sacrificed to propitiate the goddess becomes the child cooked and eaten to satisfy the cravings of the witch.

Nor are the cooking utensils lacking. The old woman has soup boiling in a big caldron. The caldron is the very emblem and recognition sign of witchery, so that no witch is thinkable without it, whether it be in *Macbeth* or in Goethe's *Faust*. But it too, like the witch herself, has undergone a sad deterioration. It was at first, and very long ago, a venerable implement of the Great Goddess as *alma mater*, as the one who suckles and feeds her children (all of creation) and from whose ever-full breasts no company parts ungrateful.[2] The caldron was then a container, a vessel of plenty, full of nourishment and life. As such it was symbolic of the goddess, who was in herself the vessel of new life. Her breasts contained the milk of life and her womb contained, nourished by her blood, the renewal of life. The Great Mother as vessel has fallen on evil times: not only are her breasts now sagging and empty, but even her caldron has become questionable. It may still be cooking meat—but perhaps the meat of babes—or it may be bubbling with poisonous potions. No longer evidence of her bountiful nature, it has become emblem of her destructiveness. As a witch, she is on the out, she is antiestablishment, and whatever she "cooks up" must be done surreptitiously, silently; even the bulldogs, fierce, passionate beasts (fierce passions) that they are, must not bark, must rage silently.

Something seems still to be lacking. But on closer inspection we find that Andersen, with unobtrusive artistry, has in fact supplied the missing pieces: The Little Robber Girl addresses her mother as "my dear nanny-goat." We are instantly reminded of the importance of the goat in the folklore of witchery as the familiar spirit and the mode of transport for the witch on her ride to the Witches' Sabbath, and of the billy goat who presides there and who is none other than Satan himself. Again, the goat—like the ibex, the bull, or the stallion—was once honorable companion to the Goddess, symbolic of male potency in the service of her abundant fertility. By the time of Greek antiquity, the goat-aspect of Pan and of the Satyrs already carried the stigma of single-minded sexual preoccupation and excess. In the Middle Ages, Satan had a goat's hoof, and at the Sabbath he ruled over an orgy of passionate sexual perversion, of sex without the promise—or danger—of procreation.[3]

Finally, should not a witch be able to fly? If Andersen intended to draw a witch, could he omit something as important as that? Well, he did not quite omit it. While reveling around the campfire, the Old Robber Woman "was turning somersaults." That isn't exactly flying, but for an old woman, and a bearded one at that, it constitutes quite a remarkable and unnatural act of levitation and one that may well have been "a terrible sight for a little girl to see."

No, there is nothing lacking; the picture is complete and reminiscent of nothing so much as Goya's *Caprichos* or paintings of Witches' Sabbaths: the grotesque, the uncanny, the shocking, and the repulsive: they are all here, and drawn with an economy of means and lightness of touch that compel our admiration.

But if the Old Robber Woman is a witch, then what is the Little Robber Girl? She must, of course, be a witch also—the alter ego of the Old Woman, her reincarnation, or her youthful avatar. As a young witch, she would most appropriately be concerned with the magic of youth—with love potions, philters, and illicit seduction. But the Little Robber Girl also carries some traits that are older by far than such medieval pettiness. She is strongly reminiscent of another type of the Great Goddesses—namely, the "Lady of the Wild Things," the virgin goddess as huntress but also as protectress and intimate of all wild animals.[4] Of these, the most famous was Artemis (Diana), who roved the hills with her band of maidens and her hunting dogs. No man could approach them without being torn to bits.

And so, quite as the Old Woman of the Garden was, like Ceres, an embodiment of nature as vegetation, so the Little Robber Girl is an embodiment of animal spirits and of animal life. Like many of the goddesses of old (and like her mother, the old witch), she can get along without a man.

But not without sex. Not for nothing does she live in a setting of silent passions, goat-presided lechery, and perverse appetites. Her intimacies with Gerda are impetuously sensual and physical, and she constantly embraces and holds her, taking advantage of her own stronger (we are

tempted to say "butch") physique. Her insistence on sticking her hands into Gerda's "soft, warm muff" (which
pleases her so much she decides to keep it) and her threat to
"stick my knife in your stomach" are sexually symbolic in a
manner that must have been fairly transparent even in Andersen's repressed age. She is alternatingly cruel and kind,
and openly derives pleasure from teasing in a frightening
and sometimes painful manner. Furthermore, just as her
mother has a man's "long, bristly beard and long eyebrows"
and thus is not purely feminine, so the Little Robber Girl
exhibits an organizational talent, efficiency, and resolve (in
the way she dispatches Gerda to Lapland) as well as an
intolerance to gentler emotions (in her contempt for Gerda's
"blubbering") that give her too a somewhat masculine cast.[5]

And so, in the light of what we said in preceding chapters,
the Little Robber Girl represents another possible defensive
stage for Gerda. Here too she could have taken refuge from
anxieties about eventual heterosexual involvement, but this
time by means of a detour into homosexuality.

This, then, would be the stage of the adolescent crush—of
a girl's seduction by or infatuation with her girlfriends or
older women. After the flower stage of narcissistic isolation,
followed by the tentative reaching out of the riddle stage
with its hiding behind all kinds of tests and demands for
proof and its thorny arbitrariness, the temporary or perhaps
permanent escape into a homosexual orientation represents,
as it were, a recoil from an evidently still too frightening
heterosexual encounter.

Again, Gerda could remain stuck here. But again she does
not, for her single-minded search for Kay pulls her through;
and once more she receives guidance from talking animals—
from her own eloquent animal instincts.

This time it is the wild wood pigeons—the doves, the
lovebirds who have always been sacred to and heraldic of
the Love Goddess herself, Aphrodite (Venus)—who remind
Gerda of her purpose and give her direction. How could
anything be more appropriate?

So the little witch fails in her own particular love magic,

and Gerda continues her quest—this time mounted on a talking reindeer. We are reminded here of Freud's metaphor of the ego and the id as a rider and horse. The reindeer, streaking north toward Lapland because it knows where Lapland is, this reindeer that carries Gerda in headlong flight without her having to direct it—it is, like the other talking animals, once again representative of the instincts and the drives, of the emotions by which we are "carried away" and that have their own purpose of which reason knows not—"le coeur a ses raisons que la raison ne connait pas." And Gerda—finally—has the courage to entrust herself to her emotions, wherever they may carry her. She is, in this regard, the opposite of Kay, who trusts only reason, measurement, and conscious intellect. On the other hand, let us note that Gerda is riding a gentle reindeer, not a lustful billy goat. She is not a witch, and though her ride is fast and headlong, she does not fly through the air. A distinction is made here between unbridled, unholy lust on the one hand and the "healthy," God-given longing for love and fulfillment that has its legitimate place in the natural order of things—or so one would tend to think. As we shall see, Andersen has his reservations even about that.

9

The Lapp Woman and
the Finn Woman

Gerda's ride, the drive of her emotions, takes her toward
Kay, but with two intermediate stops.

It is not clear—at least to me—what function these stops
are to serve. But we are introduced to two more old women,
both grotesque and ugly, both equipped with a caldron, and
both helpful. Clearly they are friendly witches, shamanistic
characters of the tundra, "wise women" of the type who, as
we have seen, had played such an important role in Hans
Christian's life.

The Lapp Woman, encountered first, lives in a little hut:
"The roof of it almost touched the ground, and the doorway
was so low that the family had to lie on their stomachs to
crawl in or out of it." In this womblike dwelling the Lapp
Woman offers Gerda food and rest, and upon hearing her
story from the reindeer, writes a message on a dried codfish
for Gerda to take to the Finn Woman who "lives up there in
the Finmark, where the Snow Queen is taking a country
vacation."

After Gerda has rested, she is tied back onto the reindeer,
and

off he ran . . . all night long. . . . At last, they came to the
Finmark, and knocked at the Finn woman's chimney, for she
hadn't a sign of a door. It was so hot inside that the Finn
woman went about almost naked. She was small and terribly
dowdy, but she at once helped little Gerda off with her mittens and boots, and loosened her clothes. Otherwise, the
heat would have wilted her. Then the woman put a piece of
ice on the reindeer's head, and read what was written on the
codfish. She read it three times, and when she knew it by

heart, she put the fish into the kettle of soup, for they might as well eat it. She never wasted anything.

The reindeer now implores her to help Gerda with her magic:

> "You are such a wise woman," said the reindeer, "I know that you can tie all the winds of the world together with a bit of cotton thread. If the sailor unties one knot he gets a favorable wind. If he unties another he gets a stiff gale, while if he unties the third and fourth knots such a tempest rages that it flattens the trees in the forest. Won't you give this little girl something to drink that will make her as strong as twelve men, so that she may overpower the Snow Queen?"
>
> "Twelve strong men," the Finn woman sniffed. "Much good that would be."

And she goes on to explain:

> "No power that I could give her would be as great as that which she already has. Don't you see how man and beasts are compelled to serve her, and how far she has come in the wide world since she started out in her naked feet? We mustn't tell her about this power. Strength lies in her heart, because she is such a sweet, innocent child."

She now instructs the reindeer to carry Gerda toward the garden of the Snow Queen, but to part company with her at a bush covered with red berries and to return promptly. Gerda is again lifted onto the reindeer and departs in such a hurry that she forgets her boots and mittens, and so, as the reindeer deposits her at the berry bush according to his instructions and takes tearful farewell of her, she is left barefoot and barehanded in the middle of icy Finmark.

She runs ahead as fast as she can. A regiment of snowflakes swirls toward her—they are large and of monstrous shape; they are the advance guard of the Snow Queen come to attack her. Gerda says the Lord's Prayer, her breath freezes in front of her mouth and condenses into angels with helmets, shields, and lances. This heavenly legion shivers the snowflakes into a thousand pieces. Gerda walks on, "unmolested and cheerful," and as she approaches the

palace of the Snow Queen, the angels warm her hands and
feet by rubbing them.

But before we hear the impending climax of our story, let
us reflect for a moment on the Finn Woman: She is so wise
that she can tie all the winds of the earth together with a bit
of cotton thread; this is a typically shamanistic skill. Andersen was familiar with it from stories told him in his childhood. Indeed, he presents just such a figure in another
story, written in 1838 (six years before *The Snow Queen*) and
entitled *The Garden of Paradise*. Regarding this story, he said,
"This was the first of many fairy tales I heard as a child. I
was very fond of it and disappointed that it was not a longer
story."[1] That it truly was the first fairy tale he had ever
heard is doubtful; no one could make such a statement with
confidence.

His first storytellers were his father and his grandmother.
The *Garden of Paradise* story tells of the mother of the winds,
an "elderly woman, so burly and strong that she might have
been taken for a man in disguise," who lives in a cave. She
is about as gentle as the Old Robber Woman, and to a visiting prince she explains why:

> "I have to be harsh to control those sons of mine [the four
> winds]. I manage to do it, for all that they are an obstinate
> lot. See the four sacks that hang there on the wall! They
> dread those as much as you used to dread the switch that
> was kept behind the mirror for you. I can fold the boys right
> up, let me tell you, and pop them straight into the bag. We
> don't mince matters. There they stay. They aren't allowed to
> roam around again until I see fit to let them."

This is not the kind of story his father, with his progressive
and literary mind, was likely to have told. So it would have
been his grandmother, or perhaps one of the old women at
the asylum. And indeed, the "almost naked" Finn Woman
evokes echoes of the asylum and recalls the "almost naked"
lady who scared Hans Christian so that "even in later years
that sight and that feeling remained within my soul."

And yet the Finn Woman, while frightening in power and
appearance, is friendly and helpful; she is an ambiguous

and ambivalent figure like all possessors of magic power, and she must represent the projection of an ambivalence about women from within Andersen's own feelings—a topic we shall have to return to.

As to her view of men, she clearly does not think much of them; when the reindeer asks her for a drink that would give Gerda the strength of twelve men, she scoffs: "Much good that would be!"

Her contempt is the typical contempt of the goddesses—and of all women—for the mere physical strength of men, a strength that can move rocks and sometimes mountains but not hearts, a strength without magic. No twelve men, explains the Finn Woman, could get the splinters out of Kay's eye and heart. But Gerda, the little girl, already has in her own little person all the strength she will need: "Don't you see how men and beasts are compelled to serve her, and how far she has come in the wide world since she started out in her naked feet? Strength lies in her heart." We cannot help, at that, to be reminded of Hans Christian himself. We have already seen some evidence of his ability to "compel men to serve him," and we know that he "started out into the wide world"—well, not literally but almost—barefoot. We shall hear shortly to what an astounding degree his "pure heart" enabled him to compel men (and women) to serve him all his life. And we may take this as a first inkling that in our story Gerda—or at least Gerda *also*—represents Andersen himself.

But to stay, for the moment, within our story. It would indeed seem that Gerda, through her love for Kay, already has all the strength needed to reach him, to reach his heart, to pull him out of his isolation. But again—as in the case of the princess who did not really marry the "bold little person" even though he passed her test—Andersen introduces a little twist that blunts and distorts his own wisdom and bowdlerizes his own story. The reindeer—Gerda's instincts—is not permitted to take Gerda all the way. Though driven (and carried) by animal instincts, she is not to prevail by carnal love; at the critical moment the flesh deserts her, and it is her innocence and her religious devotion that carry her through.

Nothing, indeed, could save a person venturing into the Arctic without boots and mittens—nothing except a miracle; and this, apparently, Gerda confidently expects. Having left her shoes behind and her gloves (the Danish word for gloves, *Handske*, means hand-shoes), she has left her ego behind altogether. Not just the red shoes, but all shoes are now gone. She goes into the Arctic as the Church Fathers went into the desert, stripped of all ego, of all self, naked and humble before God, placing their lives and their souls in God's hand in blind and unquestioning faith. Such is the degree of devotion required of Gerda. To save Kay she must be nothing less than a saint or, in Andersen's peculiar idiom, she must be an innocent child.

10

What Happened in
the Snow Queen's Palace
and What Came of It

We now return to Kay and find him sitting in the wind-swept, glacial halls of the Snow Queen's palace that is lit by brilliant northern lights. In the middle of the vast, empty hall of snow is a frozen lake cracked into a thousand pieces, all shaped alike. The Snow Queen, when home, sits in the exact center of this lake and calls it her "Mirror of Reason." It is the only one of its kind and, she thinks, the best thing in all the world. Kay, almost black with cold but unfeeling, also sits there and is deeply engaged in a "game of ice-cold reason."[1] The Snow Queen has challenged him to arrange the fragments of ice in such a manner that they spell the word *Eternity*. "If you can puzzle that out you shall be your own master, and I'll give you the whole world and a new pair of skates." Kay manages to spell all sorts of words, but *Eternity* eludes him.

What is he really trying to do?

Again, as at the beginning, Andersen's story describes a mirror that is in pieces. The first mirror belonged to the Devil, and was the mirror of criticism; this mirror belongs to the Snow Queen; it is the Mirror of Reason and, according to her, the most precious thing in the world.[2] But this time we are not told of the careless shattering and the dispersal of the fragments; we hear of the task of putting the fragments back together—a more difficult chore by far. From the re-assembly (the at-one-ment) of the fragments something good is to come, provided only that the fragments can be assembled into the word *Eternity*. But when we look at the promised reward, we realize immediately that the expected "good" is a good only in the sense of the Snow Queen (or the Devil). What she promises him—that he shall be his own master and own the whole world and a pair of skates—has a familiar ring, evokes a sinister precedent: "Again, the Devil taketh him up into an exceeding high mountain, and sheweth him all the kingdoms of the world, and the glory of them; and saith unto him, 'All these things will I give thee, if thou wilt fall down and worship me.' Then saith Jesus unto him, 'Get thee hence, Satan: for it is written, Thou shalt worship the Lord, thy God, and him only shalt thou serve'" (Matt. 4:8–10).

Kay is not serving God—he has long forgotten his prayers—he is serving another master: Reason. For it is now clear that the Snow Queen, who sits enthroned on the Mirror of Reason, is Reason herself, and insofar as Reason is critical discernment and criticism and schism, she is the Devil. Reason is the death of Faith and of childhood. Attaining the "age of reason," Andersen tells us, Kay has suffered not only the death of his childhood feelings of love—of charity—but also the death of hope and of faith. We are reminded of Paul: "When I was a child, I spake as a child. I understood as a child, I thought as a child; but when I became a man, I put away childish things. For now we see through a glass, darkly; but then face to face: now I know in part; but then shall I know even as also I am known. And now abideth faith, hope, charity, these three; but the greatest of these is charity" (1 Cor. 13:11–13).

To speak, understand, and think as a child—this is, to Andersen, the blessed state. As we grow to manhood, our world and our knowledge splinter, and we "know in part," we see "through a glass darkly"—or into a broken mirror. We risk losing "these three: faith, hope, and charity." Kay has lost them. Instead he has already, in a sense, mastered "all the kingdoms of the world," since he knows their size and population. He is now to become his own master (inde-

pendent of others and master of his own emotions, the agonized wish of every adolescent) and master of the world, if
only he can spell the word *Eternity*.

Why *Eternity?* Read, in place of it, *Immortality*—which,
after all, is much the same—and you have the chief preoccupation of mankind throughout the ages.

Of mankind, but not of womankind. Woman, by virtue of
her ability to give birth, and to nurture, and to nurse, and to
make grow—by virtue of her attunement to the vital and
organic processes of nature altogether, has also always understood and lived with the fact of death. In the eons of
matriarchal religion and world view, the cycles of the sea-
sons and of the generations—the cycle of life and death—
was the accepted scheme of things. "Eternity" was precisely
the certainty of the eternal return, the infinite back-and-forth
between day and night, between summer and winter, between the season above the black earth and the season below. "Immortality" was the immortality of the race, the self-
evident fact that men and women are born, and beget, and
die, and are born, and beget, and die, for ever and ever—a
turning of the wheel of creation in which no individual matters more than another, or is distinguishable from another.[3]
There were roles, functions, and ritualized fates to follow
and to submit to (as Thomas Mann so beautifully describes
in his *Joseph and His Brothers*), but there was no individual
who could say, "I am my own master, my own unique
self—I was never before and I will never be again."

It was man, precisely because of his peripheral and almost dispensable role in the schemes of nature, who needed
to become conscious of himself as a unique individual. Having understood his uniqueness, he could not bear to relinquish it and demanded to live forever, saying: "I was *not*
always; but *I am now* and *I want to be* for all eternity."

It was man who, in his arrogance, over and over again
insisted that the world started with him, that with *his* birth
something truly and epochally new had begun.[4] And it was
a man-god; it was, in our context, Christ Himself who came
and said: "Whoso eateth my flesh, and drinketh my blood,

hath eternal life" (John 6:54). Eternity in the Christian sense
is to be the immortality, the eventual resurrection and salvation of the soul and of the body through communion in
Jesus Christ.

But Kay is seeking immortality through the intellect. He is
looking for the Stone of the Wise like some medieval al-
chemist; he wishes to understand *rerum natura* like a philosopher of old or like Goethe's Faust. Or he hopes to
achieve the *non omnis moriar* of the writer who leaves a book
behind, a *monumentum aere perennius*. (The very temptation
to lapse into Latin quotations that overcomes me here indicates what Kay is up to.) Through scholarship and achieve-
ment he wants to acquire the fame that will make his
name—his name out of billions of others—live forever.

In this ambition he is, of course, sinning. It is hubris for
man, based on his own strength, to try for eternity, just as it
was hubris to try to build that tower into the heavens, or to
carry that mirror up to God. It is an offense both against the
Goddess, who bestows immortality of the species only
through sexual union, and against God, who bestows immortality of the individual only through communion with Christ.
And that Kay will not succeed in his frivolous endeavor is
made clear by the frivolous offer of the Snow Queen: he shall
receive not only the world, but a pair of skates. Clearly she is
mocking his childish and futile aspirations.

But he is to be saved from her and from himself by the
undaunted faith, hope, and charity of little Gerda.

She comes walking into the frigid palace, she says her
evening prayer, and the knife-edged wind is lulled to rest.
She recognizes Kay, runs up to him, embraces him. "Kay,
dearest little Kay! I've found you at last!" He sits stiff and
cold, but she begins to cry, and her hot tears wash the
splinter out of his heart. Now he looks at her, and as she
intones the verse about the Christ Child, "Where roses
bloom so sweetly in the vale," he too bursts into tears, the
splinter is washed right out of his eye, he recognizes Gerda
and cries out, "Gerda, my sweet little Gerda, where have
you been so long? And where have I been?"

The poignancy of his outcry, of his bitter regret over youth wasted, cannot be mistaken. One is reminded of Verlaine's agonized plaint:

> Qu'as-tu fait, ô toi que voilà, pleurant sans cesse,
> Dis, qu'as-tu fait, toi que voilà, de ta jeunesse?

> (What have you done, O you here, ceaseless in tears,
> Say, what have you done, you here, with your young years?)

But now the exile is over. The "children" embrace each other and their bliss is so heavenly that the bits of ice[5] dance with them and eventually drop of their own accord into a pattern that spells out the word *Eternity:* "Gerda kissed his cheeks, and they turned pink again. She kissed his eyes, and they sparkled like hers. She kissed his hands and feet, and he became strong and well. The Snow Queen might come now whenever she pleased, for there stood the order for Kay's release, written in letters of shining ice."

Hand in hand the children stroll out of the palace, talking of grandmother and of the roses back home. They find the reindeer waiting for them at the berry bush, and he carries them back past the Finn Woman and the Lapp Woman and the Little Robber Girl into a land that is now a land of spring, green and strewn with flowers. They hear church bells ringing, see a high steeple, and realize that they are entering their hometown. They walk straight to "grandmother's house" and find everything just as they left it, but they realize that *they themselves are now grown up!*

Once again they settle under the rose bushes and grandmother reads to them from the Bible: "Except ye become as little children, ye shall not enter into the kingdom of heaven." Kay and Gerda look into each other's eyes, "and at last they understood the meaning of their old hymn":

> Where roses bloom so sweetly in the vale,
> There shall you find the Christ Child without fail.

And they sit there, "grown-up, but children still—children at heart. And it was summer, warm, glorious summer."

So it ends. And we too should be feeling at peace. We should fold our hands in our laps and nod our heads and praise the goodness of Providence. But instead, we are sorely perplexed, because, on closer inspection, this happy ending just does not add up.

To begin with: Why do the pieces of ice from the Mirror of Reason so happily order themselves into the word *Eternity* just because the "children" have found each other and are joyfully embracing?

Only one form of eternity comes from the embrace of a boy and a girl—the sexual eternity, or immortality, of the race. And at that, the boy and girl must not be too "little." We do indeed hear that Kay and Gerda, upon their arrival home, are no longer little. They are "grown-up now"— young adults who could, indeed, beget children. But this is something that, though it springs from his own imagination and logically should form the happy ending of his story, Andersen cannot face. There is no "and they were married and lived happily ever after!" at the end of this tale. Like the princess and the boy in the creaking boots, Gerda and Kay never marry.[6]

They clearly have emerged from the winter of their developmental moratorium. They are now in the spring of their life, and before we know it they have even entered their summer when blossoms should be turning to fruit: that summer of life which normally means family and children and all the warmth and vigor of parent-child interaction— but Gerda and Kay are to have none of that. They are not to be parents; they live, it would seem, in a world without parents altogether.

Not only are there no parent figures in the story—with the possible exception of the Old Robber Woman, who seems really much too old to have a daughter the age of the Little Robber Girl and who has all the appearance of a grandmother—but both Gerda and Kay demonstrate neither need nor concern for their parents at any time. It is rather striking that they do not once ask themselves how their parents may be feeling about their long absence. This sounds heartless and cruel. But if we consider their entire journey a psychological voyage, the phenomenon is a familiar one. During adolescence young people go through a phase when they become strangers, when they do not live *with* their parents but only *next to them*, and when the parents feel overlooked and forgotten. The attention of the youngsters is elsewhere, but since they are in reality still living with their parents, they have no reason to worry about them. Gerda and Kay do not miss their parents because they have never left them; they merely ignore them as if they did not exist.

But in addition to their parents they ignore—we could even say they anxiously avoid—the parental condition altogether. Instead they sit together "holding hands" most chastely. They are once again informed by their grandmother (who *has left behind* the age of sex and of childbearing) that they themselves must be as little children: that they are *never to enter* the age of sex and of childbearing. It is in this sense, at last, that they "understand the meaning of the old hymn" about the Christ Child in the vale.

At any rate, Andersen states that they so understand it. We must admit that we have difficulty following him there, and that we are not at all happy with his formulation.[7] We do not understand why the story has to end this way, and we wonder whether Andersen knew and understood his own reasons. We are tempted to raise the question: did Andersen's world, the world in which he himself lived, perhaps also consist only of children and grandparents?

For an answer we must again look at his life and how he fared after he had left Odense and set out, all by himself, to conquer Copenhagen and the world.

The Fairy Tale of Andersen's Life

He arrived in Copenhagen "on Monday morning, September 5th, 1819." It sounds like a birthday and, to him, it was.[1] Here, finally, he was setting foot in the world for which he was born, and he lost no time about it. Having rented a room in a small public house, he immediately sought the theater. A ticket-seller offered him a ticket, and he "accepted his offer with thankfulness" in the childlike and devoutly matter-of-course expectation that he was being given a present. When the scalper angrily disillusioned him, he fled in confusion.

But he rallied quickly. The next day he dressed in his confirmation suit ("nor were the boots forgotten, although this time, they were worn, naturally, under my trousers") and further adorned with a hat that was too big for him he presented himself at the house of a famous dancer, Madame Schall. "Before I rung at the bell, I fell on my knees before the door and prayed God that I here might find help and support. A maid-servant came down the steps . . . she smiled kindly at me, gave me a skilling (Danish) and tripped on. Astonished, I looked at her and the money. I had on my confirmation suit and thought I must look very smart. How then could she think I wanted to beg?" (FT, 25–26). He managed to gain admittance anyway and offered by way of introduction a letter from the old printer Iversen in Odense. The only connection Iversen ever had had with the dancer was the printing of handbills for her performances, but Hans Christian had cajoled the letter out of him in the firm belief that it would serve as a proper introduction. It accomplished just that—even though the dancer "had not the slightest knowledge of him from whom the letter came, and my whole appearance and behavior seemed very strange to her." He explained his yearning for the theater. She wondered what he could do. He asked permission to take off his boots and, using his broad hat for a tambourine, began to dance and sing passages from a musical play, *Cinderella*. "My strong gestures and my great activity caused the lady to think me out of my mind, and she lost no time in getting rid of me" (*TS*, 38–39).

An attempt to find some employment at the theater resulted in another snub and a moment of despair. But "with all the undoubting confidence of a child in his father" he prayed to God and, having regained his courage, bought a gallery ticket for the opera *Paul and Virginia*. It affected him so deeply that he wept, and this in turn attracted the kind attentions of some women who sat nearby. He explained himself to them, and they fed him "bread and butter, with fruit and cakes," as well as a sausage sandwich.

Even so, the next day found him penniless, and in his extremity he looked for work. He answered the advertisement of a cabinetmaker and was tentatively accepted as an apprentice. The following morning

> I went to the workshop: several journeymen were there, and two or three apprentices; but the master was not come. They fell into merry and idle discourse. I was as bashful as a girl, and as they soon perceived this, I was unmercifully rallied upon it. Later in the day, the rude jests of the young fellows went so far that, in remembrance of the scene at the manufactory, I took the resolute determination not to remain a single day longer in the workshop.
>
> (*TS*, 41)

The master tried to reassure him, but he was "too much affected" and hastened away.

Again he knew despair,[2] and again he rallied. This time he crashed the dinner party of an opera singer he had once read about, Giuseppe Siboni, who was at that moment entertaining a number of artists and writers. Hans Christian opened his heart to the housekeeper; the good woman was moved and induced the party to see him. He sang and recited poetry for them; at the end, overcome by "the sense of my unhappy condition," he burst into tears. He was applauded. Siboni promised to give him singing lessons, and a Professor Weyse raised a small sum of money for him by subscription. To study with Siboni he needed to learn German, and a woman of Copenhagen with whom he had traveled from Odense arranged for him to receive free lessons from a language-master. Things were finally going his way, and he wrote a triumphant letter home. But within half a year, when he must have been about fifteen, his voice broke—or was injured, "in consequence of my being compelled to wear bad shoes through the winter, and having besides no warm underclothing" (*FT*, 31). This finished his singing, and Siboni counseled him to return to Odense and learn a trade.

We cannot help but raise an eyebrow. The tall, skinny boy with his long blond hair, pretty face, and soprano voice had repeatedly suffered from ribbing (and worse) on account of his girlish appearance. We would think he would have wished for an early change toward a more masculine demeanor. We would think he would know about and anticipate with some impatience the voice changes associated with puberty, and in his case already overdue. Instead, when the change does come, he considers it so unnatural that he ascribes it to a cold "in consequence of being compelled to wear bad shoes"—quite as if, had he only had proper shoes, he could have remained a soprano forever! This is passing odd. We also do not fail to notice that shoes, or boots, once again play some sort of symbolic, or magical, role. We shall have more to say about this later on.

Meanwhile, in spite or because of his new voice, Hans Christian was once again in despair. This time he bethought himself of a poet Guldberg, the brother of a colonel who had befriended him in Odense, and to this man he appealed for help. The poet received him kindly, gave him a substantial sum of money, and offered him lessons in Danish, it being apparent that Hans Christian both spoke and wrote his mother tongue rather poorly.

Needing a cheaper place to live, he took lodgings in "nothing but an empty store room, without window and light" but with permission to sit in the parlor. The landlady was a woman whom only years later he properly identified as a madam: "I found myself in the midst of the mysteries of Copenhagen, but I did not understand how to interpret them." Like the sun-god Phoebus, whose holy eye never sees the shadow, Hans Christian never spotted sin: "I never suspected what kind of world it was which moved around me" (*TS*, 46–47).

He lived in a different world. The "stern but active dame" wanted twenty rix dollars monthly for the wretched room, and he could afford but sixteen:

> This troubled me very much; when she was gone out of the room, I seated myself on the sofa, and contemplated the portrait of her deceased husband. I was so wholly a child, that as the tears rolled down my own cheeks I wetted the eyes of the portrait with my tears, in order that the dead man might feel how troubled I was, and influence the heart of his wife. She must have seen that nothing more was to be drained out of me, for when she returned to the room she said she would receive me into her house for the sixteen rix dollars. I thanked God and the dead man.[3]

He continued to play with his puppet theater and his dolls and to make doll clothes from colored fragments of material he begged from various stores—even though his voice had changed and even though he was now receiving free lessons in Latin, acting, and dancing. He was told he would never make either an actor or a dancer, but he was permitted to watch performances from the wings. Occasionally he got on stage as an extra, and finally, through the kindness of his dancing instructor, he was even assigned a little part in a ballet: "That was a moment in my life, when my name was printed! . . . I carried the programme of the ballet with me at night to bed, lay and read my name by candle-light—in short, I was happy!"⁴

Meanwhile, he was starving, and the imminent necessity of returning to Odense with his tail between his legs suggested suicide to him as a preferable alternative. But an extraordinary procession of benefactors—widows and their daughters, retired admirals, assorted officials—not only fed him in turn but listened to his first poetry and read his first dramatic efforts—largely plagiarized pieces conveying such ignorance of grammar, history, and the world that it was increasingly felt that he should be given a proper education.

One of his would-be educators was the poet Frederik Høegh-Guldberg, who went to many troubles and pains on Andersen's behalf, and among other things arranged for him to have Latin lessons. When Andersen proved anything but diligent, Guldberg lost his patience and lectured him severely. Hans Christian's reaction was characteristic:

> I realized that it was wrong of me to have neglected the Latin lessons . . . I walked homeward full of despair. He had told me that I was "a bad person," and that affected me terribly. I stood for a long time by the Pebblinge Lake . . . and the horrible thought struck me: "Nothing good can become of you . . . God is angry, you must die!" I looked into the water, and then thought of my old grandmother, who would certainly not have thought that my life would end in this way. This made me cry bitterly, but it relieved my mind, and in my heart I begged God to forgive me for . . . my sinful thought of jumping into the water.⁵

He had lost one protector, but about this time Jonas Collin, "one of the most distinguished men of Denmark" and currently director of the Royal Theatre, entered his life and began to shape it decisively. Collin was a man of grave demeanor and few words, and Hans Christian, so pitifully anxious to elicit a warm and sympathetic response from all he met, at first feared him and considered him an enemy. But Collin, sensing a spark of genius in the peculiar boy, obtained for him from King Frederik VI an annual stipend to run for several years and arranged for him to receive free instruction in the grammar school at Slagelse, a small town twelve Danish miles from Copenhagen.

In the eyes of a less astute observer than Collin, Hans Christian would, at that point, have appeared a dismal failure:

> He had been rejected as a singer, as a dancer, as an actor, and as a playwright. He was clumsy and "different," and his appearance was unfortunate in every way, and to make things worse he had grown out of his suit without being able to afford to buy a new one. His coat was too short, so he tried to pull down his sleeves all the time, his trousers too short and too narrow, and his heels trodden down. He moved awkwardly in a vain attempt to cover up the many defects in his clothing. His whole behavior was often ridiculous.[6]

When he declaimed his poetry or his plays, his listeners had difficulty not to burst out laughing. A young physician who attended one of young Andersen's performances at the elegant house of a Mrs. Belfour wrote of it later:

> In my opinion the whole performance (a reciting of plays, poems etc.) was just mediocre. But on the other hand, the great interest he took in it, the lack of restraint in his performance and his enthusiasm had such great appeal that I became somewhat indignant that they used him as a buffoon and a joker. The audience laughed at his tall, ungainly figure and his strikingly awkward appearance, which was especially noticeable in his movements and his walk. When we were going to eat he stumbled over the doorstep, tripped over his long legs, grasped the sandwich as if in a coma, lost his knife and fork, but talked incessantly. . . . But that the seeds of greatness were in him was quite clear.[7]

Andersen seems to have managed to overlook, or to reinterpret as encouragement, all the laughter; and as to the "seeds of greatness" in himself he was never in doubt. At any rate, things now were looking up. He had, in a manner, been adopted by a good father—Jonas Collin—to whom he would be able to turn with his problems and who would watch over him. And he was now, at long last, really and truly to be a student—as his poor dead father had always hoped—and so he wrote his mother a letter full of joy.

As it turned out, the next years of his life were anything but joyful. If his memory can be trusted, the year was 1822. He would have been seventeen years old when he joined a class of children aged perhaps ten to twelve. With his bean-pole figure he must have been twice the height of some of them. Nevertheless, that is not what pained him; feeling so much a child he may have fitted in uncommonly well. But he suffered bitterly from the treatment accorded him by the rector, Dr. Meisling, a well-meaning pedagogue with a sarcastic, bullying manner who never praised but criticized constantly.[8] There was nothing Hans Christian could tolerate less than criticism, and over and over again he dissolved in despair and wrote letters to his various benefactors proclaiming his unworthiness and failure. In response, he received much kindness and reassurance and so, his spirits briefly buoyed, managed to carry on. But he remained terribly vulnerable: "In my character-book I always received, as regarded my conduct, 'remarkably good.' On one occasion, however, I only obtained the testimony of 'very good': and so anxious and childlike was I, that I wrote a letter to Collin on that account, and assured him in grave earnestness, that I was perfectly innocent, although I had only obtained a character of 'very good' " (TS, 73).

Things got worse when the rector moved to a school in Helsingoer and invited Hans Christian to come along and live in the rector's house. The place was, to Andersen's perception, run like a jail: "When the school hours were over, the house door was commonly locked . . . I never went out to visit anybody . . . my prayer to God every evening was, that He would remove the cup from me and let me die. I possessed not an atom of confidence in myself" (TS, 75). He wrote one single poem during that time. It was called The Dying Child (!).

In the end, thanks to a sympathetic teacher's intervention with Collin, Hans Christian was removed from the school and permitted to return to Copenhagen. As a parting shot the rector predicted for him that he "would end his days in a madhouse." In view of his background, such a prognosis could not be taken lightly, and the boy understandably "trembled in his innermost being." Released from "jail," he took a new lease on life. An intelligent young teacher tutored him in Latin and Greek and argued religion—Hans Christian could accept God as love, but would never consent to hellfire[9]—and, bubbling like a newly opened bottle of champagne, he produced some humorous and satirical poetry that was actually published. In September 1828, now twenty-three years old, he officially became "a student" (of the University). "Thousand ideas and thoughts by which I was pursued . . . flew like a swarm of bees out into the world and indeed into my . . . work." A humorous and fantastic travel piece, self-published, had some success, and a satirical play won the acclaim of his fellow students.[10] "I was now a happy human being; I possessed the soul of a poet, and the heart of youth; all houses began to open to me; I flew from circle to circle." His first collection of poems appeared the next year. "Life lay bright with sunshine before me."

A dark cloud soon appeared—one that was to darken the remainder of his life.

In the summer of 1830, when he was twenty-five, he visited, on one of the Danish islands, the home of a fellow student, Christian Voigt. And there

> A pair of dark eyes fixed my sight,
> They were my world, my home, my delight,
> The soul beamed in them, and childlike peace,
> And never on earth will their memory cease.
>
> (*TS*, 90)

The pair of dark eyes belonged to Riborg Voigt, Christian's sister, a pretty girl of twenty who served him tea, went for walks with him, and generally showed herself attentive and interested.[11] He realized, with some dismay, that he was falling in love: "I remained in that house but three days, and when I felt what I had never felt before, and heard that she is already engaged, I departed immediately."

They met again in Copenhagen, late in the year, and he handed her a little love poem; but far from pressing his suit, he apparently took it completely for granted, and bitterly bewailed in his letters, that she would have to marry the other: "I see that I will never be happy! All my soul and all my thoughts cling to this one creature, a clever, *childlike* creature such as I have never met before . . . but she is engaged, and to be married next month. . . . I will never see her again. Next month she becomes a *wife*, then she will, then she must forget me. Oh, it is a deadly thought! . . . If only I were dead, dead, even if death were total annihilation" (Andersen's italics).[12] So he writes in January 1831. In March he still protests and, one cannot help feeling, too much: "I will never be happy in this world, I cannot; with my whole being I cling to a creature who can never become mine!—Insuperable obstacles separate us forever. Oh, God has tried me hard, almost too hard. She is the most *childlike*, the most magnificent creature I know, but engaged, the bride of another!" (Andersen's italics).[13]

He wrote Riborg a highly emotional, but typically Andersenian, love letter:

> I think you have already sensed my feelings, I am not enough of a man of the world to conceal my heart, and I dream of a hope, without which my life is lost. DO YOU REALLY LOVE THE OTHER MAN? . . . If [so], then forgive me . . . if you have been insulted by this letter, then give me permission to see you once more . . . for three months my heart and my thoughts have been obsessed . . . now I can live in this uncertainty no longer, I must know your decision. But forgive me, please forgive me! I was unable to act otherwise. Good-bye!

In the very act of declaring his love, his letter already contains resignation and farewell.[14]

By April he is, or at least appears to be, all over this infatuation.[15] His head, and his letters, are full of plans for a trip through Germany, and by May he writes travelogues about it. It was not Riborg Voigt who was to become his dark cloud; but rather it was the awkward, mysteriously abortive nature of the encounter, a failure of nerve in romantic situations, that was to remain characteristic of him, and of which we shall have more to say.

The journey itself was no doubt to serve as a distraction, but not only from the pains of love. His heart was much more vulnerable, and far more often injured, by the arrows of criticism. His happiness depended on a smile, and a frown could precipitate him into despair. "I am a peculiar creature," he writes, "so easily distrustful of humanity, I find the world cold and dark; but a single friendly word, and I am reconciled with all of you."[16] He hid his hurt feelings behind an arrogance that was considered "the most unbearable vanity . . . it was more than I could bear to hear [something] said sternly and jeeringly, by others; and if I then uttered a proud, an inconsiderate word, it was addressed to the scourge with which I was smitten; and when those who smite are those we love, then do the scourges become scorpions" (*FT*, 71).

In other words, he had become so hypersensitive and disagreeable that Collin sent him away for his own good and that of his friends. On the journey he was to rebuild his damaged pride in a manner that, again, became characteristic of him: he collected, and basked in, the attentions of famous men and women.

In the beginning these were mainly writers and artists to whom he managed to gain entry. On his first trip, in 1831 in Dresden, he met Tieck, the famous translator of Shakespeare, who "on taking leave of me, embraced and kissed me; which made the deepest impression on me" (*FT*, 72). And in Berlin he had an introduction to Chamisso (*FT*, 73), the author of *Peter Schlemiehl* and a good poet, who eventually translated some of Andersen's poems into German.[17] Upon returning to Copenhagen he promptly published his travel impressions, *Shadow Pictures*, as he eventually was to do after almost all of his journeys.

Two years later he journeyed to Paris, where one day "A man of Jewish cast came toward me. 'I hear you are a Dane,' said he. 'I am a German: Danes and Germans are brothers, therefore I offer you my hand!' I asked for his name and he said: 'Heinrich Heine'!" Together with Sir Walter Scott and E. T. A. Hoffmann, Heine had exerted the most formative influence on Andersen's youth. "There was no man I could have wished more to see and meet with" (*FT*, 88).

This is, at least in the early years of Andersen's travels, the only instance of someone introducing himself to Andersen, rather than vice versa; and, considering Heine's feelings about "being a German," the episode is somewhat questionable. Doubt seems even more justified in the light of what happened between them ten years later. Andersen reports in his diary on 26 March 1843 that he visited Heine, and he raves, "He received me graciously. He wanted me to believe that he had forgotten his German, that now all his joys and sufferings were French (his wife is a French-woman); that for him Scandinavia is the only place where the treasures of poetry can still be found; and that, were he not so old, he would study Danish. He is interested in elves and goblins."[18] But Heine raved decidedly less. He wrote later, "Andersen called on me . . . I thought he looked like a tailor. He is a lean man with a hollow lantern-jaw face, and in his outward appearance he betrays a servile lack of self-confidence which is appreciated by dukes and princes. He fulfilled exactly a prince's idea of a poet. When he visited me he had decked himself out with a big tie-pin. I asked him what it was he had put there. He replied very unctuously: 'It is a present which the Electress of Hessen has been gracious enough to bestow on me.' Otherwise he is a man of some spirit."[19]

In 1833 Andersen was not yet collecting dukes and princes, but he was rapidly heading that way. He did manage to meet Victor Hugo in Paris, the philosopher Schelling in Munich, the sculptor Thorwaldsen in Rome, and the dramatist Grillparzer in Vienna.

There followed a hiatus until, in 1838, the Danish Prime

Minister, Count Rantzau-Breitenburg, had obtained for him from King Frederick VI an adequate travel stipend. But in 1840 Andersen set out on an extended journey. Having visited the Count in his ancestral castle in Holstein, he traveled—for the first time by railway—to Leipzig. There he engaged in a little game he was to play many times later on. He had heard that Mendelssohn-Bartoldi had enjoyed one of his novels, and had issued a vague invitation for Andersen to visit him if ever he came through Leipzig. Being told that Mendelssohn was rehearsing at the Gewandthaus, Andersen sent in a note to the effect that "a traveller was very anxious to call on him." The composer emerged, sorely vexed: " 'I have but very little time, and I really cannot talk here with strangers!' he said. 'You have invited me yourself,' answered I, 'you have told me that I must not pass through the city without seeing you!'—'Andersen!' cried he now, 'is it you?' and his whole countenance beamed" (*FT*, 157). In this manner Andersen, over and over again—approaching strangers at first anonymously and then "revealing" himself—tested and heightened the favorable reception he could receive, the confirmation of his fame he could enjoy.

He continued his journey to Rome, Naples, Malta, and Athens—where he was a dinner guest of the King of Greece—and on to Constantinople, where he "found a cordial reception with the Austrian internuncius, Baron Stuermer," and crossed the Bosporus to Asia Minor to see the dancing dervishes in Scutari and Pera.[20] From Constantinople he meant to continue his journey to the mouth of the Danube and thence upstream to Vienna.

It should be pointed out that travel in those days was far from simple, far from safe, and mostly incredibly wearisome. Steamships and railways were just beginning to be built, and were sooty and most uncomfortable. Post chaises were much worse. A journey from Denmark to Italy could take weeks; the roads, especially over the mountains, were hazardous and dusty. The few existing inns were bad, their beds crawling with vermin. In the winter months heating was inadequate, and in the summer there was no defense against mosquitoes. Highwaymen were not uncommon and public conveyances often had to be accompanied by an armed guard. It was not exactly the sort of experience one would have expected someone of Andersen's finicky sensibilities to venture—much less to enjoy. In addition, his own quirks greatly aggravated the stresses of reality. He was afraid of dogs; he had such agoraphobia that he needed an escort to traverse a large square. He was so afraid of fire that he always carried a rope in his trunk so that, if necessary, he could escape through an upstairs hotel window. During the night he had to get up several times to assure himself that the candle had been properly extinguished; this in spite of the fact that he had himself, before he went to bed, carefully pinched the wick between his damp fingers.[21] He worried obsessively whether his passport was in order and had the required visas, whether he had locked the door to his room, whether he had paid the right amount in the right currency, whether someone was out to rob or murder him, and so on. "Oh, how good I am at tormenting myself!" he wrote.[22] But there was a stubborn streak in him whenever he had set his mind on something.

In this instance he was told that the proposed journey was not to be advised. The country was in revolt; it was said there had been several thousand Christians murdered. He was urged to give up the Danube route, and to return via Greece and Italy.

I do not belong to the courageous; I feel fear, especially in little dangers; but in great ones, and when an advantage is to be won, then I have a will, and it has grown firmer with years. I may tremble, I may fear, but I still do that which I consider the most proper to be done. I am not ashamed to confess my weakness; I hold that when out of our own true conviction we run counter to our inborn fear, we have done our duty. I had a strong desire to . . . traverse the Danube . . . I battled with myself; my imagination painted to me the most horrible circumstances; it was an anxious night. In the morning . . . I determined upon it. From the moment that I had taken my determination I had the most immovable reliance on Providence, and flung myself calmly on my fate.

(*FT*, 167)

There were some exciting moments, some shooting, and the discomfort and boredom of ten days' quarantine at the Austrian border, in a building "only arranged to receive Wallachian peasants," with paved rooms, horrid provisions, and worse wine. The trip from Constantinople to Vienna took three weeks. Upon his return to Copenhagen he published his travel book, *A Poet's Bazaar.*

In 1843 he again went to Paris and this time, in addition to Victor Hugo, visited Lamartine, Alexandre Dumas, Alfred de Vigny, Balzac, Scribe, Gautier, and, as mentioned, once again Heine. On the return trip he managed to take in the poet Freiligrath in the Rhine town of St. Goar and the writers Moritz Arndt and Emanuel Geibel in Bonn. 1844 took him to Berlin to meet the composer Meyerbeer, and later to Weimar: "The reigning Grand Duke and Duchess gave me so gracious and kind a reception." But it was when he met the hereditary Grand Duke and his lady—a newly married princely pair—that his heart was deeply moved. More about this later.

From Weimar he traveled to Leipzig for a "truly poetical evening" with Robert and Clara Schumann. Andersen was delighted by the reception, and by the fact that Robert had set four of his poems to music.[23] Clara said of him later, "Andersen is the ugliest man imaginable, but he looks very interesting and has a poetically childlike mind."[24] Apparently the King (Christian VIII) and Queen of Denmark thought so too, for that summer they invited him to stay with them at a spa on the North Frisian Island of Foehr: "It was just now five-and-twenty years since I, a poor lad, travelled alone and helpless to Copenhagen. Exactly the five-and-twentieth anniversary would be celebrated by my being with my king and queen, to whom I was faithfully attached, and whom I at that very time learned to love with my whole soul. . . . The reality frequently surpasses the most beautiful dream" (*FT*, 220).

This should have been the pinnacle of his success and he should have been content. But, alas, his autobiography goes on, and it degenerates into a tedious recital of royalties visited and honors, medals, and decorations received. He visited Prince Radziwill in Berlin; received the Order of the Dannebrog from the King of Denmark; visited King Friedrich August II of Saxony; was introduced to the Grand Duchess Sophie of Austria, to Archduke Stephan, and to the future Emperor Franz Joseph; and so on and so on. There was no shortage of little countries, or of big ones—and they all had royalty to be visited and to be made much of.

He is aware of the effect he is creating: "It may appear perhaps, as if I desired to bring names of great people prominently forward, and to make a parade of them; or as if I wished in this way to offer a kind of thanks to my benefactors. They need it not, and I should be obliged to mention many other names still" (*TS*, 169). And he does mention other names, such as during his visit, in 1847, to England. From there he wrote to Jonas Collin's son Edvard: "Here is a paper which says that I am 'one of the most remarkable and interesting men of this day.' Last night I made my first appearance, and that in the most select society. I was at Lord Palmerston's. I talked to the Duke of Cambric [*sic*], the Duchess of Sutherland . . . everyone knew my writing; in the end I was surrounded by fine ladies who talked of my tales . . . I grew quite giddy, but not with pride."[25]

He was lionized as never before: invitations poured in from Lord Stanley, Lord Castlereagh, the Rothschilds, and so on. He even received an invitation from Prince Albert to visit him and Queen Victoria in Scotland, but there his nerve, and his purse—he would have had to hire a valet—failed him and, under many and bitter tears, he declined.[26]

When he had chronicled all this assiduously in his autobiography, there was one friend, who knew him well, who protested. He had sent the manuscript to Henriette Wulff, an old and wise friend. A hunchbacked spinster of great intelligence and warmth, she truly cared for him. She wrote:

> To me it is a total denial of oneself, of one's own person, of the gifts God has graciously given us, such an incomprehensible self-humiliation that I am surprised when somebody like YOU, Andersen—if you do recognize that God has given

you special spiritual gifts—that YOU can consider yourself
HAPPY and HONOURED to be placed—well, that is what it
says—at the table of the King of Prussia or of some other
high-ranking person—or to receive a decoration, of the kind
worn by the greatest scoundrels, not to mention a swarm of
extremely insignificant people. Do you really place a title,
money, aristocratic blood, success in what is nothing but outward matters, ABOVE genius—spirit—the gifts of the soul?[27]

Andersen had no answer.[28]
Why indeed the parade of stars? What for? Why did he
strive so mightily to be accepted and flattered by the great?
And why does he—with all professed "humility"—make
such a show of it?

To some extent, no doubt, the description of his spectacular
ascent up the artistic and social register serves the legitimate
and well-deserved end of illustrating the laborious metamorphosis of the poor cobbler's son into a world-renowned man of
letters—the metamorphosis of the ugly duckling into a swan.
Nor shall we begrudge him a word of his triumph. However, it
is hard, in spite of his disclaimer, not to see in the recital of
famous personalities and in his attachment to them, a certain
sycophantic quality: a wish and need to derive from their
company and approval a sense of security he basically
lacked.[29] In this regard he failed completely. He continued to
play, with regard to the great, as in his far more sustaining
attachments to more faithful but less famous people (the Collin
family above all) the role of a child. The quality he was lacking,
and the lack of which he wished to conceal or to compensate
for, was manhood.[30] In this regard he had failed, at the age of
twenty-five, with Riborg Voigt. He was to try seriously only
once more—and fail finally—at the age of thirty-five, with the
famous operatic singer Jenny Lind.[31]

He was thirty-five, and she twenty, when they first met.
She was already a well-known singer in Stockholm, and he a
writer of rising fame. When he learned that she, in company
with her father, was visiting Copenhagen, he felt it proper
and appropriate to call on her. She received him "very cour-
teously, but yet distantly, almost coldly"; recoiling in his

sensitive manner, he gained "the impression of a very ordinary character which soon passed from my mind."

She was back three years later, and as friends assured him she now knew of him and had read his works, he permitted himself to visit her again. This time, indeed, he received a cordial welcome. He encouraged her to perform in Copenhagen. When she did, she was an instant success and won enthusiastic acclaim. His own view of her changed in resonance to her cordiality: she was not only the best singer and actress of her time, but "at home, in her own chamber, a sensitive young girl with all the humility and piety of a child" (*TS*, 209). We cannot help but notice the emphasis, and he repeats, so that we should not forget: "An intelligent and *child-like* disposition exercises here its astonishing power" (*TS*, 213). Must he indeed, and at all cost, see her as a child? There is, apparently, only one alternative: "Her appearance in Copenhagen made an epoch in the history of our opera; it showed me art in its sanctity—I had beheld one of its *vestals* . . . she is a pure vessel, from which a holy draught will be presented to us." If she is not to be a child, then she must be and remain "pure," a holy virgin, untouchable.

So, at least, reads the autobiography. But his diary, in the fall of 1843, when he was thirty-eight, reads: "In love," and "I love her."[32] They were meeting daily at that time, and when she left for home, he gave her a letter of which his diary records: "She must understand." She no doubt understood, but she made her position clear: she loved him like a brother. He was bitterly hurt—as he many years later expressed in some of his stories (such as *Under the Willow Tree*)—but he soon settled into resignation.

They met, off and on, in the years to follow. At Christmas 1845, they were both in Berlin. He spent a lonely Christmas Eve in his hotel. Was it, as he claims, because "every one of the many families in which I . . . was received as a relation had fancied . . . that I must be invited out [elsewhere]"? (*TS*, 263–64). Or was he hoping for an invitation by Jenny? At any rate, when she heard of his solitary Christmas, "there was (on the last evening of the year) planted for me alone a little tree with its lights, and its beautiful presents—and that was by Jenny Lind. The whole company consisted of herself, her attendant, and me; we three children from the North were together on Sylvester [New Year's] eve, and I was the child for which the Christmas-tree was lighted." This "child" was now forty years old, and apparently quite resigned to remaining a lonely bachelor for the rest of his life.

Not that he was ever really alone.

He never owned a house of its own. By preference he stayed on as a houseguest in the homes of hospitable families—as he once stayed on, for five weeks and much beyond his welcome, at the house of Charles Dickens.[33] The description of him, written years later by Dickens's son, Sir Henry Dickens, paints a vivid picture:

> He turned out to be a lovable and yet a somewhat uncommon and strange personality. His manner was delightfully simple, such as one rather expected from the delicacy of his work. He was necessarily very interesting, but he was certainly somewhat of an "oddity." In person, tall, gaunt, rather ungainly; in manner, thoughtful and agreeable. He had one beautiful accomplishment, which was the cutting out in paper, with an ordinary pair of scissors, of little figures of sprites and elves, gnomes, fairies and animals of all kinds which might have stepped out of the pages of his books. . . . Much as there was in him to like and admire, he was, on the other hand, most decidedly disconcerting in his general manner, for he used constantly to be doing things, quite unconsciously, which might almost be called "gauche," so much so that I am afraid the small boys in the family rather laughed at him behind his back; but, so far as the members of the family are concerned, he was treated with the utmost consideration and courtesy.[34]

Dickens himself poked fun at him: "We are suffering a good deal from Andersen," he wrote (in a letter). "The other day we lost him when he came up to London Bridge Terminus, and he took a cab by himself. The cabman driving him through the new unfinished streets at Clerkenwell, he thought was driving him into remote fastnesses, to rob and murder him. He consequently arrived here with all his money, his watch, his pocketbook, and documents, *in his boots*—and it was a tremendous business to unpack him and get them off." When Andersen departed, Dickens put up a card over the dressing-table mirror: "Hans Andersen slept in this room for five weeks—which seemed to the family *ages!*"[35]

Not mentioned in Dicken's description is the usual manner in which Andersen "sang for his supper" in his later years. Typically he would recite tales in the family circle after dinner or in the nursery. As his skill in that genre became renowned, he grew to resemble exactly the storyteller surrounded by children that we fancy him to have been.

When he did not stay at someone else's house or country mansion—and he appears to have stayed at more than thirty—he lived in rented rooms, or at a hotel. His popularity was such, and he knew so many ladies who were to him as mothers or grandmothers, that one or the other or several of them would invariably come to his quarters to look after him and to furnish his rooms with flowers.[36]

Through much of his life the house of Jonas Collin was his "home of homes," a place where he always felt welcome and always found understanding and loyal support. Jonas himself had directed his youth, and his son Edvard, whom Andersen regarded as a brother, became, though three years younger than Hans Christian, his business manager and practical adviser in all matters regarding publications and finances. It is characteristic of Andersen that he submitted— no doubt profitably—to this management, even though Edvard, as stern as father Jonas, grated on him: "No matter how much affection ties me to Edvard, I still feel that he cannot be a real friend to me! It may be that the very qualities which give him character become cutting edges which injure my sensibilities."[37]

When, after the death of Jonas Collin in 1861, that "home of homes" broke up, two highly respected Jewish families from Copenhagen, the Henriques and the Melchiors, became increasingly important to him and more or less "took over." Mrs. Dorothea Melchior, in particular, saw in motherly fashion after his physical and emotional wellbeing and in the end became his nurse. He died at her summer villa, just outside of Copenhagen, on 4 August 1875, shortly after his seventieth birthday.

Self-portrait of Hans Christian Andersen, n.d.

Jonas Collin. Painting by
J. V. Gertner, 1840.

Simon Meisling.
Anonymous painting, n.d.

Riborg Voigt. Daguerreotype, ca. 1845.

Hans Christian Andersen. Painting by C. A. Jensen, 1836.

Jenny Lind. Lithograph after a painting by E. Magnus, 1846.

Edvard and Henriette
Collin. Painting by
W. Marstrand, 1842.

Grand Duke Carl
Alexander of Sachsen-
Weimar-Eisenach.
Lithograph, n.d.

Hans Christian Andersen. Photograph by C. Weller, 1865.

Hans Christian Andersen in his room at Nyhaven.
Photograph by C. Weller, 1874.

12

Andersen's Literary Work

The past chapter has, in barest outline, sketched Andersen's rise to fame; it has not even mentioned that on which his fame was based, nor shall we discuss it in any detail now. But since we are primarily concerned with *The Snow Queen*, it would behoove us to look briefly at Andersen's opus insofar as it comes before or after and thereby assign *The Snow Queen* its proper place in the whole picture.

A surprise immediately awaits us, for surely most American readers are unaware that Andersen wrote anything but fairy tales, or that this unique genre did not begin to occupy him—and tentatively at that—until relatively late in his career.

We are, of course, somewhat prepared for this: we know that his chief passion was the stage, ever since his father put on plays with him before he was eleven years old, and that the most illustrious title, to his mind, was that of a poet. So it is not surprising that his first efforts aimed along those lines.

We already know of several of these early efforts. A "national tragedy," *The Robbers of Wissenberg*, was written when he was barely sixteen. It contained so many errors that, as he says, "there was scarcely a word in it correctly written," and it was returned to him by the director of the Royal Theatre with the notation: "People do not frequently wish to retain works which betray, in so great a degree, a want of elementary knowledge" (*TS*, 59). His second effort, a tragedy entitled *Alfsol*, was again rejected, but it showed enough promise to gain him financial support and entrance to the grammar school already mentioned. His first poem, *The Dying Child*, written during the unhappy days of Slagelse when he was twenty-two, is touching and sad without sentimentality and stands up remarkably well:

> Mother, I am tired, I'll drowse away.
> By your heart I'll find my sleeping place.
> Promise me you'll weep no more today
> For your salt tears burn upon my face.
> Here it's cold, outside the wind is wild . . .[1]

His first published work, it was well received.

He had two other minor successes when he was about twenty-four: a whimsical *Walking Tour from Holmen's Canal to the Eastern Point of Amager* (two locations within Copenhagen), and a parody on Schiller, a verse play called *Love on St. Nicholas Tower*. There followed travel pieces, opera libretti, and more poems. When he was twenty-eight, he produced a verse drama, *Agnete and the Merman*, which was such a flop that critics considered him "finished." His despair can be imagined, but he pulled himself together and two years later came out with a more or less autobiographical novel, *The Improvisatore*, which was an immediate success.

He wrote several more novels: two during the ensuing two years, both autobiographical (*O.T.* and *Only a Fiddler*), and three in his later years, finishing the last one when he was sixty-five. None of them, though not without some merit, would have assured him popularity in his lifetime, much less immortality. The last one, *Lucky Peer*, was eventually omitted from the first *Collected Edition* to be brought out in America—which in any case had omitted all his dramatic and lyrical efforts. The public, it appeared, was interested only in his fairy tales, not in his novels and travel books.[2] These are still read in Scandinavian countries,[3] though his operatic libretti, of which he wrote a number, have, to the best of my knowledge, vanished there also. Some of these works, though far from all, were well received in his day, but a good many met a highly critical and derogatory reception—particularly in his own country—and caused him much anguish and many a fit of deep depression.

What saved him from despair while he was alive, and

from oblivion after his death, were, of course, the fairy tales. The first batch came out while he was riding high, a month after the successful *Improvisatore*. He called it *Tales Told for Children*, and included in it *The Tinder Box, Little Claus and Big Claus, The Princess on the Pea*, and *Little Ida's Flowers*. With the exception of the last, they were Danish folktales, retold.[4] Even so, the critics declared them utterly unfit for children, full of violence and immorality, and in bad style at that.[5] The first published review of his first tales ran like this:

> Among Mr. Andersen's tales the first three, "The Tinder Box," "Little Claus and Big Claus," and "The Princess on the Pea," may well amuse children, but they will certainly not have any edifying effect, and your reviewer cannot answer for their being harmless reading. At any rate, no one can possibly contend that a child's sense of propriety is increased by reading about a princess who goes riding off in her sleep on a dog's back to visit a soldier who kisses her, after which she herself, wide awake, tells of this incident as "a curious dream"; or that a child's idea of modesty is increased by reading about a farmer's wife who, while her husband is away, sits down at a table alone with the parish clerk, "and she kept filling up his glass for him, and he kept helping himself to the fish—he was very fond of fish"; or that a child's respect for human life is increased by reading about episodes like that of Big Claus killing his grandmother and of Little Claus killing *him*, told as if it were just a bull being knocked on the head. The tale of the Princess on the Pea strikes the reviewer as being not only indelicate but quite unpardonable, in so far that a child may acquire the false impression that so august a lady must always be terribly sensitive.[6]

Andersen was admonished to stop wasting his time on such unworthy material and indeed he himself seems at first to have been in doubt as to the value of these stories. He was, after all, working almost without precedent. Up to the middle of the seventeenth century children listened to the same stories as the adults, and nothing was tailored especially for them. When the first texts for children appeared, they considered a child "a damned soul who must be saved from perdition by a rigorous pietism. Children were not born to live happily but to die holy and true. Education lay in preparing the soul to meet its maker. The result of this was a crop of seventeenth-century books zealously depicting for children the holy lives and joyous deaths of their little contemporaries."[7] The first book of fantasy especially for children was *Tales of Mother Goose* by Charles Perrault, published in France in 1697 and not in English translation until 1729. It was only the Romantics who began to appreciate folktales and who considered the possibility that children were, by nature, perhaps not all bad.[8] The Brothers Grimm were contemporaries of Andersen's (and he had his typical meeting with them, arranging first to be rejected and then admired), but they merely recorded, in anthropological fashion, orally transmitted folktales. So Andersen was indeed breaking new ground, and he had reason for apprehension.

But he persevered despite the critics and, almost, as if he could not help himself. These stories wanted to be written, wanted out.[9] In that same year of 1835 three more appeared, and from then on he published several stories each year—usually before Christmas—until he was sixty-eight years old. In 1843, when he was thirty-eight, and eight years after he had published the first tales, he wrote in a letter:

> I believe that I have now found out how to write fairy tales! The first ones I wrote were, as you know, mostly old ones I had heard as a child and that I retold and recreated in my own fashion; those that were my very own, such as "The Little Mermaid," "The Storks," "The Daisy," and so on, received, however, the greatest approval and that has given me inspiration! Now I tell stories of my own accord, seize an idea for the adults—and then tell it for children while still keeping in mind the fact that mother and father are often listening too, and they must have a little something for thought.[10]

From now on his little volumes no longer had the title *Fairy Tales Told for Children*, but simply *Fairy Tales*.

They are very uneven in quality, and if one were graphically inclined, one could construct a curve with a steep ascent on one side and a lengthy decline on the other, indicating the quality, or lack thereof, of his output. The steep ascent starts in his thirty-second year with *The Little Mermaid* and *The Emperor's New Clothes.* There follow, during the next eight or nine years, most of the stories we all know and that, all over the Western world and to this day, form an almost obligatory furnishing of any middle-class nursery: *The Steadfast Tin Soldier, The Ugly Duckling, The Fir Tree,* and *The Little Match Girl.* Two others, *The Red Shoes* and *The Snow Queen,* were written when he was forty and in love with Jenny Lind. Some twenty-five other stories written during those years may also be familiar to a good many readers: *The Galoshes of Fortune, The Wild Swans, The Nightingale,*[11] and *The Shepherdess and the Chimneysweep* among them.

But there followed, after *The Little Match Girl,* some 120 more stories spread over the next twenty-seven years. Most of these would be unknown to most readers, and many of them are repetitive, pedantic, and uninspired—some emanating a cloying and not very convincing religiosity,[12] others driven by a didactic zeal that blights what poetic or literary merit they may have. However, sparks of beauty, humor, and sheer genius flash in many of them, and during Andersen's lifetime—a time perhaps more sympathetic to instructive efforts than ours—even these stories were eagerly welcomed and read. Or was it that the masterpieces of his "golden years" had so enchanted the world that he could do no wrong, or at least was easily forgiven? However that may be, it was the stories that earned him his fame, his place at the most illustrious dinner tables, his personal and close friendship with the Danish royal family, and no end of honorary medals and titles and esoteric memberships. There was even the night when, according to the prophecy of the wise woman who predicted his great future when he wanted to leave home, Odense was lit up in his honor: on 6 December 1867, the city council declared him an honorary citizen of Odense, and at the culmination of a special school holiday a banquet and a torchlight procession were held in his honor. The ugly duckling had become a swan indeed!

But as to *The Snow Queen:* where in Andersen's life and work does it have its place? At the pinnacle, no doubt: not the pinnacle of his honors, which came late, as it should; but at the pinnacle of his creativity. Not only is *The Snow Queen* one of his longest stories; it is his most inventive and inspired.[13] It is also his most profound. The story is the best he could produce at the height of his faculties and of his craft. It is the most consummate expression of what he knew and of who he was.

Having reassured ourselves that we are, indeed, dealing with a crucial work, we shall now proceed and ask: what is it that this masterpiece has to tell us, not only about the man who wrote it but perhaps about man in general, about mankind?

PART TWO

THE YEARNING FOR REDEMPTION

13

The Psychologist

There is one thing we know already. We have pointed it out often enough, and over and over again: this story, which starts in childhood and takes its characters into adult life, is an account of the transition from the one state into the other. It is an account of adolescence and its vicissitudes.

Let us now hurry to meet the obvious objection to such a formulation. *The Snow Queen* is, of course, not just that. It is not a psychological essay. It is above all a highly imaginative, poetic tale of adventure and of faith, of love and of loyalty, and of all the wonder and magic of childhood: it is all a whopping good fairy tale should be. When we talk of it as a perceptive study of adolescence, we are talking of something below the surface, something meant not for the bright-eyed child, listening with rapt attention, but something for the pensive adult to ponder.

We have demonstrated that a dissertation on adolescence, like the skeleton within a body, underlies the story, carrying it and giving it weight. The temporary escape of the boy from his sexual-maturational storm into rude and intellectual isolation, the temporary escape of the girl from her rising femininity into the moratoria of the flower stage, the hard-to-get riddle princess, and the homoerotic "crush"—these phenomena are too frequent and important in life, and too obviously *there* in the story, to be there only by virtue of our psychologically schooled—and therefore perhaps biased—imagination.[1]

But the matter raises several questions.

We should like to know, for instance: Did Andersen know what he had produced? Did he, who died when Freud was nineteen, and twenty years before the *Studies on Hysteria*, anticipate some of the master's insights? Did he *knowingly* write an—as it were, spruced-up and fictional—account of ego defenses?

Surely, to whatever degree he had profound psychological understanding, it was not at all systematized. Any kind of systematic thinking was not only alien but totally repugnant to him. Andersen paid lip service to science and engineering and to all the industrial progress, such as steamships, railways, balloons, and telegraphic communication, that erupted in his lifetime and commanded general awe. But he dealt with these alien phenomena, insofar as they are touched on in his stories, letters, and travelogues, strictly as if they were themselves miracles and fairy tales. Thus he reacts to his visit to the technologically amazing World's Fair of 1867 in Paris by concocting the story of a tree nymph, a dryad, whose longing to see the big city is satisfied when the tree she inhabits is transplanted to a Paris square. She gets to see the city—including the marvelous sewers!—and dies of her experience.[2] Or he discusses the new transatlantic telegraphic cable in a story that tells how the fishes quarrel as to the nature of the "great sea serpent." They generally come to the conclusion that it is good for nothing, but a little fish "had his own thoughts: 'Perhaps that enormously long, thin serpent is the most wonderful fish in the ocean. I have a feeling it is' "[3]—a conclusion that is neither plausible (in a little fish) nor sound taxonomy, nor in any way related to the nature and function of the telegraph. What it does convey is Andersen's own incomprehension of technology and science (little Kay would have understood such matters better) and his evasion from system and method into fancy.

No, we must not assume that Andersen had any systematic notions of psychology. On the other hand, like all great writers, he is gifted with a psychological intuition that "surpasseth understanding." Take, for instance, the following passage from one of his stories:

> Anne Lisbeth walked on, not thinking of anything in particular, as we say. Yet, though she was not conscious of it, her

thoughts were busy within her, as they always are within all of us. They lie deep inside us, thoughts that have already shaped themselves into action and thoughts that have never yet stirred—there they lie still, and some day they will come forth. . . . Much has been said and written that one does not know—or . . . does not remember—but such things can appear before one's subconscious self, can come to mind, though one is unaware of it.

The germs of vices and virtues are alive deep in our hearts—in yours and mine; they lurk like tiny invisible seeds. . . . Walking in a daydream, one may be unconscious of many painful thoughts, but they have their being within us all the same.[4]

Both Freud and Jung are anticipated here; nor would it be hard to find other passages equally insightful. Clearly we must believe Andersen capable of any degree of intuitive understanding. As to *The Snow Queen*, he had taken his time, mulling over the story for several years. One of his early collections of poetry contained a poem by the same name (written in 1830 and set to music in 1838), but of far simpler content: The Snow Queen, riding in her grey clouds, spies a handsome young man and decides to make him her lover; he dies in her white arms.[5] From this early formulation of the Snow Queen as death it is a long way to the complex symbolism of our story; and Andersen *could* have used this time and this story to elaborate and to embody some of his understanding of human growth—whether by conscious decision or, as he put it, as a thing that "can appear before one's subconscious self, can come to mind, though one is unaware of it."

We cannot decide this matter. But as to why he should have concerned himself with such questions at all, we can give a far better answer. We have seen how, right up until his ripe old age, Andersen continued to think of himself as of a child. But there was a time—the time between the poem and the story of the Snow Queen, the thirties of his life—when he seriously considered trying to become a man, and seriously had to contemplate his inability to do so. In this regard at least, he resembled the little Kay of our story, who though he becomes fully grown yet remains a "child at heart" and, as far as we are told, never marries nor attains any form of sexuality. The "failure of nerve" in our story— its unsatisfactory, less-than-happy ending—corresponds to a "failure of nerve" in the real life of the author.[6] And because we know quite a bit about his life, and because such failure of nerve constitutes quite a frequent form of psychopathology in our day, it may not be altogether idle to speculate upon its possible psychological—and perhaps biological— causes.

Let us begin with what we—oddly—know least and therefore will say least about: the biological.

Granted that a man is born with a certain genetic endowment, and that who he will eventually become must depend on how external influences—people, events, and conditions—act upon this endowment and shape, develop, or stunt it: then what a man is made of—his bones, muscles, glands and so on—should plausibly be given more attention than in current thinking it is generally paid. As to Hans Christian and his bones, we know this: that he and they grew early and long, and kept on growing until he was longer than most men. But there is a relation between the growth of long bones and the production, within the body, of sex hormones, in such a way that an outpouring of sex hormones during a period of growth of bones will terminate that growth. Conversely, continued growth would suggest a belated appearance of the sex hormones. The matter is far less simple than here presented, and numerous other hormones—the growth hormone itself, chief among them—are involved. But with regard to Hans Christian, we do know that he had a lovely soprano voice right into his fifteenth year, when it finally broke: an onset of puberty well on the late side of the normal range. And it is, I believe, a matter of general clinical impression that those who come to sexual urgency relatively late lose it relatively early; and that tall and lanky individuals or, in Kretschmer's terms, asthenic individuals—brilliant though they may be intellectually and possibly strong willed and capable of manly action in most regards—approach sexuality with a certain diffidence and hesitation, with a sensibility easily discouraged and detoured, especially by comparison with their more squat and square, pyknic or mesomorphic compeers.[7] This is, of course, a vague generalization, which must never be foisted blindly on any given individual. But with regard to Hans Christian, it is pertinent to speculate that by virtue of his bodily makeup he was less driven by the urgencies of sex, more delicate, and more vulnerable to interpersonal wind and weather, than had he been a stouter fellow.

Be this as it may. We have mentioned the matter to indicate that, in our opinion, the detrimental influences we will now discuss impinged upon a man singularly ill armored against them; but whether such mention was wise or foolish the biochemical research of the next few years will probably demonstrate.

14

The Fathers

Speaking now of influences that went into shaping our frail hero, let us start with the proposition that what sort of man a man is going to be is likely to relate in some fashion to what sort of man his father was: a proposition that must surely be granted some plausibility. And let us ask, therefore, in what manner his father may have influenced Hans Christian, not so much in the choice of his calling, for that we know already—it was his father who implanted in him his love for poetry and for the theater—but with regard, specifically, to his image of and growth toward manhood.

And there we are struck immediately by a certain lack of strength. Apart from stubbornly holding some rather free-thinking opinions, and eventually acting on them by going to war in the service of Napoleon, Mr. Andersen Senior was anything but assertive; and we have seen that his venture at becoming a fighting man got him nothing but sickness and frustration. Certainly at home, with a robust and resolute wife fifteen (or at least seven) years his senior, he cut a poor figure. Withdrawn, moody, and mostly silent, he appears suffering rather than active. Even the imaginative and delightful playtime with Hans Christian assumes, in this setting, the aspect of an escape from everyday drudgery. For he loathed his work and was, apparently, not too good at it. At one time a chance was offered him for full-time and secure employment with a rich country family. But the pair of dancing shoes he cobbled as a test piece was found wanting, and the thing fell through.[1] Life had denied him the chance to become a scholar; he made a poor shoemaker, and he failed as a soldier. By coming to grief in the world, he also failed to deflate his wife's phobic world view. Indeed he must have shown to his son what a frail and vulnerable thing it is to be a man—a place and a position in life to be dreaded rather than sought after.

Hans Christian did, indeed, feel extremely vulnerable all his life. He was beset by fears of illness, animals, and strangers; on his actually rather adventuresome travels he was said to be in the habit of leaving a note by his bedside, "I only seem dead," for fear of being buried alive.[2] But how deeply he had nevertheless been attached to his father is attested to not only in a general way by his dedication to literature, which was clearly his father's "territory," but more specifically by the importance of shoes and cobblers as protagonists and symbols in his writings and in his life.

We recall, for instance, the creaking boots he was so proud of when he first wore them for his confirmation. There was a quality of self-assertion in wearing them to church that fitted well to an occasion that represented a "rite of passage" from childhood to a more adult condition. Boots were much worn in an age and place that knew few sidewalks, but even so, shoes were more common in civilian life and boots had something military. The soldier in *The Tinder Box*, Andersen's first fairy tale, of course wore boots, and he stuffed them full of gold (just as Andersen stuffed his valuables into his boots in London!). Hans Christian's father must have donned boots when he asserted himself and went off to war. Hans Christian felt cocky at his confirmation and wore his boots *outside* his trousers, so everybody should see them (*TS*, 30). He felt afraid and helpless in Copenhagen when he went to appeal to Madame Schall for assistance, and so, "naturally" (*TS*, 37), he now wore these same boots *under* his trousers. We may not be stretching the point too far if we call this a rather fateful decision. For the remainder of his life Andersen always wore his boots, metaphorically speaking, under his trousers; he remained forever an "applicant," forever insistently ingratiating, but never frankly asserting himself.

Even though he never mentions his father directly or indirectly, except in the account of his childhood, one gains the impression that he felt let down by him. Thus he attributes his change of voice to "bad shoes"; and in the story *She Was Good for Nothing* (1853) the heroine, a washerwoman clearly modeled after his mother, dies because her wooden shoes, lined with straw, are washed away by the river.[3] Andersen's mother had to become a washerwoman because of her husband's death; the poor, inadequate wooden shoes floating away down the river seem symbolic of the state of poverty and insecurity to which his death had relegated her and her child. There is also a strong suggestion in the story that Hans Christian was bitterly ashamed of the lower-class stigma that now fell on him. As the saying goes, "The family of the shoemaker is left to go barefoot." His father, it would seem, did leave Andersen ill shod in terms of material goods, education, and manly qualities. He did, however, give his son a form of footwear that lasted him through life. In *The Galoshes of Fortune* (1838), Andersen tells the tale of a pair of galoshes that instantly grant every wish to anyone who wears them; they literally make dreams come true—one must merely be gifted for dreaming. Andersen, thanks largely to his father, was a great dreamer; his dreams became the vehicles, the magical galoshes, that carried him to fame.

Yet another deprivation was inflicted upon Hans Christian by his father's death—one he surely was not aware of. Among the important roles a father plays for his adolescent son is that of an opponent. No man, and no boy, can properly fight a woman and not suffer a diminution of his manhood. A boy asserting himself against his "poor mother" is a mean, heartless brute, and no matter how justified or necessary his rebellion may be, it earns him no glory. But a father, particularly if he be strong of will and principle and firm in purpose, is a worthy opponent. His son may attack him, safe in the conviction that his father can withstand the onslaught, and that the counterattack will be severe but measured. To attack such a father is not destructive, to be defeated by him not shameful; to win against such a father means earning one's manhood, quite as the slaying of a dragon makes a man a hero.[4] But Andersen's father while alive was too depressed, too sick and weak, ever to be a worthy enemy; at any event the boy was then too young. After his father's death, Hans Christian had no one on whom he could exercise his growing manhood; nor did he develop the mettle that would have enabled him to stand up to a man, face to face, whether with weapons or with words. In his more or less autobiographical novel, *The Improvisatore*, an exasperated friend says to him: "I would cudgel you if I only knew that, by so doing, I could excite a little gall in you. If you would only for once show some character—strike me in the face with your clenched fist when I laugh at you, then I could be your most faithful friend; but now I must give up every hope of you!" It was, in truth, quite easy to excite some gall in Hans Christian; but if ever he did fight back, it was from ambush—through satire and ridicule.[5]

There were, of course, other men in Andersen's younger years. Some, like his stepfather, passed through his life briefly and without apparent effect; some, like the good-natured but vulgar journeymen in the manufactory or the anything but good-natured teacher at Slagelse, terrified him by manly qualities he could never hope nor wish to possess. Others such as Jonas Collin took the aspect of illustrious benefactors and were by that very fact rendered unsuitable for emulation or competition, since the relationship structured once and for all the one as the giver, the other as the recipient. And so it would seem that Hans Christian lacked both proper models and proper opponents. Part of his "failure of nerve" could be attributed to this: that no one had shown him, in a way he could understand and accept, the way to becoming a man.[6]

But should he need to be shown?

Surely it helps to have a model. But if, for whatever reason, the masculine model is lacking, should there not sound from the other side, as it were, an evocative call to virility? Should not femininity cajole and arouse and challenge and inspire a man to assume his biological part? Cannot a man become a man because a woman demands it of him?

Surely again: this can happen, and has. But it did not happen to Andersen. Let us look at the women in his life.

15

The Mothers

His mother—his mother was the one who kept the little house spick and span: "the walls covered with pictures . . . over the workbench a cupboard containing books and songs; the little kitchen . . . full of shining plates and metal pans" (*TS*, 3). She was responsible for what well-being there was, but she was also the constant squelch: "I had a good memory, learned entire comedies by heart and performed them all alone in the shed; for this I would receive a beating: my mother, a pious but simple and kindhearted woman, considered my activities a form of insanity."[1]

Her "piety" was largely fear and superstition. We know already what an important role the "wise women"—the witches—played in her scheme of things. Her world was full of signs and ill omens. Thus Andersen writes in one of his stories: "A little boy and his mother stayed inside their room. The tallow candle was burning and the mother thought she saw a bit of wood-shaving in the light. The tallow formed a jagged edge around the candle, and then it curled. The mother believed these were signs that her son would soon die. The wood-shaving was circling toward him. This was an old superstition, but she believed it. The little boy lived many more years."[2]

To be ill and to be nursed by such a mother must have been frightening indeed; on the other hand, the mother-and-sick-child image presented in the poem *The Dying Child* is tender, if still anxious:

> Mother, why do you so press my hand?
> And why do you put your cheek to mine?
> It is wet, but burns me like a brand.
> I will always be yours, true and fine,

But no longer, mother, sigh such sighs;
If you cry, I'll cry as easily.[3]

The anxiety was always there, and at times one senses aversion or, at any rate, avoidance.

Thus when, at eighteen, Hans Christian manages to visit Odense for the first time since his departure four years earlier, he writes to the printer Iversen: "Since I know that my mother, living in modest circumstances, has no bed for me, I am taking the liberty to ask whether, for a few nights, you could put me up."[4] He had slept, during his father's absence and again after his death, in the same bed with his mother— probably lying crossways at her feet.[5] That in itself could be a sticky arrangement for a boy aged eleven to thirteen; it may have been rendered overwhelmingly physical by the circumstance, suggested in his story *She Was Good for Nothing*, that his mother, then a washerwoman, was drinking heavily. Under such conditions, modesty and propriety are likely to be neglected; and the excessive closeness, the frighteningly incestuous stimulation of such an arrangement may well be a potent repressive force of sexual awareness later in life.

We know that Hans Christian never heard, or understood, sexual jokes or allusions, that he managed to live in a whorehouse without realizing what was going on there. His extraordinary sensibility to certain bed-connected stimuli is conveyed in a letter, written when he was twenty-four. He had arrived at a coach station late at night and drenched by rain; dead tired, he had to wait another hour before they assigned him room and bed, but since "it was still warm from a lady who had lain in it, I had to be content to change clothes and lay me down on top of the bed, where I slept some few hours."[6] Such finickiness was hardly compatible with travel in his day, and he traveled a lot! But was the warm bed in which "a lady . . . had lain" too much *mother*, too much covered by the incest taboo to be treated as anything but mother?

Be this as it may. At the time he wrote to Iversen his

mother would in any case have been living with her second husband, in circumstances less modest than before. In that same new house Hans Christian had lived from age thirteen to fourteen and had had a bed of his own. It is still possible that there was no bed there for him now; it is also possible that he wished to avoid his stepfather, not his mother. But one cannot escape the impression that he did not wish to stay under her roof.

He did maintain contact—after a fashion. An avid and voluminous letter writer, he wrote to his mother only on special occasions, and economized at times by asking others in Odense to pass on to his mother letters he had written to them.[7] A few years later his mother, once again widowed, once again took to drink and made growing financial demands on him.[8] She died when he was twenty-eight, and he received the news by mail while in Rome. He reacted to it in the postscript of a long letter to one of his numerous intimate friends, Henriette Wulff: "Yesterday evening [!] I received a letter from father Collin reporting the death of my old mother. Her circumstances had been strait, and I had been able to do almost nothing for her.[9] That often saddened me back home, but I could not talk about it! Now our dear Lord has taken charge of her, and I owe him a childlike gratitude. But it has moved me deeply after all. So now I am truly quite alone—no living thing is impelled by Nature to love me."[10] Following this passage, he goes right on to discuss the probability that his latest work, *Agnete and the Merman*, may run into hostile criticism.

We have no reason to judge him. Yet we cannot help but observe that he sounds more glad to be rid of a responsibility than guilty of having failed to meet it. And he does not so much miss his mother as suffer the loss of someone "by nature obligated" to love him.

A nasty little epilogue appears, many years later, in his correspondence with Horace E. Scudder, his American publisher. Scudder had mentioned in a letter, on 10 April 1871: "There is a pleasant little story travelling through our newspaper that an enthusiastic friend of yours had purchased the little house at Odense in which you were born and had given it to you. I hope it is true!" To which Andersen replied on 2 May 1871: "There is no suspicion of anyone having bought and presented me with my birthplace in Odense, nor do I entertain any such desire."[11] Granted that he was now sixty-six years old and entitled to being crotchety, it is still hard to see how he could more succinctly or more icily have rejected any further interest in what was not just his mother's house, but the very memory of her.

In his fiction mothers do appear. On two occasions they give birth with great pain, and one of them dies in labor; they are washerwomen; they have sick children.[12] Only once is a mother rewarded: her son buys her a fine house[13]—something Andersen obviously was not able to do for his mother, even had he been willing. Only one mother is truly admired. In his episodic story *Picture Book Without Pictures* he offers a glimpse of the House of Rothschild in the Jew's Alley of Frankfurt. Here sits a respected old lady, the mother of famous sons:

> But I thought about the old lady in the narrow, miserable street. A single word from her, and she could have had a magnificent house on the bank of the Thames; one word from her, and she could have had a villa on the bay of Naples. "If I should desert the humble house from which the fortunes of my sons have sprung, then perhaps fortune might desert them!" This was a superstition, but one that, to those who know the story . . . two words of postscript will give the full meaning—*a mother* [his italics].

In other words, the Rothschilds too had a superstitious mother, but *theirs* made them rich! This is not a "nice" sentiment in our hero; but perhaps what he really resents is not that his mother failed to make him wealthy but that *she* did move from her house. She moved because she remarried, and it is the remarriage that Hans Christian may have resented so vehemently that he left home shortly thereafter and never forgave his mother. That she was "unfaithful" and "left" him—that, perhaps, was her supreme sin in his eyes. And we shall see how the experience of being jilted by a woman, and left for another, remained and recurred as the chief and ever insuperable trauma of his life.[14]

But before we proceed to adult disappointments, let us complete the survey of important figures in Andersen's childhood. Obviously there was his grandmother—father's mother, for on his mother's side all was uncertain and unknown. She acted powerfully upon his imagination, through her own fancy and rich folkloric memory as well as by introducing him to the pungent world of superstition and emotion that was the old-age home and insane asylum. She seemed to him often the impersonation of kindness and maternal warmth, and indeed seems to have given him more attention and love than did his mother. But she too had a dark side: we know how ready she was to prophesy death or to wish it for him. In a cheery Halloween poem Andersen shows her as a witch:

> The full moon casts on bush and hedge its sheen.
> Hush! It's the merry night of Halloween
> Hush! Hush!
> Grandmother mounts her broomstick,
>   what a horse
> It is! She flies fast as the wind across
> Dark clouds, dark air. She flies up,
>   she flies down,
> She flies to join the gayest dance in town.
> Hush! Hush![15]

We said "a cheery poem," but grandmother's flight over "dark clouds, dark air" resembles too much the flight of the Snow Queen; her participation in "the gayest dance in town" too much the somersaults of the Old Robber Woman. In fact, later lines of the same poem introduce images of doom:

> The hemlock's swaying in the wind tonight.
> . . . .
> Death laughs behind the cool stone of a tomb.
> A thief is hanging from the gallows.[16]

Neither Halloween nor grandmother as a witch is to Hans Christian a truly gay occasion. On the contrary, behind the facade of gaiety and kindness there lurks for him, at all times, the terror of a Witches' Sabbath and of death. Love and death are interwoven, woman and magic are one and the same, and man—"a thief . . . hanging from the gallows"—is forever the plaything and victim. While grandmother was a witch, she was not mad. It was her husband, the whittler of monsters and the witless mock of the street urchins, who was mad and in need of being supported by her. She was the strong one, he the weak, and who could tell but that she had driven him insane? For the story of the burnt farm was not true. . . .

Have we now exhausted the number of family members who shaped the boy's youth? To read his own account of his childhood, it would appear so. We exclude certain men and women living in Odense who befriended and encouraged him during his last year or so in that town. They were helpful in furthering him without shaping his character, and they were not of his blood.

But there was one other, whom he never mentions in his autobiography, though she appears in his stories, one who, while absent during his childhood, still seems to have left a deep mark: his half-sister, his mother's illegitimate daughter.

16

The Sisters

She had been born six years before Hans Christian, and put out to nurse.[1] I do not know when or how he found out about her, but she does seem to have become in his mind the symbol of a wild, sinful, and un-Christian strain in his family. As he shuddered to be of the same blood with his insane grandfather, so he quaked at the thought that this dark strain was also part of him. What is the evidence? Reginald Spink writes:

> Anne Marie (Hans Christian's mother) was illegitimate herself, one of three daughters her mother had borne to three different men, all out of wedlock. Andersen called on one of these half-aunts soon after his arrival in Copenhagen, but failed to get any help from her. If only her half-sister, Hans Christian's mother, had sent her a little girl, he records her as having said. The lady, in short, ran a brothel.[2] Fears that these disreputable relations might one day turn up to embarrass him used to haunt Andersen in the years of his success and social respectability. None of them did, however, except that on one occasion during the last years of his life, his half-sister and her lover called on him discreetly to beg money, and she turned out to be, not, as he had feared, a prostitute, but a respectable if wretchedly poor washerwoman.[3]

He closed his eyes to sex as best he could. Blind to the plastic arts, he reports with amazement how, at twenty-eight, he for the first time "saw" a "classical statue":

> I had never had an eye for sculpture; I had seen almost nothing at home; in Paris I had certainly seen many statues, but my eyes were closed to them; but here [Florence] when visiting the magnificent galleries, the rich churches with their monuments and magnificence, I learned to understand the

beauty of form[4]—the spirit which reveals itself in form. Before the 'Venus de Medici' . . . a new world of art revealed itself to me, and I could not escape from it.

(*FT*, 104)

But escape he did—after his fashion. Having managed to see the voluptuous, naked Greek goddess of love, accompanied by her little Eros, as "spirit revealed in form," he later proceeded to see her as the impersonation of "divine" as contrasted to "earthly" love.[5] But when, at thirty-eight, he visited the Rubens collection at the Brussels museum, he felt revolted: "I don't like Rubens," he wrote in his diary, "I find those fat, blond women with coarse faces and bleached dresses very boring."[6] (But was this not—with all due respect be it said—the very type of femininity he was likely to encounter at home?)

And there were "boring"—meaning upsettingly stimulating—sights that he could not avoid, which came right up to him. Thus he once wrote to Christian Voigt from Paris:

I can tell you that Paris is the most lecherous city under the sun, I don't think there is an innocent person there, things go on in an unbelievable way; publicly in the street I have been offered during the daytime in the most respectable streets 'a lovely girl of sixteen'; a young lady with the most innocent face, the most acceptable behavior, stopped us . . . yesterday and in the most lovely manner asked us to visit her, saying that she would subject herself to any kind of examination first, that there was nothing the matter with her, etc. Everywhere there are bawdy pictures, everywhere lasciviousness is referred to as something demanded by nature, etc., so that one's modesty is almost deadened. All the same I can say quite candidly that I am still innocent, though it is hardly believable to anyone who knows Paris.[7]

What kept him "innocent" was his horror of these women:

We believe no longer in ghosts; we believe no longer that the dead in their white garments appear to the living at the hour of midnight. [But] we see them yet in the great cities. By moonlight, when the cold north wind passes over the snow, and we wrap ourselves closer in our cloaks, we see white-garmented female beings in light summer dresses, beckoning, float past us. The poisonous atmosphere of the grave breathes from these figures: trust not the roses on their cheeks, for the death's head is painted, their smiles are the smiles of despair or of intoxication. They are dead, more horribly dead than our deceased ones. The soul is interred; the bodies go like evil spirits hither and thither, seeking for human blood like the vampire, that they may nourish themselves thereby. They therefore hang even upon the poorest man, upon the coarsest churl, on those from whom even men draw back. They are horrible, unhappy ghosts, which do not descend into their graves with the morning twilight. No, for then they are followed home by the dreams of despair, which sit like nightmares on their breasts, and sing to them of the scorn of men and of a better life here on earth—and tears stream down their painted cheeks. . . . "Save me! I am yet only half dead!" . . . but everyone flies away horrified . . . and she, the half-dead one, has no longer strength to throw from her the coffin-lid of her circumstances and the heavy earth of sin.

(*Only a Fiddler*, 134–35)

Only late in life was he capable of more kindly thoughts. In 1868, when he was sixty-three years old, he was once again in Paris and this time, together with his young travel companion, he repeatedly visited brothels and talked to the prostitutes: "Fernanda, the little Turkish girl . . . she was the loveliest of them, we spoke about Constantinople, her native city . . . she was very insistent *pour faire l'amour*, but I told her I had only come to talk, nothing more."[8] He was, by then, presumably past the urgencies of sin; half a lifetime earlier, at thirty-two, the issue was still fraught with terror:

Does it lie in him that he shall be a thief, or have an inclination for the girls, this instinct will not be repressed; he may be brought up among the most honest people, they may instill the most honest principles into him, yet, if this evil is in him, it will break forth. We may certainly keep it back somewhat, but, when he has attained some years, it will break forth all the more strongly. The wild beast is in all men; in one it is a ravening wolf, in another a crawling serpent, which knows how to crawl on its belly and lick dust. The beast is born within us; the only thing is whether we or this wild beast possess the most power, and the power no one possesses of himself. . . . God protect us from the power of the evil one!

(Only a Fiddler, 67)

Such were his fears in real life. From his fiction we learn more:

We have already encountered the sinful girl in the story of *The Red Shoes*. We shall, by now, boldly assert that any of his stories containing shoes as prominent features is particularly "close to his own skin." We have already pointed out that Karen *chose* to wear her red shoes—sin—the way Gerda *chose* to sacrifice hers. In this sense they are the white and the black, the good and the bad versions of the same figure. This Karen-Gerda figure is feminine, but insofar as Karen is Hans Christian's half-sister she is a possible variant of himself—and, therefore, so is Gerda. We have already seen that Hans Christian used to play amid the flower boxes on the roof of his house all by himself, never with another little child. He is, therefore, not only Kay, but also Gerda. Kay and Gerda are possible opposites, are opposite potentialities in his own self. In just this same way so are, along a different psychological axis, Karen and Gerda opposite potentials within the writer. (In the novel *O.T.*, one of Andersen's many works of autobiographical fiction, the hero, who is of course Hans Christian, is told by his evil genius that he has a deformed and depraved *twin sister* [213]. This turns out in the end not to be true, but a twin sister is even more one's own flesh and blood than a half-sister. She is practically one's alter ego; she is another version of oneself.)[9]

Or let us consider the story of *The Girl Who Trod on the Loaf*, one of the few powerful stories Andersen wrote after *The Snow Queen* (in 1859, when he was fifty-four). Inger, a poor girl, pretty, proud, and cruel to animals, is sent by her mother to serve with rich people. She is terribly ashamed to have for a mother a poor, ragged woman who gathers sticks for burning, and she is reluctant to visit her. But after some time her mistress sends her home for a visit, giving her a loaf of white bread to take along as a present for her mother:

So Inger put on her best dress and *her fine new shoes* [italics mine] and lifted her skirts high and walked very carefully, *so that her shoes would stay clean and neat*, and for that no one could blame her. But when she came to where the path crossed over marshy ground, and there was a stretch of water and mud before her, she threw the bread into the mud, so that she could use it as a stepping-stone and get across with dry shoes. But just as she placed one foot on the bread and lifted the other up, the loaf sank deeper and deeper, carrying her down until she disappeared entirely, and nothing could be seen but a black, bubbling pool![10]

Inger sinks down "to the Marsh Woman, who brews down there . . . the meadows begin to reek in the summer when the old woman is at her brewing down below . . . a cesspool is a wonderful place [by comparison]." That very day, the Devil and his Great-Grandmother have come to visit and the latter "was sewing bits of leather *to put in people's shoes* [italics mine] so that they should have no rest. She embroidered lies, and worked up into mischief and slander thoughtless words." She takes a liking to Inger and carries her along to Hell. There Inger stands like a statue, but still proud: " 'This is what comes of trying to have clean feet,' she said to herself. 'Look at them stare at me!' " She thinks she must be pretty to look at, but in fact her clothes have become covered with slime, "a snake had wound itself in her hair and dangled over her neck; and from every fold of her dress an ugly toad peeped out, barking like an asthmatic lapdog."

We have, it appears, another sinful girl. Her sin is the sin of cruelty and pride, of hubris; and it is symbolized in her shoes, which she intends to keep clean and shiny even if she has to step on "God's gift," the loaf of bread. By way of punishment she sinks down into a malodorous underworld of swamp and slime, ruled over by women—the Marsh Woman and the Devil's Great-Grandmother. We are reminded here of the Flower Garden of the Woman Skilled in Magic, who also ruled in the underworld. The Devil's Great-Grandmother works at corruption by means of magical "bits of leather to put in people's shoes"—and since shoes represent character and character as fate, this would seem to be an appropriate employ for her energies.

But the slime and the toads and snakes are new—at least, to us. They were, since the late Middle Ages, symbols of sexuality and corruption—in short, of sin. Statues of "Frau Welt" ("Mistress World") or similar characters showed "pretty" women not just beset but penetrated by assorted reptiles and amphibians.[11] In Danish-Nordic folklore, there are furthermore the figures of the "Ellefruwen," the elf maidens[12] (whose aunt, according to Andersen, is the Marsh Woman) and of the "Skogsnuva," seductive creatures bonnie in front but rotting behind like old tree trunks.[13]

As to the stench, it reappears in Andersen's story *The Psyche* (1861), which tells of a sculptor who, having been jilted by his love, is advised to seek available consolation: "Why don't you stop your eternal dreaming! Be a man like your friends. Don't be an idealist; if you do you'll have a breakdown. Get a little tipsy; then you'll sleep well. Let a beautiful girl be your doctor. The girl from the campagna is as beautiful as your princess in the marble castle. They are both daughters of Eve, and you can't tell them apart." The sculptor follows this suggestion (as Andersen did not); he goes to a tavern with his friends, and they pick up girls and take them home. "In Angelo's room their voices became quieter, but no less fiery. 'Apollo! Jupiter! Into your heaven and glory I am carried! The Flower of life has blossomed forth in my heart this very moment!' Yes, it blossomed— broke, withered, and a nauseating fume whirled from it, blinding his sight; his thoughts went blank. . . . 'Shame!' This came from his own mouth, right from the bottom of his heart." He eventually dies of the experience.[14]

The stench of the "decaying flower of life," the cesspool-smelling swamp with its slime and its reptiles: all stand, in a purely physical way, for those dangerous and contaminating elements in women's bodies that caused Andersen to keep a safe distance from them.[15] In a more general sense they symbolize—just like the shiny red shoes!—sexual and moral corruption. What strikes us as peculiar in this instance is that Inger sinks into this morass for the sin of *wanting to keep her shoes clean*, for which, as Andersen says, "no one could blame her"! This symbolic complication will have to occupy us some more later on.

At any rate, right now Inger is in sin and in Hell, and is punished not only by filth but by hunger (obviously because she degraded the "bread of God"). Her salvation is eventually accomplished through the tears of good people. Her mother's tears are, in this regard, insufficient: "A mother's tears of grief for her erring child always reach it, but they do not redeem; they only burn,[16] and they make the pain greater." Inger is first moved from her frozen, statuelike pride and suffering (she is "frozen" into an immobile statue just as Kay is immobile and frozen on the Lake of Reason) by the tears of pity shed by "an innocent little girl" whose mother has told her the story of "wicked Inger." This same little girl, grown into an old woman and called to heaven, finally saves Inger by crying for her once more. Inger is released from her petrified state, becomes a little bird, and atones for her wrongs by collecting grains of corn for other little birds during a cold winter "until [the grains] would have equalled in weight the loaf upon which little Inger had stepped to keep her fine shoes from being soiled." At that moment she turns into a white bird and flies straight into the sun.

The Girl Who Trod on the Loaf is thus another story of a wicked girl. Inger is clearly a double of Karen of *The Red Shoes*, of Andersen's own mysterious half-sister, perhaps of Andersen himself. But the tale is also a story of redemption and atonement, and by far not the only such story Andersen wrote. We shall have more to say about this later on.

For the moment let us drop the theme of woman as sin, and of sin and salvation, and pick up a thread we left dangling: the theme of the woman jilting her lover.

We already know of Andersen's infatuation with Riborg Voigt. We saw how hesitantly he went about it, so that he never properly declared himself and, unwooed by him, she went on to marry another. Considering he never proposed, he could hardly feel jilted—though he may have managed to feel so anyhow. But there followed a similarly half-declared "love" to a girl he saw much of in his "home of homes," Louise Collin. She already loved another, and as soon as she sensed what was stirring in Andersen, she saw to it that they were never alone together. She was married soon thereafter.[17] He had no better luck with Sophie, the sixteen-year-old daughter of his friend Ørsted, who "became engaged just at the time that Andersen got his stipend from the King, and felt sufficiently well-to-do to propose to her."[18] And we already know of the greatest—and last—love of his life, Jenny Lind, who so insisted on calling him and treating him as—her brother.

Jean Hersholt, his loving translator, writes: "In all these cases, a more worldly, more handsome and less knotty man than Andersen might well have swept all obstacles before him. But he was unworldly, and ugly, and knotty, so he remained a bachelor. He was not nearly as happy about it as the psychiatrists may suppose. The bridal kisses of his stories he had to imagine, and as he said when he came to be old, 'I have imagined so much and had so little.'"[19] Well! Speaking as a psychiatrist, I must say that I do not suppose he was happy at all; and as to "the bridal kisses of his stories," there are precious few of them! But why he "had so little"—that is precisely what we called his "failure of nerve," and the question that is occupying us now. Perhaps we can find some answers in his stories dealing with jilted lovers? Let us take them in chronological order, one by one.

17

The Jilted Lover

When he was thirty-two, Andersen wrote *Only a Fiddler*, a novel as miserably maudlin as the title suggests. The hero, Christian, entertains a lifelong unhappy love for his childhood sweetheart, Naomi. She runs off with a circus rider, eventually marries a count, and lives happily ever after; he barely makes a living as a mediocre violinist, and eventually dies at a young age from poverty, illness, and despair. The contrast between her indomitable, impudent self-assertiveness, on the one hand, and his timid, vacillating, ineffective longing for good luck, on the other, forms the essence of the book. She is so clearly superior, her interest in him so sporadic, cruel, and insincere, that his death comes as a relief not just to him, but also to the reader: it is the only solution to a hopeless predicament.

When Andersen was forty-eight (1853), and the matter with Jenny Lind had been long decided, he wrote a lengthy story called *Under the Willow Tree*.[1] It is the tale of a *shoemaker*'s apprentice's unhappy love for his childhood sweetheart, a poor girl who goes off and becomes an opera singer (just like Jenny Lind!). Initially the girl loves him and knows that her love is returned, but "he is a man, so he must speak first." He does not speak first—not as a boy, not as an apprentice; and he does not write to her while she becomes a singer in a big town. When, as a journeyman, he finally visits her and actually declares himself, she answers: "Dear Knud, don't make us both unhappy. I shall always be a loving sister to you, one in whom you may trust, but I shall never be anything more." Upon parting, she "repeated the word 'brother.' Yes, that was supposed to be a great consolation!" In his despondency he travels far and wide (as An-

122

dersen had done), but he remains miserable. Finally, one winter, he is seized by the urge to return to his homeland. Tired after a long march through the snow, he sits down under a wayside tree such as the one he and his love had played under as children. He has a dream of happiness and freezes to death.

In this story rejection (and, in effect, "castration" to the nonsexual role of brother) leads to nothing but icy death. The same fate, no doubt, would eventually have overcome Kay had he not been rescued by Gerda.

Two years later, having perhaps "worked through" some of these feelings, Andersen manages to give the same theme another twist. *Ib and Little Christine* (1855) again tells the story of two children who love each other.[2] An old gypsy woman offers them the choice of three wishing nuts. Christine asks for the two golden ones, which turn out to contain, respectively, a golden coach and beautiful clothes. Ib takes the black one, which the gypsy woman tells him contains "the best of all things for you." In accord with the magic of the wishing nuts, the girl soon goes off and marries a rich young man; Ib, *who makes wooden shoes,* is left poor and bereft. But Christine and her husband soon squander their wealth, while Ib eventually finds a treasure of gold in his field.[3] Now wealthy, he travels to Copenhagen, and there takes pity on a poor little girl who is crying. The girl, who strangely reminds him of Christine, leads him to the attic of a wretched, tumbledown house, where, in the heavy and almost suffocating air of the room, her mother lies dying. The sick woman is, of course, Christine. Her husband, having lost his money, had drowned himself. Now she is tortured by the thought that she has no one to whom she can entrust her little daughter. "Ib . . . lit a piece of candle he found in the room . . . he looked at the little girl and remembered how Christine had looked when she was that age, and he felt that for her sake he would love this child." When the mother dies, Ib adopts her little daughter. "Ib had money, said people, gold from the black earth, and he had his little Christine, too."

Here, clearly, the tables are turned, and the jilted lover can, as it were, "have his cake and eat it too." Although the faithless girl dies in well-deserved misery, her loyal lover can "have" her in the person of her reincarnation, her daughter. (He can, in fact, have her the way Andersen likes his women best—as a little girl.) Regarding this story, Andersen commented: "My mind is heavy, and I have not been able to do much work, but I have written a little story. It is not bad, but there are no sun rays in it, because I have none myself."[4] Indeed, it is illumined only by the pale fire of revenge.

Five years later, the theme has become even more somber. *A Story from the Sand Dunes* (1860) has an apparently joyful beginning.[5] For the first time, we see a happily married young couple. Their only regret is the lack of children. But as the young husband is offered a brilliant diplomatic post, his wife becomes pregnant. They travel by ship from their Portugal homeland to the St. Petersburg court where he is to serve, and as they round Denmark they suffer shipwreck in a storm. Although the husband drowns, the wife is saved—for the moment. No sooner is she made comfortable in a poor Danish fisherman's hut than she breaks into "screams of pain and fear." "After hours of suffering and struggles" her child is born, but she dies. The infant, Joergen, is raised by the poor people in whose hut he was born. His life is one of poverty and backbreaking labors. He loves, and eventually declares his love to, a childhood sweetheart, but she loves another and calls Joergen her brother (!). He helps her and her lover (a friend of his) find a house to live in, then leaves on extended travels. Eventually life seems willing to smile on him and once again he loves. But this time the girl he loves suffers shipwreck before his eyes. He swims out to save her, fails, and himself survives a battering by the sea only as a brain-damaged idiot. After a somewhat unconvincing religious illumination, he dies in a lonely church that is being buried by sand during another storm.

Andersen says of this tale of woe and the injustice of fate that it was meant to convey the necessity, hence certainty, of compensation during the life eternal.[6] There is little sense of compensation in the story. What we do see is the case of a struggling and noble-hearted man, who is jilted by one girl and dies in the attempt to get another. The happy couple of the beginning apparently belongs at the end of a progressive series of disasters of love. Andersen seems to say: if you declare yourself to a girl, you will get rejected; if you struggle hard for her, it will be your death. If by any chance you should get her, trust not the semblance of bliss. You may be childless, or if not, your wife may die in childbirth. Or you yourself may not live to see your child, or to raise it. Life is nothing but a draught of bitter gall. (What a far cry from the smiling teller of fairy tales we imagine Andersen to have been!)

A year later, *The Psyche* (1861) tells the story of a young sculptor in love with the girl whose likeness he sculpts.[7] Since she is of high birth, she scorns him when he declares his love, even though she admires his art. As we already know, he tries to console himself by debauch, but the "nauseating fume" of reality drives him to become a monk. He stops sculpting and eventually dies. The girl dies too; only the statue of Psyche—art—survives.

More rejection stories follow, but by 1865 (when Andersen was already sixty years old!) we see the first uplift, the first indication of sublimation. In *Golden Treasure,* another jilted lover reacts by becoming a famous violinist; the girl who jilted him becomes a councilor's wife—mild punishment indeed![8]

Five years later in *Lucky Peer* (1870), Andersen wrote yet another autobiographical story.[9] This time he gave away a secret: when the hero receives the letter from his beloved in which she informs him of her betrothal to "the fat councilor," he "felt as if he had been pierced through the heart. At that moment it became clear to him that, during all the vacillation of his soul, she had been his steadfast thought. He cared more for her than anyone else in the world. Tears came into his eyes; he crumpled the letter in his hand. It was the first great grief of heart he had known since he had heard, with Mother and Grandmother, that his father had fallen in the war."[10] The secret slipping out here is obviously that Andersen never truly felt his infatuations until after they had become hopeless; only after he had been waved off did he elaborate his feelings into something resembling passionate love.

The hero in *The Improvisatore* says of a woman: "It is admiration for her which fills my soul. I worship her loveliness, her understanding. . . . Love her? the thought has never entered my mind." And his friend responds: "You are not in love! no, that is true indeed. You are one of those intellectual amphibious creatures that one cannot tell whether they rightly belong to the living or the dream-world—you are not in love, not at least in the same way as I am, not in the same way as everybody else—you say so yourself, and I will credit you; but still you may be so in your own particular way" (vol. 1, 234).

No—he knew he could not love "in the same way as everybody else." Very late in his life (27 March 1874, a little over a year before his death) he wrote to his American publisher, Scudder: "You are now in your best years of vigor, and as I see from your letter of February, a married man. You have got yourself a home, a loving wife, and you are happy! God bless you and her! At one time I too dreamed of such a happiness, but it was not to be granted me."[11] He is deceiving himself; or rather, this is at best a very partial truth. If indeed he ever dreamed of marriage, his dreams were not happy dreams but rather nightmares. At best, he could have wished and dreamed to be the sort of man who wore boots and was unafraid of all that marriage may imply, but he hid his boots—or had no boots at all—and was afraid.

But are we not shamelessly psychologizing and overlooking some perfectly simple, *practical* reasons why he never married?

Hersholt, in the paragraph we quoted in the preceding chapter (note 18) suggests that Andersen would not have been *financially* able to afford marriage until after he had received his stipend from the king. And sure enough, An-

dersen himself had thought of blaming poverty for his loneliness. In *The Galoshes of Fortune,* published in 1838 and
therefore written after at least the first two of his "disappointments" in love, he has a poetic young lieutenant write
a poem called *If Only I Were Rich.* The last two stanzas contain these lines:

> If only I were rich, is still my heavenly prayer.
> My little girl of seven is now a lady fair;
> She is so sweet, so clever and so good;
> My heart's fair tale she never understood.
> If only, as of yore, she still for me would care,
> But I am poor and silent; I confess I do not dare.
> It is your will, oh Lord!
> . . . .
> You, whom I love, if still you understand
> Then read this poem from my youth's far land,
> Though best it be you never know my pain.
> I am still poor, my future dark and vain,
> But may, O Lord, you bless her!¹²

The implication—though with typical restraint an implication only, not a frank statement—is that he would have
proposed had he only been rich.¹³

Twenty-seven years later, he still quips in the brief and
rather charming story *In the Children's Room* (1865): "There is
nothing in [his] pockets, and that's very interesting, for
that's why the course of true love doesn't run smoothly."¹⁴
And in his letters too the theme crops up. Thus in December
1837 he writes to Henriette Hanck:

> My loneliness is increasingly oppressive to me. You write
> that I would certainly not keep it a secret from you if I were
> to become engaged; no, that I would not; but, by God, I am
> not thinking of it! . . . I am too clever to take an ill-considered
> step (and God grant that I remain so!). I earn but a poor
> living and have no prospects. My wife would have to live as
> she had been accustomed to in her circles, and you must
> therefore see that I can never become engaged; like my poor
> Christian in the novel [*Only a Fiddler*] I shall die a lonely man.
> Do not believe that I am romanticizing; no, I shall open my
> heart to you like a brother. Yes, if I were well-to-do, if I could
> expect some day to receive one- or two-thousand per year,

then I would fall in love! There is a girl here, pretty, intelligent, good and lovable, from one of the spiritually most elevated families of Kopenhagen; but I have no means and—I don't even fall in love! She is, besides, exactly half as old as I. Thank God, she has no inkling that she more than pleases me, and . . . she may, one of these days, tell me: "Andersen you must congratulate me, I am engaged!" But she will not say this; I do not know a girl more timid than her.[15]

According to her age, the girl in question must have been Sophie Ørsted, and we already know that she shortly did just what he declares her incapable of. As to his excuse for "not even falling in love" (could a full-blooded man, no matter how sensible, really stop himself?), it sounds sensible enough at that stage of his fortunes. But by the time he met Jenny Lind he had a comfortable income and the fame that would ensure its continuation. True, she did in fact reject him. But why, oh why, were there no others? Why was he, after the age of forty, even past having to defend himself against love?

Kai Friis Möller believes that "his three abortive wooings may without difficulty be attributed to his notorious uncomeliness . . . [which] filled his ever-self-absorbed mind with its own depressing image."[16] Andersen would have agreed quite eagerly. In 1834 he wrote to his friend Christian Voigt:

> I often think: if only I were handsome *or* rich and had a little office of some kind, then I would get married, I would work, eat, and finally lie down in the churchyard—what a pleasant life that would be; but since I am ugly and will always remain poor nobody will want to marry me, for that is what the girls look for, don't you know, and they are quite right. So I shall have to stand alone all my life as a poor thistle and be spat at because it happened to fall to my lot to have thorns.[17]

He even wrote a story, *What Happened to the Thistle*, in which a thistle, growing just *outside* a garden where a betrothal is taking place—the garden of marriage—wants very much "in," but only the thistle's flowers (his stories) make it across the fence (the bride wishes to be decorated with them); the thorny thistle remains forever outside.[18] Yes, he thought of himself that way. But surely: he, the sharp observer, must have seen that many a man, as ugly as he or worse, was found attractive and marriageable by the fair sex.

He was, in fact, quite aware that he had something very precious to offer. In *The Toad* he gives another version of his own "family romance."[19] Mother toad had fallen into a deep, dark well, where she gave birth to her children. "She's thick, and fat and ugly," said the young green frogs, "and her children will be just as ugly as she is." "That may be," retorted the mother toad, "but one of them has a jewel in his head." One of the little toads "had an immense desire to get to the edge of the well, and to look over; she felt such a longing for the green, up there." She jumps into the bucket as it is being raised. "Ugh, you beast!" said the farm laborer who emptied the bucket, "you're the ugliest thing I've seen for a while." The frogs near the well are friendly. "You are welcome! Are you a he or a she? But it doesn't matter; you are equally welcome." Having come up so far, the little toad is intent on going ever higher and higher: "She always felt a longing for something better . . . 'I must go higher up, into splendor and joy! I feel so confident, and yet I am afraid. It's a difficult step to take, and yet it must be taken. Onward, therefore, straight onward!'" She encounters a naturalist and a poet. The former calls her "so wonderfully ugly," and the poet retorts, "Is there not something beautiful in the popular belief that just as the toad is the ugliest of animals, it should often carry the most precious jewel in its head? Is it not just the same thing with men? What a jewel that was that Aesop had, and still more, Socrates!" Noticing storks high on a roof, the toad wishes to go to Egypt with them. It is, of course, she who has the jewel. "That jewel was the continual striving and desire to go upward—ever upward. It gleamed in her head, gleamed in joy, beamed brightly in her longing." She goes to Egypt—in the belly of the stork—but a sunbeam carries the jewel from the head of the toad up into the sun, "into the glories which God has created." Here Andersen not only portrays himself as the son of a "fallen" woman who climbs to social heights despite his ugliness, but compares his shining genius to that of another great storyteller, Aesop—and even to that of Socrates.

Yes, he knew he had something of great value to offer. And his "uncomeliness" presented him not with an obstacle to marriage but—like his poverty and his lowly origins—with an excuse. But there were graver complications, and he hints at them in a letter to Henriette Wulff on 16 February 1833:

> I am sitting alone in my shabby little room and torture myself—perhaps more than I should; but it is a torture all the same!—There are leaves in the diary of the heart that are so stuck together, only our Good Lord could pry them open; and on these leaves are written sufferings the cause of which, no matter how hard I tried to be honest, I could never even hint at. This cause lies within me, in a sentiment for which I have no fitting name!—I have remained a child long beyond childhood; yet I have never known what it really means to be young! I feel such an infinite yearning for it, a desire to tear myself away from my melancholy thoughts and my habits, and to enjoy life like a sensible human being; there is so much I would like to forget, in order to learn something better.[20]

Earlier still, in 1830, he had written to Henriette Hanck: "You think that I *pretend* my misery? . . . consider that certain scenes are being enacted, not just in my heart but in reality, into which no one is initiated and which I *must* not reveal . . . much, much has happened . . . events have intruded upon the drama of my life which are not phantasy."[21]

He is hinting at a dark secret, but what could it be? Surely if, in the latter passage, he were referring to his unrequited love for Riborg Voigt, he could afford to be more open; or if, the matter still being fresh and perhaps undecided, he did not feel free to discuss it right then, he could with perfect propriety have discussed it in the former letter, when Riborg was good and married? No, he seems to be hinting at something darker and undisclosed, a sentiment for which he has no word and that renders him miserable. And so, in view of the halfhearted, ambivalent interest in women we have discussed above, we must now examine the possibility that his "nameless" secret, "enacted not just in my heart but in reality," may have been homosexuality.

18

A Confusion of Loves

Now that is a difficult topic to discuss, and we had better clarify our terms.

We mean by homosexuality only overt sexual intercourse between individuals of the same sex. We may speak of homosexual feelings when there is a conscious wish for such actual activity. And we are willing to consider that friendship can be invested with strong but diffuse sensual feelings that we may call homoerotic, but that it frequently lacks such coloring. We shall further state emphatically that homosexuality and effeminacy are not congruent, that many homosexuals are not effeminate and some effeminate men are not homosexual. Nor does the active-passive axis in any way coincide with the homosexual-heterosexual continuum, since there are obviously both active and passive individuals of either sexual orientation.

Keeping these distinctions and cautions in mind, let us now look for whatever evidence we may find regarding Andersen's possible homosexuality.

We know already that Hans Christian was a "pretty boy." On two occasions, once in the Odense manufactory and once in the cabinetmaker's shop in Copenhagen, small groups of "coarse" apprentices and journeymen made fun of him and treated him, by mockery and perhaps by not-so-gentle physical indiscretions, as if he were a girl, or at least as if he were in need of demonstrating that he wasn't. These incidents prove not only that he was effeminate in appearance (his long, blond hair and his soprano voice must have contributed heavily to giving such an impression) but also that he in no way strove to seem otherwise. There are effeminate-looking men whose resolute and perhaps belligerent behavior forbids the kind of pleasantries Hans Christian was exposed to. (Off-hand, the "pretty," almost girlish-looking medal of honor winner of World War II, Audie Murphy, comes to mind.) That Hans Christian was twice treated the way he was would indicate that in some fashion he was asking for it, that on an unconscious level he may have been longing for the rough manhandling he received.

Perhaps this was so. At twenty-four Hans Christian writes to Madam Iversen: "We recently put on some plays. . . . I acted Columbine with long flaxen tresses and naked arms, a curious spectacle!"[1] What with his having been twice "burnt," one would expect him to overreact against his girlish appearance; instead he, at least on this occasion, exploited and exaggerated it and clearly enjoyed himself.[2] But all sorts of people like to act, and occasionally to cross-dress, without this having any psychopathological significance; so we should guard against making too much of it.

Things get a bit more precarious when we hear about his friendship with Ludwig Læssøe. Apparently Ludwig was a high school student—perhaps around thirteen when Hans Christian was twenty-five. All I know of him and Andersen's friendship with him comes from two letters.

In the first of these letters, of 22 June 1930, Andersen, then on a tour through Jutland, responds to a letter of Ludwig's, which had been a long time catching up with him: "In Veile I expected definitely to find a letter of yours, and I cannot deny that I was somewhat hurt that you had forgotten me altogether; but now I see that you are innocent." He continues with a description of his travels and finds occasion to say, "From Viborg across the heath of Aarhuus I drove all night in a pouring rain, so that my clothes clung to my body and all my pretty shapes became apparent"—a statement not only vain but allusive to the point of lubricity.[3]

This first letter is addressed "Dear Læssøe." The second one, apparently at Ludwig's request, starts, "Dear Ludwig!" a change that, to Germanic or Nordic ears, indicates more closeness. It was written three weeks later, discusses Andersen's latest writings, and refers to Ludwig's mother in a manner that clearly proves Andersen's relationship to have been with the whole Læssøe family. Then he answers what must have been a request by suggesting to Ludwig various themes for school essays, such as patriotism, the most important moments in the life of Moses, and so on. His sixth suggestion is "to find all those passages in biblical history when Woman acted in a fashion less noble or good.—Actually, one should, by way of contrast, enumerate all those passages where men acted as shining heroes; but that would lead too far, so let it be enough with woman. By the way: I suppose your sister will say of this sixth essay that I am disgusting?"[4] The same letter continues two days later: "Upon my arrival [in Odense] I received your friendly letter; but, my dear friend, it was cruelly brief; not more than nine lines and a blot on the first page! Next time you must really write more closely and on all three pages!" And he closes after a lengthy travelogue: "But write soon, very soon; I am really longing for a letter, for the last one was nothing." And then comes a postscript: "This letter can stand for four of yours, so do not be brief! The last one I received drove me to despair; it was as short as a sneeze . . . write, write more! Tell me of this or that, about things at home or elsewhere, or about me, since you know so well how much I love that. Right? Fare well!!!!"[5]

There is an unmistakably flirtatious tone to these letters, and one cannot help raising an eyebrow. As Ludwig's parent one would feel like discouraging such a relationship. But perhaps this was not necessary. No further letters to Ludwig follow, whereas a correspondence with his mother continues, on and off, for many years. Did Ludwig himself put a stop to this?[6] We do not know. But the already quoted letter to Henriette Hanck referring to "scenes enacted not only in the heart but in reality" follows shortly upon the correspondence with Ludwig. And so, as to what may or may not have happened between the boy Ludwig and the young man Hans Christian we are left to guess.

But whatever did or did not happen, what followed shortly thereafter was the infatuation with Riborg Voigt, and we must now consider in the present context a character previously mentioned only in passing—her brother Christian. Andersen writes in a letter to B. S. Ingemann in January 1831: "Consider my situation! I shall never get to see [Riborg] again, I must not, I cannot! But I have a consolation, I have won her brother, he knows everything and feels and suffers with us, he loves both of us so heartily, through him I can hear of her."[7] And in a letter to C. H. Lorenzen of March of that year, discussing his daily habits and life-style:

> From one to three I visit people, like a cosmopolitan butterfly; but I don't spend the entire two hours just strolling around; most of that time belongs to my heart and my friendship; every day I go to see my dear Christian Voigt, him to whom I feel drawn more than to all others; I don't even notice how time passes [when I am with him], even though I am almost always so heavy-hearted, so sad. It is as if he had bewitched me, I do not know myself why I think so much of him![8]

What do we make of this?

The most obvious interpretation, on the face of it, would be that Andersen was fond of Christian because Christian was, so to speak, all that was left him of Riborg; that he was fond of the brother because he had loved the sister, that some of his love for her was transferred onto the brother, by way of holding on to what was left of the glow.

But *if* there had happened more between Hans Christian and Ludwig than was permissible (and we do *not* know that), then there are two further possibilities: Andersen could have pushed himself (more or less unconsciously, to be sure) into an at first halfhearted and then gratefully exaggerated and dramatized "love" for Riborg by way of "proving" his "normality"—in effect using Riborg as a defense against Ludwig. In this process Christian may have appeared as an unexpected but blessed bonus and a retreat into more familiar territory. Or, conversely, the congenial familiarity with Christian could, in the first place, have enabled Andersen to "cross over" (as over a bridge) by way of the brother to the sister.[9]

Lest this seem farfetched, we may refer to a similar situation earlier in Andersen's life, one he spelled out himself. In his late teens, "to keep up with his 'already wildly-infatuated comrades'" he imagined he was in love with the poet Oehlenschläger's daughter, Lotte, a girl of thirteen or fourteen years. "I worshipped Oehlenschläger, and I thought that this worship might be transferred to his daughter. I found it poetic to love his daughter, and I decided to do so. I gazed at her; I wanted so much to be in love, but I could not. Yet my glances were observed, and it was said: 'He loves Lotte'. I myself believed it, although I remember well that I wondered that one could be in love at will! Ah well, I loved Lotte, but it was really her father I meant. It was of short duration."[10] Perhaps even his love for Sophie Ørsted rested on a similar basis, or at least contained an element of it. Her father, the scientist H. C. Ørsted, had been one of his earliest patrons and became a lifelong friend and adviser, a man Andersen revered. If he could not be his son, could he not at least become his son-in-law?[11]

More closely to the point—since we are considering not a father-son but a peer attachment—is Andersen's own treatment of the topic in his novel *O.T.* Otto and Wilhelm are close friends at the University. Otto has "noticed"—is carefully developing an infatuation with—Wilhelm's beautiful sister, Sophie. And Wilhelm is in love with a pale, delicate but "pure" servant girl, Eva, who resembles Otto a good deal and who, it turns out eventually, is Otto's long-lost sister. At one point the students put on a festivity, which entails (since women are not admitted to the University) that some of the young men dress up as girls.

> Many of the youngest students who had feminine features were dressed as ladies; some of them might even be called pretty. . . . Otto was much excited. . . . A young lady, one of the beauties, in a white dress, and with a thin handkerchief over her shoulders, approached and threw herself into his arms. It was Wilhelm! but Otto found his likeness to Sophie stronger than he had ever before noticed it to be; and therefore the blood rushed to his cheeks when the fair one threw

her arms around him, and laid her cheek upon his: he perceived more of Sophie than of Wilhelm in this form. Certainly Wilhelm's features were coarser—his whole figure larger than Sophie's; but still Otto fancied he saw Sophie, and therefore these marked gestures, this reeling about with the other students, offended his eyes. When Wilhelm seated himself on his knee, and pressed his cheek to his, Otto felt his heart beat as in fever; it sent a stream of fire through his blood: he thrust him away, but the fair one continued to overwhelm him with caresses . . . [and] flew dancing with him through the crowd. The heat, the noise, and, above all, the exaggerated lacing, affected Wilhelm; he felt unwell. Otto led him to a bench and would have unfastened his dress, but all the young ladies, true to their part, sprang forward, pushed Otto aside, surrounded their sick companion and concealed her.

Later a toast is proposed to the ladies; they rose, but

"No, no," whispered Otto to Wilhelm at the same time pulling him down. "In this dress you resemble your sister so much, that it is quite horrible to me to see you act a part so opposed to her character!" "And your eyes," said Wilhelm, smiling, "resemble two eyes which have touched my heart. A health to first love!" he cried, and struck his glass against Otto's so that half of the wine was again lost. . . . "I wish you would put on your own dress!" said Otto. "You resemble, as I said before, your sister"—"And I am my sister," interrupted Wilhelm, in his wantonness. "And as a reward for your charming readings aloud, for your excellent conversation, and the whole of your piquant amiability, you shall now be paid with a little kiss!" He pressed his lips to Otto's forehead; Otto thrust him back and left the company. Several hours passed before he could sleep; at length he was forced to laugh over his anger: what mattered it if Wilhelm resembled his sister? The following morning Otto paid her a visit. . . . He related how much Wilhelm had resembled [her], and how unpleasant this had been to him; and they laughed. . . . Otto could not forbear drawing a comparison. How great a difference did he now find! Sophie's beauty was of quite another kind! Never before had he regarded her in this light. Of the kisses which Wilhelm had given him, of course, they did not speak; but Otto thought of them, thought of them quite differently to what he had done before, and—the ways of Cupid are strange!

(162ff.)

The attachment between Otto and Wilhelm is prior, in time, to their love for each other's sister—and each sister looks like her brother. That the friends love the sisters *because* of this resemblance could not be spelled out more clearly than in the preceding passage. As it turns out in the end, Eva fades away and dies, and Sophie marries a jolly landowner; thus neither of the friends "has to" marry, and they presumably can continue to travel together as they have been doing—though there is a faint hint that Otto considers marrying Louise, Wilhelm's second sister.

Returning to Andersen's confessed "bewitchment" by Christian Voigt, it remained, as far as we can tell, a matter of the heart, a friendship perhaps lightly tinged with homoerotic feeling; there is no evidence of anything having happened "in actuality."

What more?

Very little. Three years later he writes to Signe Læssøe, Ludwig's mother: "I almost believe that I am myself the dissonance in this world; too many tears have fallen upon the strings of my love; it can no longer resound harmonically nor can I reach what I longed for. You probably do not understand me, but I *may* not speak more clearly."[12] Why not? If he were referring to Riborg or Louise or Sophie, he could easily be more clear. Does he wonder whether Mrs. Læssøe had sensed his feelings for Ludwig?

Shortly thereafter he writes to Henriette Wulff: "O God, Jette, you do not know how my happiness in Italy has been disrupted; since my spirit became ever more manly there, it was hurt by the fact that a younger man than myself treated me as if I were a boy. I am offended by a person to whom I have confided every thought and who is now co-responsible for this indescribable fear of going home."[13] He goes on to express suicidal thoughts. What has happened? Did he, in a letter to Christian, reveal too much? Did Christian, who must have been about five years younger than Andersen, rebuff him and put him in his place? Does this explain why the man by whom he declared himself "bewitched" is heard from no more?

Let us admit: this is all meager evidence and brittle guess-work. But the topic is intriguing. In 1901 Albert Hansen published a paper in which he claimed to furnish "proof" of Andersen's homosexuality.[14] In fact, though he could draw on letters and diary entries not available to me, he does not come up with anything more substantial than Andersen's foppish vanity, his fear of aggressively seductive women, and his exuberantly affectionate language toward his men friends; in the end he concludes that "Andersen's heart did not know love." We may take it that the expression "heart" here stands as *pars pro toto* for "body"; for if "heart" is to mean "soul" or "sentiment," then Andersen's heart was quite capable of infatuations—almost certainly toward *either* sex.

Still, Hansen's "verdict" demanded further investigation, and in 1927 Hjalmar Helweg published *H. C. Andersen. En psykiatrisk Studie,* followed in 1929 by a German paper, "H. C. Andersen und die Behauptung seiner Homosexualität."[15] Helweg, unlike Hansen, was a psychiatrist, and his refutation is both clinically astute and thorough.

He begins by pointing out that Hansen (in a manner that then as now may have been in vogue) painted all four great Danish writers—Holberg, Andersen, Kierkegaard, and Jacobsen—with the brush of homosexuality, but that it was all unsubstantiated guesswork. He then proceeds to draw a pathography of Andersen based on his published works, his letters and diaries, and on the writings of people who had known him personally and well.

Andersen, relates Helweg, was a sickly child, given to faints and convulsions, some of which may have been hysterical in nature. These fits ceased when he was about thirteen. He was a daydreamer and did not play with other children. His dolls were not like those girls play with, but rather stage figures. He began to keep diaries when a schoolboy, and so it is possible to follow his life, day by day, over a period of thirty years. He frequently felt tired and weary, sometimes to such a degree that he could barely walk. At times he records inexplicable moments of wellbeing. He would faint under the impact of strong psychic impressions. He often felt dizzy and was plagued by irritability and nervous restlessness. He could not sit still, suffered when the streets were deserted on Sundays, and lost his composure when the weather was bad or some remark had injured him. Depressive periods, which he himself interpreted as illnesses, recurred. He labored under hypochondriac fears of cancer and rheumatism, had food fads, suffered from agoraphobia and obsessive doubts, and spent hours in railway stations so as not to miss a train. All his life he feared poverty and was exquisitely sensitive to insult. His puberty came late, but when it did, his voice became virile. Even so, he was imbued with inferiority feelings.

According to his diaries he masturbated from the onset of puberty until his forty-second year. He considered this a sin and fought against it. Friends tried to introduce him to normal heterosexuality, but these efforts failed due to his shyness and his moral scruples. Yet he was not without sex drive. In 1834 he wrote in his diary: "In Naples . . . sensuous mood, I am fighting with myself . . . my blood is burning, dreams are boiling within me. It seems that the South demands its rights. . . . Happy the man who is married." And in 1842, "Sensuous mood. An almost animal passion in my blood, a wild desire to kiss a woman and to hold her in my arms, quite as in the South." And in 1847, "Greatly tempted to commit some foolishness, my blood is prickling . . . repeatedly walked up and down the street and then, as before, back home: I am foolish, my heart is beating. Old fool!"

In spite of such moments of temptation, writes Helweg, Andersen never satisfied his inclination toward women. He rejected with a sense of disgust those worshipful ladies who offered themselves to him. Instead, he was seized by an unconscious passion for playing the role of the unhappy lover. There is no doubt that he remained a virgin all his life, but at his death the only letter Riborg Voigt had ever written him was found in a leather pouch on his chest.

By way of compensation, continues Helweg, Andersen entertained glowing friendships, and indeed his assertions of love and affection often seem exaggerated and a bit sticky. But such was the language of the day. And as to the young men who accompanied him on his travels (Jonas Collin, William Bloch, Nic Bøgh), he needed them for practical assistance. He was frail and in poor health, and his peers were too busy; nor would they have been willing to subordinate themselves to him and his idiosyncrasies. (One could add that the young men did not subordinate themselves to him all that easily either. He frequently found them inconsiderate and ungrateful, and one in particular, Harold Drewson, a grandson of the elder Collin, was "boring, silent, surly and irritable"[16]—obviously the worst kind of nuisance.)

Helweg concludes: Andersen was a sensitive-hysterical psychopath with sexual inhibition except for masturbation, but he was definitely heterosexual.

Spink, who published his biography of Andersen in 1972, adds this consideration: "The Collins knew Andersen intimately. He had grown up in the family and had been under their daily observation for many years. Perfectly normal, as well as eminently respectable themselves, they were also intelligent and perceptive. Had there been the merest shadow of suspicion of homosexuality in Andersen, they would never have allowed their young sons to accompany him on long journeys abroad."[17]

Yes, that stands to reason. But there is still something else, something that stared everyone in the face, then and since then, without being noticed, something that was with Andersen since he first came to Copenhagen, and it stayed with him until his death; namely, his relationship with Edvard Collin. The scholars have only recently "discovered" it, and we must now give it its due.

When Andersen first entered the Collin house, during his Christmas vacation in 1825, he would have been twenty years old, and Edvard seventeen; Andersen did not care for Edvard, who would not speak to him.[18] Edvard also did not much care for Andersen. Edvard was a sober and methodical young man who disapproved of young Andersen's disor-

ganization. He wrote about him later: "He had a 'split personality'—half poet, half schoolboy, a person who at times
felt like a caged bird, but at others could think of nothing
but his school reports. . . . He was diligent, he read much;
but how did he read? He learned many things, but 'he never
learned to read properly.' " If this was really what Edvard
thought of Hans Christian when Edvard was seventeen,
then Edvard had the mind of a schoolmaster. And Andersen
reacted accordingly: "Edvard seemed to me so cold, so for-
bidding, that I really believed that he could not stand me,
that he was arrogant, and even my enemy."[19] Not a propi-
tious start.

But Andersen sensed a strength in Edvard that he needed;
and Edvard sensed that Andersen needed him, that such a
muddlehead had to be firmly taken in hand. In the course of
the next years they gradually came closer, and by 1830 were
intimate enough that Andersen could confide his infatuation
with Riborg Voigt. By that time Andersen had adopted Jonas
Collin as his father, a role Jonas calmly accepted, so that
when he visited the Collins' home (which he did daily when
in town), he naturally regarded Edvard as his brother. Or
almost his brother, just as he himself was in truth only *almost* a
member of the Collin family. He sometimes called himself a
"swamp-plant," a boy from the slums who could forever only
almost make it into the upper crust of society.[20] This "almost"
caused him bitter grief, and the more being "in" seemed
impossible, the harder he tried for it.

In June 1830 he wrote to Edvard: "There is no one to
whom I feel attached more closely than to you, and if you
are prepared to forget the conditions of birth and always be
to me what I am to you then you will find in me the most
candid and cordial friend." And when Edvard in his reply
signed himself "Your sincere friend," Andersen was over-
joyed.[21] Edvard had, indeed, already proven himself a
friend: he had helped Hans Christian with his Latin composition for the university entrance exam and had corrected
his spelling. He had also begun what he did for the rest of

their friendship—take charge of all the practical matters, financial and otherwise, for which Andersen was totally incompetent. In return, he felt free to lecture Andersen on his behavior and to criticize him mercilessly. Like a good pupil, Andersen attempted to absorb such preachings without too many tears and to comply with them even if it involved—oh bitter pain—giving up reading his poetry to everyone who was willing—or unwilling—to listen. "Believe me," he wrote to Edvard, "it was hard to resist, and quite honestly, I would have liked to do it very much [he had been invited to recite his poems at Odense Theater]—again my sinful vanity! But your letter made me decide to refuse the invitation categorically."[22]

In 1831, while on his first journey, Andersen managed to present in writing a request he would not have dared utter face to face: "You alone are the one person of my own age to whom I feel closely attached. I have an important request, perhaps you will laugh at me, but if sometime you really want to make me happy, to let me have true evidence of your respect—if and when I deserve it—then—oh! please do not be angry with me—say 'Du' to me! . . . If you have any objections, then please do not ever mention this matter to me and I shall never ask you again, of course. . . . You have no idea how my heart is beating while I am writing this."[23]

But Edvard did have objections. His style was the formal 'De.' And he concluded his reply by making his rejection impersonal: "There are many insignificant things against which people have what I believe to be an inborn dislike; I have known a woman who felt such a dislike against wrapping paper that she was sick whenever she saw it—how are such things to be explained? But when I have known for a long time someone whom I respect and like and he invites me to say 'Du,' then this unpleasant and inexplicable feeling arises in me."

The matter was not as absurd as it may sound to American ears. In Scandinavian and Germanic countries the intimate 'Du' comes easily only with close relatives and school friends—or at any rate individuals whom one has known since childhood and who are of roughly equal age. A switch from the formal to the intimate address in adulthood carries with it a strong emotional charge and occurs—except in a drunken stupor—but rarely.

About five years after the exchange of letters we have just quoted, Andersen has one of his protagonists in *O.T.*, Otto Thostrup, offer the 'Du' to his friend Wilhelm. Otto is a moody young man of lowly and murky origins and clearly an impersonation of the author, Wilhelm is a count who, in this relationship, takes the place of Edvard. Otto writes: "Wilhelm, in the future we will say *thou* to each other; that is more confidential!' 'He is the first to whom I have given my thou,' said Otto, when the letter was dispatched. 'This will rejoice him: now, however, I myself have for once made an advance, but he deserves it.' A few moments later it troubled him. 'I am a fool like the rest!' said he, and wished he could annihilate the paper" (76). But when Wilhelm for the first time addresses him with the 'Du,' Otto has a strange reaction: "It seemed to him as though the spiritual band which encircled them loosened itself, and Wilhelm became a stranger. It was impossible for Otto to return the 'thou,' yet, at the same time, he felt the injustice of his behavior and the singularity, and wished to struggle against it; he mastered himself, attained a kind of eloquence, but no 'thou' would pass his lips" (132). And eventually Wilhelm, acknowledging, "You cannot make up your mind to say *thou* to me; therefore let it be" (146), lets Otto off the hook. The intimacy Otto had sought was, once granted, more than he could handle.

This ambivalence may explain why Andersen was not totally undone by Edvard's refusal, nor was he totally discouraged. He continued to assert his love. "Oh! How I wish you were my brother in the blood as you are indeed in my heart and my soul, then perhaps you might be able to understand my love for you!" And he kept right on campaigning, off and on, for the 'Du'; frightened by his own courage, he even added something like "Please be my dear and kind Edvard as you are indeed every now and then!"[24]

And then a curious thing happened—the Voigt story in reverse, as it were. Andersen began to tell his sorrows to Edvard's sister Louise, who listened patiently and tried to comfort him. And gradually he began to realize that he was now in love with *her*! We already know that nothing came of this. He wrote her some urgent letters in which he pleaded for her to be kind to him; the parents took notice and set up an older sister to censor his letters before giving them to her. But there was really no need; he himself made his wooing innocent and impersonal, writing that his impatience between visits was "due to the fact that I am very lonely, have no home and look for it in the family which is dearest to me." On New Year's Day, 1833, Louise became engaged to a Mr. Lind, and Andersen was quickly resigned.

But that threw him back on Edvard, and Edvard was as standoffish as ever. Yet when Andersen left to go abroad in April 1833, Edvard wrote a letter to him, to be handed him by the ship's captain once they were at sea; in this letter he revealed a sudden crack in his armor, one that would stir Andersen deeply. "Believe me," he wrote, "I am truly saddened by your departure, I shall miss you terribly, I shall miss not seeing you any more coming up as usual to my room to talk to me; I shall miss you on Tuesdays at your place at the table, and yet, you will miss us even more, I know, for you are alone." It must have sounded to Andersen like love returned, and it made him cry.[25]

Henceforth his letters to Edvard became increasingly emotional. He excused himself on the basis of his "half-womanliness" (1833) and wrote that he felt toward Edvard "as tender as a woman" (1834); and in 1835: "I long for you as though you were a beautiful Calabrian girl."[26] All along he felt bitterly humiliated by the lopsided nature of the affair: "I feel there is something begging, something degrading in [my] constant demand for pity, but my pride succumbs because of my love for you."[27] That same year, in a deliberately emotional letter to Collin he once more declared his love and wrote: "Our friendship is like 'The Mysteries,' it should not be analyzed"; and in a draft not intended to be sent he used the familiar 'Du,' and rhapsodized that their friendship would attain perfection after death, when they would say 'Du' to each other.[28]

In reality, things went the other way. In 1836 Edvard Collin was married; Andersen did not attend the wedding, but sent his friend a letter of farewell—his last love letter.[29] And he converted his suffering into literature. The novel *O.T.* is the story of a friendship between lowly born Otto and brilliant Wilhelm, a friendship in which Wilhelm fulfills all the expectations for affection that Andersen had entertained toward Collin. The question of 'De' or 'Du' comes up, and the limits of social acceptability are approached but never transgressed. In the last pages there is the suggestion of a liaison between Otto and Wilhelm's sister—Louise! A little later he wrote one of his masterpieces, *The Little Mermaid*. It tells the story of a creature not fully human, neither man nor woman, who decides to assume the shape of a woman in order to gain the love of a prince. The prince does not return her love and so deprives her of an immortal soul. A sentence originally included but stricken by Andersen before publication has the mermaid saying, "I shall strive to win an immortal soul *myself* . . . so that in the world beyond I may be re-united with him to whom I gave my whole heart!"[30] This formulation is almost identical to the one in the draft letter addressed to Edvard.

And afterward—what became of their relationship? It went on as before, if only in a somewhat attenuated form. Andersen continued, off and on, to appeal for the 'Du,' and Edvard continued to deny it.[31] Edvard kept right on, without much tact, to tell bitter truths as he saw them, and Andersen, as ever, felt deeply wounded and got over it. But what became an obsession with him was to have the Collins—and Edvard in particular—finally acknowledge his growing fame as a writer.

Edvard was impressed by other achievements. After Andersen had reached Constantinople he wrote to him, "You are a damned good traveller! The way you have managed to carry through this journey is something not many others could have done, and if you haven't got courage then at least you have shown a firm determination, which is equally good; that certificate will be given you by yours faithfully, who is not in the habit of flattering you."[32] Halfhearted praise indeed!

Nor did Edvard spoil him by answering every one of his letters, and when he did answer, it was often "as cold as a law book . . . in place of friendship he has offered me willingness to render services." And when Andersen wrote of the reception given him by the Grand Duke and Duchess of Weimar and their son, Edvard replied, "What a hell of a fuss they make of you." Edvard, and for that matter his father—Andersen's "father"—Jonas, just refused to be impressed. In 1846 Andersen wrote, "I think of your father and believe that I have given him gratification . . . and yet—? He does not realize it, he does not see it like that. Even to those closest to me at home I am only—Andersen, the harmless person, with a certain amount of talent, someone who thinks very highly of himself . . . no one at home is proud of me, I seem to be the rejected corner-stone."[33] Edvard replied:

> You are popular in Germany, in Weimar you are being kissed and hugged by all the distinguished people there. We who are your friends here at home and who happen not to like the idea of kissing one another, we do not melt away in sentimental joy over this. . . . First you are being embraced by the Weimar court for having read fairy tales, and now you are sitting alone in a hotel room. The same here: yesterday in the Casino Square the pile drivers shouted "Hurrah!" for me to make me give them Schnapps, and today I am sitting at home in my old velvet jacket with a tummy ache. We have to put up with the ups and downs of life.[34]

What a comparison! What a sermon! And yet—at the same time Edvard volunteered to proofread and copy, in his own hand, Andersen's entire autobiography!

Edvard continued to be Andersen's "manager," taking care of finances, contracts, and such, and in 1873 the sixty-eight-year-old writer voiced his appreciation: "I have many

friends . . . but you . . . are the earliest of my friends, right
back from the time you helped me with my Latin composition, when you seemed to me a little too much of a mentor,
until these last few years when everything was resolved. . . .
On every occasion your many wonderful qualities stand
out. . . . You are infinitely dear to me, and I shall pray to God
for you to survive me, for I cannot think of losing you."[35]

He never lost him. Edvard survived him and wrote a
book about their relationship.[36] In it he states that "Andersen was happy among [the Collin family], happy to see himself treated like a son of the house, but not without sadness
for not being one . . . he did not find his works sufficiently
appreciated *by us;* that sadness was bound to increase as he
was gradually being recognized by others." His summation:
"I have looked into the depths of his soul, and I have not
allowed myself to be put off by the excesses of his imagination. . . . I know that he was *good.* This simple testimony
will not be misunderstood by those who really knew him."[37]
In other words: *Honi soit qui mal y pense!*

Thus cautioned, how are we then to evaluate the matter?
Von Rosen, the latest scholar to address it, concludes: In the
first half of the nineteenth century, before the "discovery"
of homosexuality by the early sexologists and the ensuing
awareness and apprehension of it, friendship had a far
wider scope than it was to have later on. A tender friendship had its place within the conventions of society. "Andersen was not a 'homosexual': he only fell in love with men—
and with women too, possibly—and most of all with Edvard
Collin. Even if this did not develop into the tender friendship that Andersen longed for in the 1830's, it did become a
fine and life-long friendship, for one thing because Edvard
Collin was a fine person."[38]

That even high society tolerated affectionate intimacy between men is illustrated by the last such relationship we
need to mention—a curious one indeed, the one between
the "swamp-plant," Hans Christian Andersen, and His
Royal Highness the Hereditary Grand Duke of Weimar.

When they first met, Carl Alexander was a young man of

twenty-six, married to a Dutch princess, and Andersen was thirty-nine. On 26 June 1844, Andersen wrote: "The young duke was extremely kind. I could have chosen him as a friend if he weren't a duke . . . I really love the young duke, he is the first prince towards whom I have felt truly drawn; I wish he weren't a prince, or else that I was one." When they met again, in January 1846, "The hereditary grand duke rushed towards me, pressed my hands and said: 'I cannot receive you here the way I would have liked to at home, oh! my friend, I have been longing for you!' His consort also received me graciously." And the next day: "I went to the hered. grand duke, in those splendid rooms. He came towards me, pressed me to his bosom, kissed me several times, thanked me for my love for him; arm in arm we walked to his room, sat talking for a long time until he was called to the Council of State, then he walked, arm in arm with me, to the furthermost door." The next day: " . . .went to the hered. grand duke . . . sat 'in my seat' as he called it, on the sofa; he said we must always remain friends . . . 'Give me your hand!' He held it so firmly in his, told me that he loved me and pressed his cheek to mine." And again: "At the table (with the grand duke and grand duchess present) I sat on the right side of the hered. grand duke, who pressed my hand under the table. He told me that when his consort was in labor she had told him she wanted to be the steadfast tin soldier." And later on: "Went to the hered. grand duke at 8 o'clock in the morning, he received me in his shirt, with only a dressing-gown over it: 'I can do that, we know one another.' He pressed me to his bosom, we kissed one another. 'Think of this hour,' he said . . . 'we are friends for life.' We both wept."[39] The friendship was troubled when, in 1848, Carl Alexander led a contingent of Weimar volunteers to join the war against Denmark in Schleswig-Holstein. For a while Andersen stopped writing to him. But by 1854 the rift was healed, and at the unveiling of a monument to two other great friends, Goethe and Schiller, the "usual" cordial embracing and kissing of cheeks and holding of hands between Carl Alexander and Hans Christian resumed.[40]

Enough of that. It was all out in the open, and if society—

and in particular aristocratic license—permitted it, we are left only to note that Andersen clearly wanted, even craved, this kind of license, but that his emotional transports, which seem so turgid to us today, were more ingratiating than sexual.

However, yet another aspect of his emotional makeup has recently come under scrutiny, and its pertains to his attitude regarding children.

For a bachelor, he saw quite a bit of them.

> In Copenhagen he moved a good deal in circles where there were children; he made friends with them and told them stories which he partly invented and partly told in a different form . . . what was most certainly his own about them was his manner of telling, the exuberant life and daring childishness of it, his wild and mad caprices, his many grimaces, antics and gestures, which fascinated the children . . . and made them scream with delight. He formed, in the telling of his tales, their graphic, crooning, living, dancing, jumping style . . . before he made any attempt at writing them down.[41]

In this passage Brandes, who had known him personally and could speak from observation, not only confirms the image of Andersen surrounded by children that we all have in our mind's eye, but he underlines the importance of such contacts by saying that they were, in effect, dress rehearsals for what would "play" and what wouldn't, and that Andersen could not have written his fairy tales without such an audience.[42]

But a curious event served to reveal a different truth. Apparently his fellow citizens, finally alerted and aware of his great fame, could not wait for his death to erect him a monument. One day a sculptor with a commission for a statue presented to Andersen a sketch of what he had in mind—namely, exactly the scene just described. Andersen flew into a rage. In a letter to Jonas Collin the younger, dated 6 June 1875, he described his reaction:

> My blood boiled and I spoke out plainly and explicitly, saying that none of the sculptors knew me, that nothing in their

proposals indicated they had seen or recognized the characteristic feature of me: that I could never read aloud when someone was sitting behind me or close to me (leaning up against me), and even less so if I had children on my lap or on my back, or young Copenhageners lying close up against me, that it was only a manner of speaking to call me 'the children's writer', my aim being to be a writer for all ages, so that children could not represent me; the naivity was only one part of the fairy tales, the humor however their salt, and that in my written language I relied on the popular idiom that was my Danish heritage.

And in his diary he had written, a bit more explicitly, on 29 May: "Visit by Saabye, whose sketch for my statue I cannot stand, for it reminds me of old Socrates and young Alcibiades. I couldn't tell him that but refused to pose or speak to him altogether today. I was more and more enraged." He objected in particular to what he called "the tall boy who is lying right up against my crotch."[43]

When the statue was finally erected, it showed Andersen all by himself, reading from a book to an invisible audience. But we are left wondering, why the vehemence of his reaction? Why the hypersensitivity to physical contact? Why the special pique against the "tall boy" who, surely, was only *apparently* "lying right up against [his] crotch?" And why the allergic reference to Socrates and Alcibiades?

Phyllis Greenacre recently discussed the matter from a psychoanalytic point of view and, having reviewed his childhood as have we, she ponders his aversion to being physically close to anyone, such as in a crowd; his preference for having the children listen at a respectful distance; and his concern, in that regard, primarily for the boys; and concludes, admittedly in a speculative way, that he must have felt himself genitally underequipped and that he probably once had been—or thought he had been—sexually attacked by an older boy.[44]

This may be so, but we have no direct evidence. Could it not be simpler? Could it not be that an old man—after all, at the time of the statue episode Andersen was close to seventy and close to death—could it not be that such an old man, who had always been frail, hypochondriacal, and afraid of injuries, infections, and even of having his careful attire ruffled: could not such a man, apprehensive of any touch, be particularly anxious about those members of the human race who approach most energetically and whose touch, no matter how affectionately meant, is quite likely to be rough, perhaps even hurtful—namely, boys? Are not most old people apprehensive about properly rambunctious boys? But, one might argue, it was not so *only* in his old age! True enough. Though I am not aware of any description or statement attributing to him paedophobia in his middle years, we do know that in his youth he was roughly handled by some boys—was the "inspection" he underwent in the cloth manufactory a "sexual attack"?—and that he preferred to play with girls—little girls, for, as has already been quoted, he had no use for big ones.

Of this preference for prepubertal girls, we can say with reasonable assurance that it stayed with him. The hero in *The Improvisatore,* called Antonio but in truth an Andersen-alias, has this to relate of a visit to the temples of Paestum:

> One young girl there was, scarcely more than eleven years old, lovely as a Goddess of Beauty . . . I could think of nothing else but the Medicean Venus . . . I could not love, but admire, and bow before the form of beauty. She stood at a little distance from the other beggars; a brown square piece of cloth hung loosely over one shoulder, the other breast and arm were, like her feet, uncovered. . . . Modesty, soul, and a singular, deep expression of suffering, were expressed in her countenance. Her eyes were cast down . . . raising them, I saw that she was blind. . . . I grew quite warm at the sight . . . bowed myself involuntarily, and pressed a hot kiss upon her forehead. . . . She sprung up like a terrified deer.
>
> (Vol. 2, 121–26)

Six years after that first encounter Antonio meets the girl again in a totally different setting. She has regained her sight and has been taken up by a wealthy family. Antonio, still in love with her, actually marries her in the last few pages of the novel and—one is tempted to ask how—has a child by her.

This ending, so un-Andersen, rings totally untrue. But the encounter at Paestum was true enough. It is related just so, almost verbatim, in his autobiography:

> Later I visited Pompei, Herculaneum, and the Grecian temple at Paestum. There I saw a poor little girl in rags, but an image of beauty, a living statue, yet still a child. She had some blue violets in her black hair; that was all her ornament. She made an impression upon me as if she were a spirit from the world of Beauty. I could not give her money, but stood in reverence and looked at her, as if she were the goddess herself appearing from the temple upon the steps of which she was seated among the wild figs.
>
> (*FT*, 118–19)

Verbatim? Well—not quite. The *real* girl was not blind— and Andersen (considering that she could see him? See how ungainly he was? See through him and know that he was not a man?)—Andersen did not kiss her. But he spun out the fantasy of an eventual marriage and made a book of it.[45]

To summarize, finally, the vexed question of Andersen's heart, we think the matter must be judged as follows. That he never engaged in any overt sexual acts, heterosexual or otherwise; that he probably had no explicit, conscious sexual desires of an "improper," socially unacceptable nature, with the possible exception of some occasional ogling of prostitutes; that the secret deed committed "in actuality" consisted of masturbation (little plus-marks [+] in his diaries, following passages speaking of sensual arousal, suggest as much);[46] but that he was capable of strong erotic (sensual, not sexual) feelings toward either sex, including children; and that therefore, without sexual or sensual outlet of any kind, he was left with the feeling of being incarcerated in an icy, depressing, eventually deadly jail made of his own frustration.[47]

19

The Dream of Redemption

Why did he never break out?

Why did this man, who by his very innocence and child-like charm compelled men and women to serve him just as men and beasts were compelled to serve Gerda, remain essentially lonely? Why was he, who constantly appealed to and always successfully aroused the interest and compassion of society, essentially excluded from the society of man?

Andersen started as an ugly duckling and became the resplendent swan of the *salon* and the house party; but, contrary to the ugly duckling of his famous story, he never truly *believed* that he was being accepted by the other swans, that he had truly become a swan himself.

The ugly-duckling complex, the deeply ingrained inferiority complex, is very common. And every time, over the past many years, when I listened to some of my ugly-duckling patients and was told how, once again, in spite of all insight and reason, they had fallen victim to it, had acted like swans and yet felt like ugly ducklings—every time I heard this I found fault with Andersen's story. I could believe that the swans would accept the new swan; I did not think it *true* that he would so easily accept their acceptance. Now I know that Andersen shared my misgivings. True, in objective terms he had won fame, he had "arrived." Subjectively, though, in terms of his inner experiences and beliefs, it was sheer wishful thinking. He himself never ceased to consider himself an ugly duckling, an unacceptable outcast, and he "knew" there was nothing he could do about it. . . .

Except, of course, to dream—to dream wish-fulfilling dreams, to dream of some sort of salvation.

We know, after all, how he acted in all other matters. He

preferred to be done for rather than to do for himself. When we hear that he "yearned to tear himself away from his habits,"[1] from his accustomed mode of relating, we may suppose that here too he would probably rather be torn free. Rather than liberating himself, he would *dream to be redeemed.*

And so, coming finally back to *The Snow Queen* and looking at it from this particular aspect, we can discern a new meaning. We recognize a theme we have briefly struck before. *The Snow Queen* is not only, as we have pointed out so far, the story of adolescent moratoria, but it is, above all, *the story of the redemption of a lonely, inhibited intellectual by the love of a woman.*

This is, of course, one of the great and recurring themes of mythology and world literature. Thus Isis, when Osiris was stolen from her by the evil force of Seth, went in search of him. Having finally found him, she "redeemed" him by conceiving on his dead and rigid body the sun god Horus, reincarnation and avatar of his father, Osiris. Thus Ishtar journeyed into the dark vastness of the underworld to seek and return to life her son-lover, Tammuz. And in the Gilgamesh epic—the oldest recorded story we know—a (sacred) prostitute redeems Enkidu, who was like a lonely, wild animal, and through her (physical) love transforms him into a civilized man:

> . . . him, Enkidu, who eats grass with the gazelles / drinks with the game at the drinking-place, / whose heart delights with the animals at the water, / him, the wild man, the prostitute saw, / the savage man from the depths of the steppe. / . . . The prostitute bared her bosom, she opened her womb, and he succumbed to her loveliness. / She did not hesitate to approach him; / she aroused desire in him, which is the task of women, / and he impressed upon her his love. / Six days and seven nights Enkidu lay with the harlot. / After he was sated with her charms, / he set his face toward his game. / But when the gazelles saw him, Enkidu, they ran away; / the game of the steppe fled from his presence. / It caused Enkidu to hestitate . . . no longer could he run as before. / But he had intelligence, wide was his understanding. / He returned and sat at the feet of the courtesan, / looking at the courtesan, / and his ears listening as the courtesan speaks, / the

courtesan saying to him, to Enkidu: / "Wise art thou, O Enkidu, like a God art thou; / why doest thou run around with
the animals on the steppe? / Come, I will lead thee to Uruk,
the city, / to the holy temple / . . . / He listened to her words
and accepted her advice; / the counsel of the woman / he
took to heart. / She tore her garment in two; / with one she
clothed him, / with the other she clothed herself. / She takes
his hand / and leads him like a mother / to the table of the
shepherds / . . . / The milk of the wild animals / he was accustomed to suck. / Bread they placed before him; / He felt
embarrassed, looked / and stared. / Nothing does Enkidu
know / of eating bread, / and to drink strong drink / he has
not been taught. / The courtesan opened her mouth, / saying
to Enkidu: / "Eat the bread, O Enkidu, / it is the staff of life; /
drink the strong drink, it is the custom of the land." / Enkidu
ate bread / until he was sated; Of the strong drink he drank /
seven goblets. / His soul felt free and happy, / his heart re-
joiced, / and his face shone. / . . . / He anointed himself with
oil, / and he became a human being.[2]

Beauty and the Beast dramatizes this same theme.[3] A
coarse, wild, beastly man can be "saved" (and turned into a
handsome prince) only by the devotion of a woman who
loves him *in his beastly state,* a woman so understanding and
persistent that she recognizes and knows the prince within
the beast; and has the heart—meaning: the courage, the
faith—to "thaw him out," just as Gerda had the heart to
thaw out Kay.

Similarily, in the myth of *The Flying Dutchman* (in Wag-
ner's version of it, at least) a man is condemned to roam the
empty vastness of the oceans (comparable to the empty vastness of the Snow Queen's palace) until, on one of his rare
visits ashore, a woman shall love him. In Dostoevski's *Crime
and Punishment* the murderer, Raskolnikov, is finally redeemed from a state of nihilistic alienation (suffered in the
night and ice of Siberian exile) by the love of the saintly
prostitute, Sonia. Hermann Hesse's Steppenwolf is liberated
from near-psychotic isolation (again, the Steppe invokes Si-
beria) by the whore Hermine. Other works of Hesse strike
similar themes. Nor would it be hard to find many more
examples from world literature.[4]

Of course, the opposite—the redemption of woman by man—also exists. A man, by his valor, may redeem a woman from a dragon and marry her, as Perseus saved and married Andromeda. A man, by his superior strength, may redeem a woman from her own Amazonian superiority and isolation and make her fit to be married, as Siegfried did for the Valkyrie, Brunhilde. Or a man may, by virtue of being decent and true to his word, save a woman from ugliness, as Sir Gawain did when he granted Dame Ragnelle's wish and married her though she was a repulsive hag—and was rewarded for doing his conjugal duty by seeing the lady freed from evil bewitchment, a radiant damsel once more.[5] In all of these stories the hero, as savior, has to suffer much hardship and prove himself in many a harrowing adventure; he must, in short, prove himself a hero before he can re-deem a woman.

But a woman redeems through love. She may, like Raskol-nikov's Sonia or like Gerda, have to follow her man into icy exile and suffer hardship along the way; she may even have to go to Hell, as Ishtar did to rescue Tammuz (Adonis).[6] But in so doing the woman does not need to pass tests, she does not need to become a hero, and she does not need to become more than she has been. She proceeds with the unswerving purpose of a sleepwalker, and in the process only becomes more—what she already is. Gerda, like Sonia and all the other women who saved men, did not have to learn and to become—the way a hero has to learn and become a hero; they were all adequate to their task from the start; they save simply by being women and by loving.

Woman redeems through love—through *physical* love—which is why the redeeming woman is so often shown as a prostitute. There are exceptions: if the man has lost himself because he has corrupted and dissolved his manly spirituality and will power in an orgy of sensuality—as Tannhäuser did in the Mountain of Venus—then salvation must come through a pure saint—for Tannhäuser through the saintly love of Elis-abeth.[7] But by and large the man in need of redemption (the man who writes redemption stories), whether he suffers the rude loneliness of the wild animal or the icy remoteness of the intellectual, dreams of being rescued by a love that is to be magical, spiritual, gently maternal, wildly passionate, and above all—physical.

Or at least most men's thoughts and most myths run that way. But not Andersen's. His particular loneliness was neither that of the beast nor that of the thinker. His loneliness was that of the child left behind, deserted by everyone.

He has told us that he was a child, but never a youth. Nor was he ever a man, and so no woman could save him. That which, according to the Gilgamesh epic, is "the proper task for woman"—to arouse desire in men—is precisely what he dreaded. He felt inadequate to it, and he considered it evil. He attributed it to Karen of *The Red Shoes* and to Karen his "wicked" half-sister. He called upon it the wrath of God and vented upon it all the icy cruelty of which sanctimonious piety is capable. *His* deliverance was to come through a pure little girl, just as the deliverance of the world came about through the Christ *Child*.

20

The Shadow

Poor Andersen! Did he ever, even for a moment, consider that it would have been Karen—or one like her—who could in fact have saved him? Did he ever reflect that his sin might be, not masturbation, but pride—in this case a pride both timid and spiteful, the hubris of purity?

Perhaps he did. You recall the wicked girl Inger, the Girl Who Trod on the Loaf. She was wicked even before she stepped on God's gift. Not only did she despise her poor mother, but, "when but a very little child, she found pleasure in catching flies, to pull off their wings and make creeping insects of them. And she used to stick Maybugs and beetles on a pin . . . so that the poor animals clung to it, and turned and twisted as they tried to get off."[1] Compare this with her effort to keep her fine new shoes clean and neat, an effort for which, as Andersen states, "no one could blame her." He does not tell us the color of her shoes, but surely they were not red, they were white: for whiteness goes with cleanliness and with purity, and with excessive purity goes puritanism and all the cruelty to what is "vermin"—flies and insects, the creations of the Devil that symbolize sin—all the cruelty that is part of the essence of puritanism.

Yes, this too was an aspect of Hans Christian Andersen. He does not tell us whether he ever tortured flies, but we do on occasion get the impression from his letters that he could be cheerfully indifferent to the hardships of others.[2] But what concerns us here is his anxious, almost frantic intent to "keep his shoes clean." We are interested, too, in the degree to which he was aware of it and the degree to which he could recognize it as a fault and a weakness within himself—if not as an outright sin against the "bread of God."

He was not often in danger of getting "dirty." The dirt all
around him, as when he lived in a whorehouse, did not wet
him any more than water wets the proverbial duck's back.
As far as we know, only once, during his youth, did anyone
ever try to seduce him. Mrs. Meisling, the schoolmaster's
wife at Slagelse, apparently climbed right into his window.
She came, she explained, for the butter that was kept in
Hans Christian's room.[3] At another time she told him she
was beginning to lose weight and he should feel how
loosely the dress was hanging around her body. He remi-
nisces: "I bowed many times before my headmaster's wife;
she gave me some excellent punch, was extremely kind and
good—but, I don't know, I was on tenterhooks, I might be
wrong in my suspicions . . . but she made me think badly of
her, and I hurried away as soon as I could . . . she used to
say: 'You're not really a man!' "[4] But her "shameless ero-
tomania"[5] went so far that she pursued him years later in
Copenhagen to tell him of her unhappy marriage and to
invite him to pay her a "tender visit" in her lodging house.
He of course refused the invitation.[6]

His thoughts about her are perhaps given vent in *The
Improvisatore*, where Mrs. Meisling may have become the
Italian peasant girl and artist's model, Mariuccia:

> With the exception of my mother, I could not endure
> women. . . . I do not myself know why, but I had an antipa-
> thy to all women, and, as I expressed this unhesitatingly, I
> was bantered by every girl and woman who came to my
> mother's. They all would kiss me: in particular was there a
> peasant girl, Mariuccia, who by this jest always brought tears
> to my eyes . . . [she] always told me that she was my bride,
> and that I was her little bridegroom, who must and should
> give her a kiss; I never would do so, and then she took it by
> force.
>
> Once when she said that I cried childishly, and behaved
> myself exactly like a child that still sucked, and that I should
> be suckled like any other baby, I flew out, down the steps,
> but she pursued and caught me, held me between her knees,
> and pressed my head, which I turned away with disgust,
> ever closer and closer to her breast. I tore the silver arrow out

of her hair, which fell down in rich abundance over me and
over her naked shoulders.

(Vol. 1, 59–60)

In his many works of autobiographical fiction, Andersen
never invented; they are all merely permutations of events
that did, in fact, occur. This scene too must have occurred,
and most likely at Meislings'. At any event, it conveys very
clearly how he felt about women as a youngster, and how
he dreaded their approach.

Even so, this does not fully explain his dread of Karen,
the "wicked" half-sister. Surely *she* would not have tried to
seduce him? And his fear of social embarrassment, should
she appear on the scene, does not seem to encompass, to
our satisfaction, the entire scope of his dread. Something
more must lie behind it.

Perhaps we are on the right track if we consider that, in
later life, Andersen experienced a considerable fascination
for Karen's supposed fellow professionals, the whores of the
red-light districts of Naples or Constantinople or other "sinful" cities he visited. According to entries in his diary, he
haunted such places with a mixture of curiosity and repul-
sion, and it would have been at such times that he was most
aware of the liberation he could possibly find there.[7] But he
never "succumbed."

Why not? Here we are in the realm of guesswork, and I
should guess as follows: I think the fuss about Karen, whom
as a boy he saw very seldom if at all, is quite overdone. I
think he concentrated his dread on her in order not to have
to think of where this dread really arose—with his mother.
The protestation in the passage from *The Improvisatore* just
quoted, to the effect that he "could not endure women with
the exception of my mother," should undoubtedly be read
that he could not endure women *because* of his mother. Thus
he is condemning his half-sister in order not to have to
condemn his mother.

That which, in his eyes, so tarnished Karen—her illegitimacy—was in truth a "spot" on his mother. The mother,

not the girl, was responsible for the illegitimacy. We do not know when he found out that his mother also, together with her two sisters, had been born outside of wedlock. We also do not know when it dawned on him that he himself had been conceived a good seven or eight months prior to his parents' marriage (and that possibly his legal father had not begotten him!).[8] But whenever he realized all this, the knowledge must have superimposed itself on the awareness that his half-sister, at any event, was born "in sin," and that his mother was, by this account, a loose woman.

Again, I do not know just how traumatic in those days and in those social circles such a realization would have been. Most boys, provided they were robust and happily involved in the life of the streets, would likely not have given it a second thought. But Hans Christian was not robust; he was always home, thinking and dreaming. Moreover, he slept in his mother's bed. The closeness of her (perhaps inebriated) body; the awareness of her moral laxity; and his own pubertally stimulated imagination must have created a degree of incestuous tension beyond his feeble endurance.[9] He would have reacted to it by developing a veritable horror of his mother—a feeling quite incompatible with his pious upbringing as well as with his total material and emotional dependence on her. Needing to shift this horror somewhere, he shifted it, conveniently, to a woman he hardly knew, hardly ever saw: Karen. And so his loathing for all women—as described in the passage from *The Improvisatore*—was an extension of his loathing for Karen, and she in turn was nothing but a screen in front of his mother, the true source of the aversion.[10]

Such a hypothesis is in no way incompatible with the other one, put forward earlier, that he resented his mother for having "deceived" him by marrying her second husband. On the contrary, what was offended here and aroused his jealous resentment was precisely the same incestuous attachment that would have given rise to the revulsion. Furthermore, the remarriage could not fail to offend the sensibilities of the adolescent boy by virtue of the inevitable, demonstrative re-

assertion of his mother's sexuality. In view of all this, it is no
wonder that he had to get away; and it is no wonder that, all
protestations to the contrary, he thenceforth shunned her,
maintained minimal contact, avoided only flagrant indiffer-
ence, and thanked God for her death.

So his mother—or his image of her and his feelings about
her—stood between him and other women. And how this
could have worked is perhaps again most plausibly illustrated by the previously quoted passage about Mariuccia.
What she does to him and what horrifies him so: to push his
head against her breasts—this is as close as one can come to
repeating the infant's sucking at mother's breast (in fact Mariuccia herself places it in this context)—or, somewhat later,
to the affectionate cuddling of the boy's head against the
maternal bosom. It is both a sexual gesture—"I was her little
bridegroom"—and a maternal gesture—"I should be suckled
like any other baby." This mutual contamination of the sexual
with the maternal is precisely the problem Andersen could
never overcome and which he attempted to sidestep by remaining a child. He hung on to the desexualized mother, the
grandmother, and surrendered his claim to sexuality.

It was from this predicament he needed to be redeemed;[11]
and because the sexual woman frightened him so, he
dreamed of redemption by the "pure" woman or, better
still, the "pure child," Gerda. In real life, considering when
The Snow Queen was written, this would have been Jenny
Lind. She refused to play the role. Nor could she, in any
event, have played it. To save him from the sin and the hell
of his purity, only an "impure," a sexual woman, would
have been able.

I know nothing of Jenny Lind's love-life (except that she
eventually did enter into an apparently happy marriage).
But had she even been willing to reveal her sexuality to
Andersen, he would surely not have been saved thereby.
He would merely have seen her purity blemished, and he
would have fled.

Andersen actually imagined such a scene in *The Improvisatore*:[12]

She drew me towards her: her lips were like fire that flowed into my very soul! Eternal Mother of God! Thy holy image, at that moment, fell down from the wall where it stood above my head. It was not a mere accident! No! thou touchest my brow: thou didst seize me as I was about to sink in the whirl-pool of passion! "No! No!" exclaimed I, starting up: my blood was like seething lava. "Antonio," cried she, "kill me! kill me! but do not leave me." Her cheeks, her eyes, her glance and expression was passion; and yet she was beautiful—an image of beauty, painted in flame. I felt a tremor in all my nerves; and, without replying, I left the apartment and rushed down the steps as if a dark spirit had pursued me. . . . "Never again will I see her," I firmly determined in my heart. "I will fly the serpent of beauty which shows to me the fruit of knowledge. Thousands would ridicule me for do-ing so; but rather their laughter than the lamenting cry of my own heart!"

(Vol. 2, 93)

But his heart lamented anyway: "And what does the world give me for my virtue? For my childlike temper? Ridi-cule, and time brings bitterness and grey hairs. . . . There are combats, thoughts even, which the most mortal dare not express, because the angel of Innocence in our breast re-gards them as sinful. . . . I felt that in myself—in my own corrupt nature—there abode no good thing."[13] In his diary he is more accurate and more honest regarding his "inno-cence": "I'm sure experienced people will laugh at my inno-cence, but it isn't really innocence, it is an abhorrence of this thing for which I have such a dislike."[14]

He did hear seductive, challenging advice:

Be gay and wild in thy youth, so that thou mayest become satisfied when thou growest older. The sins of youth men pardon; the man, however, they judge more severely. Seize on the joys of life whilst thou canst, so that when thou art an old man thou mayest not weep because thou hast no sins; for they belong to life, as salt does to meat. Better is it to have enjoyed life too much, than later to sigh because one has not enjoyed it as one could. Write that in your wandering-book! God, or the devil, in whose soever regiment thou mayest enter thyself, be a good master to thee!

But Christian, the fiddler to whom that advice is given, "understood the demon-like sentiment of these words, attached himself more closely to his God, and prayed 'Deliver us from evil!' "[15]

No, Andersen never accepted the "evil" in himself, just as he never accepted the doctrine of Hell, never accepted that man and God must include both Good and Evil. As Nyborg writes with reference to *The Snow Queen*: "The realization of 'God's other face' was lost to Andersen."[16]

His relationship to God was, in any case, somewhat peculiar. As Brandes put it:

> The foundation of Andersen's religiosity was a burning gratitude for prosperity. In prosperity and honor . . . he traced a Providence, and not an indefinite and universal but a special Providence that had watched over him constantly, guided his footsteps, led him to kindhearted people, benefactors, helpers, patrons, had allowed him to be born in humble circumstances that his greatness might appear the more dazzling against the dark background of poverty and abandonment, in short had granted him redress and appreciation and at last crowned him with glory. As the first lines of his autobiography have it: "There is a loving God who makes all things work out for the best." And as there cannot be a God unless we receive everything from Him and owe everything to Him, all the honours that were ultimately showered upon him made Andersen not haughty, but humble.[17]

And what if things went wrong? Then, despite his childhood declaration that "people at first have an immense deal of adversity to go through and then they will become famous," he could never believe—since God had no "other face"—that any misfortune befalling him could also have been planned by Providence. At such moments he doubted God, doubted his existence.

He called God, Father. And we recall that his own, earthly father, the one who had set him on his way to literature, had "deserted" him when he was but eleven. His adopted father, Jonas Collin, while in fact always solidly supportive, regularly instilled doubts and fears in Andersen because he failed to be properly impressed by his accomplishments and his fame, and was in that sense not totally "there" for him.

But was Andersen himself totally "there"? Can a man who, denying the "other face" of God, then also denies, or at least rejects, his own—can a man who denies and rejects sensuality and sexuality feel, or be, completely "real"? Must he not forever be an onlooker at other people's feasts? Must he not feel left out, excluded from the essence and inner sanctum of human experience?

In his story *The Fir Tree* Andersen conveys just that: The fir tree, at any moment of its life, always hopes that the next experience will finally validate him, fulfill him, make him glow. He lives in hope—until he lives only in memory. He never realizes the moment.[18] Others live, but the fir tree is only a witness and a victim of their lives.[19]

Andersen gave himself several reasons for being, forever, an outsider: his lowly origins,[20] his ugliness, and his poverty. Like Thomas Mann after him, Andersen considered even artistic genius as somehow disreputable and suspect—something not "solid" and not integrated into society.[21] But basically it was his failure to achieve sexual love that for him, as for the Little Mermaid, eventually resulted in a kind of "invisibility and disembodiment." It also gave him his unique and painful insight into the reality, or rather unreality, "of the upstart, the outsider, the deviant, the loser, the impossible lover and the false role-player."[22]

He was an outsider who desperately wanted to be "in," and who pursued this goal with aggressive determination.[23] Just as, upon first arriving in Copenhagen, he attacked the closed doors of society and crashed through one after another, just so he "networked" later on to inject himself into the company of writers, artists, aristocrats, and royalty—as if he could acquire legitimacy through association. But the touchstone of acceptability was, for him, not to be found in the wide world through which he flitted, but at home in Denmark, in the Collin family, and most particularly with "father" Collin. Over and over again he besieged

him with letters such as the following, written at Christmas
1845:

> You know that my greatest vanity, or call it rather joy, con-
> sists in making you realize that I am worthy of you. All the
> kind appreciation I get makes me think of you. I am truly
> popular, truly appreciated abroad, I am famous—all right,
> you're smiling. But the cream of the nations fly toward me, I
> find myself accepted in all families, the greatest compliments
> are paid me by princes and by the most gifted men. . . . Oh,
> no one at home thinks of this among the many who entirely
> ignore me. . . . My writings must have greater value than the
> Danes will allow for. . . . You must know, you my beloved
> Father must understand that you did not misjudge me when
> you accepted me as your son, when you helped and pro-
> tected me.[24]

Jonas had in fact "adopted" him long ago, but Andersen,
knowing himself to be "unreal," could never believe the
reality of his inclusion in the Collin family. Only once did he
come close. In May 1845, Jonas wrote to him: "My dear
Andersen,—My wife is very ill. All the children are here.
Yours, Collin." Andersen was jubilant:

> I have realized how firmly I have grown into the family, felt
> that in your circle I am a son, something which has made me
> proud in the good sense of the word. The fact that on that
> Sunday night you called me home together with the other
> children, that in one of the most serious hours I was placed
> among yours, has filled me with happiness and apprecia-
> tion. . . . I feel strangely moved by this, I wish I could ex-
> press my feelings in words, show it, show that I love you,
> love you with the soul of a son.[25]

It did not last. The Danish critics cut and ridiculed him,
and the Collins refused to be awed by his fame. In his sensi-
tivity and insecurity he took this as rejection, and felt least at
home where he most yearned to "belong." Hence his many
journeys.[26] He traveled, of course, to gain new impressions,
and to have something to write about, since his travel books
made money. But he traveled, above all, as he had traveled
the first time, to get away from the hurts he suffered—or
imagined—at home.[27] His trips enabled him to get away

from rejections, to avoid being an outsider, and to harvest applause abroad where, legitimately an "outsider," he was very much "in" (the camaraderie of all expatriates). Like Peer Gynt, that restless wanderer created by his younger colleague Ibsen, Andersen always knew that his salvation lay at home. But he always again fled it, sensing that even if some Solveig were waiting for him lovingly there, he could not live up to the implications of such a love.

In the most primitive and anatomical sense, the male act or mode is intrusive; this phallic, intrusive mode colors all male functioning. Andersen was intrusive, he wanted "in" in every other way except that very basic one that would have entitled him to a "legitimate" place in society, that would have made him a "member" as a man. He struggled to be accepted, at least, as a son; and finally had to be contented with being fussed over as a child.

The Little Mermaid

There remains an ambiguity both in Andersen's writings and in our presentation of them. For example, we have said of Karen, the girl of *The Red Shoes*, that she was Karen the half-sister; but we have said of Inger, in *The Girl Who Trod on the Loaf*, that she was an aspect of Andersen himself. In other words, some characters in his stories are taken from life, and some are projections of his own self.

Or again: pointing out that the rooftop garden scene in *The Snow Queen* was taken from real life, we said that in fact Hans Christian had played up there by himself. Therefore, both of the children in his imagination, both Kay *and* Gerda, would have to be seen as representations of himself.

In both these instances we did not hesitate to assume that Andersen could feel, or present himself, as a woman. Lest this should raise eyebrows, let us cite a salvation story we have not discussed so far, though it is perhaps the most famous of his stories: *The Little Mermaid.*

Of this story it has been said by many critics and scholars—though, as far as I know, not by Andersen himself—that the Little Mermaid represents *him,* whereas the rejecting prince stands for Louise Collin.[1] What their evidence may be I do not know, but we can adduce some "internal" evidence of our own.

The Little Mermaid lives at the bottom of the sea with her father, the sea king, and her sisters. She is being raised by the king's "*old mother,*" who is extremely fond of her *granddaughters*—the mother having died long ago. As mermaids, the girls have *no feet.* (They have, in fact, not much of anything. They have no soul, and in case of death dissolve into foam. They are insubstantial, they have no real personality, they are not real persons. What can you expect, after all, of creatures who lack not only shoes, but feet to put them on?) At fifteen they are permitted an excursion to the world above (as Andersen was at fourteen). The five older sisters are not much taken by what they see up there and prefer to return home, or else to lure sailors to the deep by singing to them with their *beautiful voices.*

When her turn comes, the youngest one falls in love with a prince whom she spies aboard a ship. The ship founders in a storm; the mermaid saves the prince and pulls him ashore. There a princess finds him the next morning, and he thinks this princess has rescued him. The mermaid, unable to leave the sea, pines away yearning for him; but she finds his seaside castle, watches him whenever she can, and finally decides that she wants to become a human being in order to be with him all the time. She consults her grandmother, who explains that a mermaid can acquire a soul and become immortal only "if a human being loved you so much that you meant more to him than his father and mother." (The plot thus follows the familiar theme of redemption by love, but, in the light of what we have said before, this is not the proper princely way of redeeming a woman through heroic action, but a woman's way of redeeming through love. It is the opposite of what the story—classically—should call for.) "If his every thought and his whole heart cleaved to you so that he would let a priest join his right hand to yours and would promise to be faithful here and throughout all eternity, then his soul would dwell in your body, and you would share in the happiness of mankind."[2]

But the grandmother is not willing to help her attain this goal, so the Little Mermaid decides to visit the *sea witch.* This is a terrifying undertaking, for the sea witch lives surrounded by predatory polyps like hundred-headed snakes, and the ground is littered with the skeletons of men. The sea witch herself lets a toad eat out of her mouth and has an "ugly, fat watersnake" as a pet. (These symbols of sexuality are familiar to us from the fate of wicked Inger.) The witch is willing to give her a draught that will change her fishtail into

legs, but "every step you take will feel as if you were tread-
ing upon knife blades so sharp that blood must flow." Her
life and immortality will depend on whether the prince marries her; if he does not, but marries another, then her "heart
will break on the very next morning" and she will become
foam of the sea. In return for the draught, the sea witch
takes from the mermaid her *sweet voice*. (Andersen, too, lost
his at fifteen.) She cuts out the mermaid's tongue, so that
she *becomes speechless*.

As the sun rises, the mermaid takes the draught on a
beach by the prince's palace, and there he finds her. She
now has "the loveliest pair of white legs any young maid
could hope to have," but she can neither sing nor talk.[3] She
wins the prince's heart by her beauty and, later, by her
graceful dancing. (Andersen made his debut on the Copenhagen stage as a dancer; and he too was always speechless—
tongue-tied—when it came to declaring his love.) The
prince, however, eventually locates the princess he had encountered on the beach after his shipwreck, and she is the
one he decides to marry.

At the wedding the mermaid dances wonderfully, even
though her feet feel as if they were pierced by daggers. That
night her sisters rise from the ocean and tell her she can
save herself from death only if she strikes a knife into the
prince's heart, a knife the sea witch has given them and
which they present to her. She must kill him before sunrise,
but as she ponders the prince and princess asleep in their
tent on the deck of their ship and then the sharp blade in
her hand, *she cannot deliver the thrust that would save her*. She
throws the knife overboard and jumps after it. Instantly her
body dissolves in foam. She should, at this point, have
ceased to exist; but there follows a contrived happy ending
that is both unworthy and, alas, characteristic of Andersen:
in the long run, it will be the goodness of children that will
save her after all.[4]

This, then, is another tale of unrequited love. Or, rather,
it is the first in that long series of such tales Andersen wrote.
But this time it is the girl who is being scorned.

Or is it?

This girl, the Little Mermaid, has all the characteristics of Hans Christian: she has the beautiful voice, and she loses it. She tries to appeal through dancing, and fails; she is in love, but has no tongue to declare herself. She lacks the true flesh-and-blood personality that would make her human (she acquires, ever so painfully, human legs, but we never do hear that she wears shoes), and she recoils in horror from delivering the loving thrust that would draw blood but make her *real*. Like Andersen, she remains insubstantial. She must join the "daughters of the air," hoping to gain within the next three hundred years a soul that will never die—either through her own good deeds (but what good deeds could such a wraith perform?) or through the goodness of children. She also has, just like Andersen, an "old grandmother," whose double (or shadow) is a frightening old witch who turns out to be helpful. There is enough autobiography in all this to make us agree with the verdict of the critics: the mermaid is Andersen himself; and so we must also accept that he had the ability to project himself into his stories in the shape of either sex.

From there it is only a short step to the assumption that each and every main character in his stories represents not just someone he may have known in real life, but also, and perhaps above all, an aspect of himself. And in this sense, all the adventures and conflicts as well as all the yearning for redemption become *inner* events and processes; and the hoped-for salvation of the personality is to be accomplished by an aspect of itself.

22

The Lonely Oyster

It is not at all an outlandish assumption to say, as we did in the preceding chapter, that the main characters in Andersen's stories may have been aspects of himself. When analyzing dreams, we commonly assume that every person appearing in them is an aspect of the dreamer. In daily life we may readily say that someone's intelligence had better rule his passions, or that his heart should mitigate his reason. In each instance we are saying that an aspect of the personality can and should act upon another.

Looking at things in this manner, let us start—since we must start somewhere—with Kay. Such a resolute, rambunctious, scientific type—if that is how we see him; or such a hard-thinking, deep-pondering type—as he may eventually appear to be, sitting on his mirror of cold reason: such a fellow would do quite well as an ego-representation for a man, as symbolic of that part of a man's function that he most readily supports and furthers with all the will power at his command—that part of him he knows most about and for the sake of which he most esteems himself—a real manly part. But with Andersen, poor little Kay gets no such endorsement. There is something wrong with him, we hear. He is bewitched. (Or, at any event, bedeviled.) He is, in that sense, alien. He would, were he to be around and not so far away up North, surely be a bad influence.

But such ambivalence toward—what shall we call little Kay by way of a generic term: the *logos*?—such ambivalence toward the logos does not behoove a man. It would better befit a woman, forming part of her masculine side, that problematic and contentious masculine aspect of woman to which Jung gave the name *animus*.[1] Yes, little Kay might well be a suitable animus-representation for a woman; but it so happens that he is Andersen's animus. Andersen so fears this alien, un-Christian masculinity in himself that he relegates it to the loneliness of outer space[2] and considers it much in need of reconversion, redemption, and rescue.

Rescued he must be, for without him the self of even such a man as Andersen could not function. And so, out to search for him goes Gerda. Since she represents Hans Christian's feminine aspect—that considerable part of him that is in touch with nature and animals, with instincts, and with the unconscious altogether—we may as well once again use Jung's terminology and call her an *anima* figure: that aspect of man which, if any, is inspired and creative. That aspect, that anima, that Gerda, now goes on an adventurous quest through many dark and magical places, driven by the restless energies of those instincts that we may as well summate under the technical term *libido*.

Whenever some great work is to be accomplished—and the more so, the more it depends on an element of inspiration and intuition—a man may well shrink back, doubtful of his strength, and feel the need for some sort of magical assistance, for some infusion of strength from some primal source.[3] At such times, he sends his receptive-fertile self, his anima, on a long voyage through the night of the unconscious. The period she spends below, like Persephone in Hades, is felt as a time of incubation and germination, during which a man may be restless and remote, turned in upon himself, like a pregnant woman. One day the anima returns, and his libido, so long dormant, awakens to renewed fruitfulness—as when Persephone returns to earth in the person of Core, the maiden, adorning the world with flowers and all the new growth of spring.[4]

Of such a renewal Andersen was, while writing *The Snow Queen*, sore in need: his last, highest hope for inspiration by a living, flesh-and-blood muse (Jenny Lind), had failed. He was left, not only with the prospect of final bachelorhood, but without the tensions and emotional resources that must stir and fuel creative activity.[5] Lacking inspiration, he was thrown back upon his intellect, which sat as pitifully and blue-with-cold on the blank but unrevealing mirror of reason as did Kay, and produced nothing.

So Gerda was sent out to fetch back poetry—quite as Faust was sent to the realm of "the mothers" to fetch back Helen.[6] Indeed mother-figures dominate every part of Gerda's journey and, appropriately, all important developments occur at night. Mother and womb are symbolic for each other, as are womb and feminine creation; and the whole creative process of incubation and germination, whether in the womb or in the soil or in the unconscious, is associated with darkness and requires it.

This journey through the night is strangely seductive and has its risks. We were all, apparently, in grave danger when Persephone, held in Hades against her will, yielded to temptation and nibbled on some pomegranate seeds. Because she had partaken of this—for the living—forbidden food, she was not permitted to leave the underworld altogether. For nine months she was to regain the light of day, to join her mother Demeter and fructify the earth; but back to Tartarus she must go for three months out of every year, during which time the earth lies barren. It was a close call. How easily could she have been caught forever in Hades, and the world condemned to death![7]

Just so, as we have pointed out, is Gerda constantly in danger of accepting too much hospitality, of getting stuck in the wonderland of the (inner) world in which she travels. At each stage she is invited to stay, and each stay must appear to her as more comfortable and infinitely more safe than the continued journey. And yet, if both Kay and Gerda are aspects of the self, though far removed from each other, and if the integration of the self, the reenergizing of the self, is to be expected from bringing them back together, then the quest must continue. The stages, which before we had discussed as moratoria in the development of a girl, now appear as traps in the progress of a soul in search of salvation.

Gerda manages not to get trapped, but she also manages not to learn anything. She goes through all her adventures essentially untouched and unimpaired, but also unenriched; she has, in fact, a veritable aversion to learning.

We know this already, since we know that she failed to learn from her grandmother the language of infants and of animals. In the garden of the Woman Skilled in Magic she fails to pick up any vegetation magic: she never gets her hands dirty with the good dirt of the earth, she makes nothing grow, and she helps nothing to grow. And at the court of the princess or at the lair of the robbers she learns nothing about sex or violence. She does manage, for a while, to understand the language of the gentler animals, but we doubt whether she retains that skill; and she picks up none of the sorcery of the Lapp Woman or of the Finn Woman. Even though all of these people and all of the animals so obviously try to be helpful, she insists, in last analysis, on getting along on the strength of her religious faith alone.

We realize: what she refuses to learn, what she, in effect, represses, is what Andersen repressed. It is the very part of himself he had to deny. That part of him contained all he had always found unacceptable in himself. And because all his life those rejected qualities and emotions hung over him like some gigantic, ominous shadow, we shall, once again, adopt one of Jung's terms and refer to these qualities, once they are projected upon and rendered concrete in a person, as his "shadow." But while, theoretically, the shadow should make its appearance in the guise of a person of the same sex, we shall have to face the patent fact that for Andersen it always appeared as a girl—such as Karen, the diabolic half-sister and the girl of *The Red Shoes*.[8]

Now while the shadow may represent all that we dislike, all that we cannot stomach in ourselves, it nevertheless also contains great value. In Jung's words: "Libido is by nature demonic: it is both God and devil. If evil were to be utterly destroyed, everything daemonic, including God Himself, would suffer a grievous loss; it would be like performing an amputation on the body of the Deity."[9] And so one must not cast out the devil altogether, but one must come to terms with him and draw strength from him, as Faust did with his shadow, Mephisto.

This is exactly what Andersen never managed. To his mind, unacceptable evil was crowding him, as it were, from both sides. He was threatened on one side by Kay's critical intellect, because it killed faith, and on the other side by all organic processes, whether vegetable or animal, because they deny the spirit. All these were anathema to him. True integration of his personality not only would have required the union of Gerda (anima) with Kay (logos), but would have had to include also, as in a new trinity, Karen (the shadow).

Such integration, such "at-one-ment," he never conceived of, much less reached. True—more than most men he was in touch with his own feminine aspect, and through it he dipped deeply into the unconscious and brought forth from his night-journeys a wealth of imagery and symbolism comprehensible to anyone. True also, his anima "saved" his logos to the extent that he could be creative—not only potentially but in fact, producing a body of work that without the disciplining, organizing, structuring capability of the logos would never have seen the light of day. But because the shadow remained unintegrated, therefore even his best stories remained flawed, as *The Snow Queen* is flawed by its timorous, inconclusive ending. His worst stories, those pietistic or pseudo-progressive tales he tortured out of the logos alone, without the grace of his poetic anima, are total and dreary failures. And the whole body of his work, to the extent to which it survives, has been relegated by the brutal and perhaps justified verdict of time to the realm of "children's literature."

With this we return to the beginning—to the beginning of *The Snow Queen* and of this study—and ask again: what is the basic sin symbolized by the devil's mirror, the sin that forms the theme of our story?

As we pointed out initially, there are really two sins involved: the sin of impertinence, hubris, or the desire to ascend to the gods to be like unto them; and the sin of criticism. But as to the latter, we now understand that no mere literary criticism can be meant, even though Andersen suffered from his critics deeply and often tried to get even with them.[10] No, what we are dealing with must be criticism, *krisis*, in a deeper sense—namely, the sin of dividing and of keeping apart. But in what manner could it have been of crucial importance to Andersen?

And there, we must truly marvel. Just as in the practice of psychotherapy we often find that the patient presents us with the decisive clue to his problems right in the first interview—though it may take us weeks or months to understand it—just so Andersen gave us the key to the story, and to his personality, right at the outset—though we failed to grasp it.

He tells us the mirror converted a good, pious thought into a (carnal) grin. But that is what Andersen did with any sexuality, since in his view there was no good physical love but only "carnality" with all that the term implies of wickedness and "dirt." And so the hubris of the poor devils who tried to get up to heaven to be like unto the angels was the same as the hubris of Inger who wanted to stay "clean," and it was the same as Andersen's hubris when he declares all sexuality a "carnal grin." In so doing, he tries to divest himself of "evil," to remain "clean"—as if he could thereby become an angel or, better still: once again a child.

He did not succeed in this. What he did accomplish was to "perform an amputation on the body of the Deity." With his childlike goodness he castrated God, and he castrated himself, and he castrated, finally, his own body of work. I think he knew it and suffered deeply from it. It was this castration that constituted the basic misery and failure of nerve in his life, and from which he so badly needed to be redeemed.

No woman ever came to redeem him—or so he professes and complains, over and over again. We do not know, for we are never told, how many, in fact, would have been willing to try. The type of the *caballero de la triste figura*, the

Don Quixote type whom Andersen, in his own way, so greatly resembles, usually attracts a great many willing or would-be redemptresses. But if love was offered him, he lacked the courage to meet it.

In one of his poems he speaks of love as the pearl that causes the oyster to die.[11] In fact it was not love but his *failure* to love that caused his protracted, lingering emotional death. But it was from his very failures, from the very flaws of his loving, that Andersen—poor, lonely oyster that he was—created the pearls he has left us.

Epilogue

Well then: We have finished. And now that the story is done, do we know any more than we knew before?

Not very much, perhaps; and yet again—not all that little.

We know, of course, a good deal more about the man Andersen—who was born in obscure poverty and rose to fame; whose father inspired him but failed him and left him fatherless; whose mother and grandmother cared for him devotedly but terrified him; who fled into the wide world when still a child in the firm belief that the world would love him; who was loved by all the world, but never found love; and who died, in the midst of friends and admirers, essentially a lonely man.

But what is Andersen to us, or we to Andersen, that we should weep for him?

Nay, weep for him we need not—not unless, by some of his words, he makes us weep for ourselves. And there the brittle, self-centered, in many ways superficial man that was Andersen exhibits an astounding gift. It is hard indeed to read one or the other of his stories and not be profoundly moved. A strong, well-established man reading Andersen tales to his children may find himself choking up and may be dismayed by the watering of his eyes before he is done. A magic is at work. What causes it? How does it function?

It lies, I believe, not only in all that Andersen knew about the human heart and what moves it, but above all in what he did not know he knew and what we do not know we know about ourselves.

Take, for instance, the Ugly Duckling. The term has become indispensable to us; we really have no better way to designate the unhappy, unloved, and unrecognized creature we all at one time or another imagine ourselves to be. Nor could we think of any prouder image for what we would yearn, some day, to become than a swan. But there are harmonics at work in the term that evoke more than we commonly let ourselves know. The Ugly Duckling does not just feel itself misunderstood, since it does not yet know that it can become a swan. But the Ugly Duckling thinks the world justified in treating it badly, for it knows itself to be ugly, meaning: defective, evil, unworthy, and hence cast out beyond the pale, beyond community. Seen in this light, the term denotes what, in a Christian context, has been called the Original Sin: the feeling, often unaware but psychodynamically powerful, that we are not worthy by birth alone; that we must in some manner either prove ourselves or, more likely, be redeemed. The Ugly Duckling of the story proves itself simply by surviving the cold winter—by bearing the burden of its unworthy state. What ends this state of unworthiness is surely an act of redemption, an act of grace: the totally unlooked-for, unhoped-for, improbable, incredible, undeserved, and hence doubly awesome growth of white plumage, the acceptance into community, into love, into God.

One can write volumes of psychology, moral philosophy, and theology on this theme and still not get any closer or any deeper into the understanding of the phenomenon than Andersen manages to do with his inspired symbolism. His consciously writing mind here touched an unconscious truth—an archetype, if you wish—which, being common heirloom, resonates a similar unconscious truth in each of us. With a few words a key is struck, with one stroke a whole cluster, a whole ramified complex, a *Gestalt* is struck, and we are—moved.

And as to *The Snow Queen*? The theme is the same with an important difference. The theme is once again redemption, but not through a natural process such as growing up or growing white plumage through the grace of God. This time it is redemption through the love of woman. The proposition is far from new or unique. But I submit that it is most timely.

We live in an age . . . ah, but it behooves me to be careful: what nonsense has not been written by observers of their own age! And yet how can we *not* attempt to define the present, and how else can we guide our steps? Well then: We live in an age that would please the Devil greatly. The splinters from his distorting mirror must have been recycled, since there are so many of them about. Division is everywhere, society has fallen into ever smaller factions, and each faction—no doubt rightly—feels maltreated, and—no doubt rightly—seeks its own redress. And in the course of all these rightful struggles over important details, some great truths stand to get submerged.

One of these partisan struggles being waged in the Western world today is the struggle for the liberation of woman. It is a cause of such undoubted merit that one must wish it well. And yet—one cannot help but fear that all this concern with independence will submerge a truth basic to human nature: that men, at any rate, cannot get on without women.

I do not mean this in the obvious, biological sense, which would cut both ways. I mean it in the psychological sense, in the way Andersen meant it. Without the validating love of woman, without the love of *his* woman, *for whom* he works and hunts and fights and *to whom* he brings his victories and his wounds—man in himself would be an empty shell, an ephemeral accident unrelated to the grand purposes of God and world, an idle display.

If Kay were not rescued, were not redeemed by Gerda, he could continue his frigid intellectual games amid the vacuous light show of the aurora borealis forever—and he would never *come alive*. The most moving passages of the story are those relating the reunion of Gerda and Kay. Speaking to what we deeply know but do not know we know, they remind us how lonely we are or have been; how, if we are men, we need the validation, the confirmation, the redemption by woman; and if we are women, how the redemption of such a lonely man is one of the magic feats, one of the miracles a woman can perform.

We live in an age when, in the strife of causes and liberations, in the divisiveness that increasingly fractures the bonds between men and women, such a basic truth stands to become submerged. To the degree to which this is happening, we are all further impoverished. To the degree to which Andersen moves us, reminds us how much we could be for each other, we owe him a debt of gratitude.

APPENDIX: THE TEXT

The Snow Queen

A Tale in Seven Stories

FIRST STORY

WHICH HAS TO DO WITH A MIRROR AND ITS FRAGMENTS

Now then! We will begin. When the story is done you shall know a great deal more than you do now.

He was a terribly bad hobgoblin, a goblin of the very wickedest sort and, in fact, he was the devil himself. One day the devil was in a very good humor because he had just finished a mirror which had this peculiar power: everything good and beautiful that was reflected in it seemed to dwindle to almost nothing at all, while everything that was worthless and ugly became most conspicuous and even uglier than ever. In this mirror the loveliest landscapes looked like boiled spinach, and the very best people became hideous, or stood on their heads and had no stomachs. Their faces were distorted beyond any recognition, and if a person had a freckle it was sure to spread until it covered both nose and mouth.

"That's very funny!" said the devil. If a good, pious thought passed through anyone's mind, it showed in the mirror as a carnal grin, and the devil laughed aloud at his ingenious invention.

All those who went to the hobgoblin's school—for he had a school of his own—told everyone that a miracle had come

From *The Complete Andersen*, trans. Jean Hersholt (New York: Heritage Press, 1942), 196–228. Courtesy of The Limited Editions Club, New York.

to pass. Now, they asserted, for the very first time you could see how the world and all its people really looked. They scurried about with the mirror until there was not a person alive nor a land on earth that had not been distorted.

Then they wanted to fly up to heaven itself, to scoff at the angels, and our Lord. The higher they flew with the mirror, the wider it grinned. They could hardly manage to hold it. Higher they flew, and higher still, nearer to heaven and the angels. Then the grinning mirror trembled with such violence that it slipped from their hands and fell to the earth, where it shattered into hundreds of millions of billions of bits, or perhaps even more. And now it caused more trouble than it did before it was broken, because some of the fragments were smaller than a grain of sand and these went flying throughout the wide world. Once they got in people's eyes they would stay there. These bits of glass distorted everything the people saw, and made them see only the bad side of things, for every little bit of glass kept the same power that the whole mirror had possessed.

A few people even got a glass splinter in their hearts, and that was a terrible thing, for it turned their hearts into lumps of ice. Some of the fragments were so large that they were used as window panes—but not the kind of window through which you should look at your friends. Other pieces were made into spectacles, and evil things came to pass when people put them on to see clearly and to see justice done. The fiend was so tickled by it all that he laughed until his sides were sore. But fine bits of glass are still flying through the air, and now you shall hear what happened.

SECOND STORY

A Little Boy and a Little Girl

In the big city it was so crowded with houses and people that few found room for even a small garden and most people had to be content with a flowerpot, but two poor children who lived there managed to have a garden that was a little bigger than a flowerpot. These children were not brother and sister, but they loved each other just as much as if they had been. Their parents lived close to one another in the garrets of two adjoining houses. Where the roofs met and where the rain gutter ran between the two houses, their two small windows faced each other. One had only to step across the rain gutter to go from window to window.

In these windows, the parents had a large box where they planted vegetables for their use, and a little rose bush too. Each box had a bush, which thrived to perfection. Then it occurred to the parents to put these boxes across the gutter, where they very nearly reached from one window to the other, and looked exactly like two walls of flowers. The pea plants hung down over the boxes, and the rose bushes threw out long sprays that framed the windows and bent over toward each other. It was almost like a little triumphal arch of greenery and flowers. The boxes were very high, and the children knew that they were not to climb about on them, but they were often allowed to take their little stools out on the roof under the roses, where they had a wonderful time playing together.

Winter, of course, put an end to this pleasure. The windows often frosted over completely. But they would heat copper pennies on the stove and press these hot coins against the frost-coated glass. Then they had the finest of peepholes, as round as a ring, and behind them appeared a bright, friendly eye, one at each window—it was the little boy and the little girl who peeped out. His name was Kay and hers was Gerda. With one skip they could join each other in summer, but to visit together in the wintertime they had to go all the way downstairs in one house, and climb all the way upstairs in the other. Outside the snow was whirling.

"See the white bees swarming," the old grandmother said.

"Do they have a queen bee, too?" the little boy asked, for he knew that real bees have one.

"Yes, indeed they do," the grandmother said. "She flies in the thick of the swarm. She is the biggest bee of all, and can never stay quietly on the earth, but goes back again to the dark clouds. Many a wintry night she flies through the streets and peers in through the windows. Then they freeze over in a strange fashion, as if they were covered with flowers."

"Oh, yes, we've seen that," both the children said, and so they knew it was true.

"Can the Snow Queen come in here?" the little girl asked.

"Well, let her come!" cried the boy. "I would put her on the hot stove and melt her."

But Grandmother stroked his head, and told them other stories.

That evening when little Kay was at home and half ready for bed, he climbed on the chair by the window and looked out through the little peephole. A few snowflakes were falling, and the largest flake of all alighted on the edge of one of the flower boxes. This flake grew bigger and bigger, until at last it turned into a woman, who was dressed in the finest white gauze which looked as if it had been made from millions of star-shaped flakes. She was beautiful and she was graceful, but she was ice—shining, glittering ice. She was alive, for all that, and her eyes sparkled like two bright stars, but in them there was neither rest nor peace. She nodded toward the window and beckoned with her hand. The little boy was frightened, and as he jumped down from the chair it seemed to him that a huge bird flew past the window.

The next day was clear and cold. Then the snow thawed, and springtime came. The sun shone, the green grass sprouted, swallows made their nests, windows were thrown open, and once again the children played in their little roof garden, high up in the rain gutter on top of the house.

That summer the roses bloomed their splendid best. The little girl had learned a hymn in which there was a line about roses that reminded her of their own flowers. She sang it to the little boy, and he sang it with her:

> Where roses bloom so sweetly in the vale,
> There shall you find the Christ Child, without fail.

The children held each other by the hand, kissed the roses, looked up at the Lord's clear sunshine, and spoke to it as if the Christ Child were there. What glorious summer days those were, and how beautiful it was out under those fragrant rose bushes which seemed as if they would never stop blooming.

Kay and Gerda were looking at a picture book of birds and beasts one day, and it was then—just as the clock in the church tower was striking five—that Kay cried:

"Oh! something hurt my heart. And now I've got something in my eye."

The little girl put her arm around his neck, and he blinked his eye. No, she couldn't see anything in it.

"I think it's gone," he said. But it was not gone. It was one of those splinters of glass from the magic mirror. You remember that goblin's mirror—the one which made everything great and good that was reflected in it appear small and ugly, but which magnified all evil things until each blemish loomed large. Poor Kay! A fragment had pierced his heart as well, and soon it would turn into a lump of ice. The pain had stopped, but the glass was still there.

"Why should you be crying?" he asked. "It makes you look so ugly. There's nothing the matter with me." And suddenly he took it into his head to say:

"Ugh! that rose is all worm-eaten. And look, this one is crooked. And these roses, they are just as ugly as they can be. They look like the boxes they grow in." He gave the boxes a kick, and broke off both of the roses.

"Kay! what are you doing?" the little girl cried. When he saw how it upset her, he broke off another rose and then leaped home through his own window, leaving dear little Gerda all alone.

Afterwards, when she brought out her picture book, he said it was fit only for babes in the cradle. And whenever Grandmother told stories, he always broke in with a "but—." If he could manage it he would steal behind her, perch a pair of spectacles on his nose, and imitate her. He did this so cleverly that it made everybody laugh, and before long he could mimic the walk and the talk of everyone who lived on that street. Everything that was odd or ugly about them, Kay could mimic so well that people said, "That boy has surely got a good head on him!" But it was the glass in his eye and the glass in his heart that made him tease even little Gerda, who loved him with all her soul.

Now his games were very different from what they used to be. They became more sensible. When the snow was flying about one wintry day, he brought a large magnifying glass out of doors and spread the tail of his blue coat to let the snowflakes fall on it.

"Now look through the glass," he told Gerda. Each snowflake seemed much larger, and looked like a magnificent flower or a ten-pointed star. It was marvelous to look at.

"Look, how artistic!" said Kay. "They are much more interesting to look at than real flowers, for they are absolutely perfect. There isn't a flaw in them, until they start melting."

A little while later Kay came down with his big gloves on his hands and his sled on his back. Right in Gerda's ear he bawled out, "I've been given permission to play in the big square where the other boys are!" and away he ran.

In the square some of the more adventuresome boys would tie their little sleds on behind the farmers' carts, to be pulled along for quite a distance. It was wonderful sport. While the fun was at its height, a big sleigh drove up. It was painted entirely white, and the driver wore a white, shaggy fur cloak and a white, shaggy cap. As the sleigh drove twice around the square, Kay quickly hooked his little sled behind it, and down the street they went, faster and faster. The driver turned around in a friendly fashion and nodded to Kay, just as if they were old acquaintances. Every time Kay started to unfasten his little sleigh, its driver nodded again, and Kay held on, even when they drove right out through the town gate.

Then the snow began to fall so fast that the boy could not see his hands in front of him, as they sped on. He suddenly let go the slack of the rope in his hands, in order to get loose from the big sleigh, but it did no good. His little sled was tied on securely, and they went like the wind. He gave a loud shout, but nobody heard him. The snow whirled and the sleigh flew along. Every now and then it gave a jump, as if it were clearing hedges and ditches. The boy was terror-stricken. He tried to say his prayers, but all he could remember was his multiplication tables.

The snowflakes got bigger and bigger, until they looked like big white hens. All of a sudden the curtain of snow parted, and the big sleigh stopped and the driver stood up. The fur coat and the cap were made of snow, and it was a woman, tall and slender and blinding white—she was the Snow Queen herself.

"We have made good time," she said. "Is it possible that you tremble from cold? Crawl under my bear coat." She took him up in the sleigh beside her, and as she wrapped the fur about him he felt as if he were sinking into a snowdrift.

"Are you still cold?" she asked, and kissed him on the forehead. *Brer-r-r.* That kiss was colder than ice. He felt it right down to his heart, half of which was already an icy lump. He felt as if he were dying, but only for a moment. Then he felt quite comfortable, and no longer noticed the cold.

"My sled! Don't forget my sled!" It was the only thing he thought of. They tied it to one of the white hens, which flew along after them with the sled on its back. The Snow Queen kissed Kay once more, and then he forgot little Gerda, and Grandmother, and all the others at home.

"You won't get any more kisses now," she said, "or else I should kiss you to death." Kay looked at her. She was so beautiful! A cleverer and prettier face he could not imagine. She no longer seemed to be made of ice, as she had seemed when she sat outside his window and beckoned to him. In his eyes she was perfect, and she was not at all afraid. He told her how he could do mental arithmetic even with fractions, and that he knew the size and population of all the countries. She kept on smiling, and he began to be afraid that he did not know as much as he thought he did. He looked up at the great big space overhead, as she flew with him high up on the black clouds, while the storm whistled and roared as if it were singing old ballads.

They flew over forests and lakes, over many a land and sea. Below them the wind blew cold, wolves howled, and black crows screamed as they skimmed across the glittering snow. But up above the moon shone bright and large, and on it Kay fixed his eyes throughout that long, long winter night. By day he slept at the feet of the Snow Queen.

THIRD STORY

The Flower Garden of the Woman Skilled in Magic

How did little Gerda get along when Kay did not come back? Where could he be? Nobody knew. Nobody could give them any news of him. All that the boys could say was that they had seen him hitch his little sled to a fine big sleigh, which had driven down the street and out through the town gate. Nobody knew what had become of Kay. Many tears were shed, and little Gerda sobbed hardest of all. People said that he was dead—that he must have been drowned in the river not far from town. Ah, how gloomy those long winter days were!

But spring and its warm sunshine came at last.

"Kay is dead and gone," little Gerda said.

"I don't believe it," said the sunshine.

"He's dead and gone," she said to the swallows.

"We don't believe it," they sang. Finally little Gerda began to disbelieve it too. One morning she said to herself:

"I'll put on my new red shoes, the ones Kay has never seen, and I'll go down by the river to ask about him."

It was very early in the morning. She kissed her old grandmother, who was still asleep, put on her red shoes, and all by herself she hurried out through the town gate and down to the river.

"Is it true that you have taken my own little playmate? I'll give you my red shoes if you will bring him back to me."

It seemed to her that the waves nodded very strangely. So she took off the red shoes that were her dearest possession, and threw them into the river. But they fell near the shore, and the little waves washed them right back to her. It seemed that the river could not take her dearest possession, because it did not have little Kay. However, she was afraid that she had not thrown them far enough, so she clambered into a boat that lay among the reeds, walked to the end of it, and threw her shoes out into the water again. But the boat was not tied, and her movements made it drift away from the bank. She realized this, and tried to get ashore, but by the time she reached the other end of the boat it was already more than a yard from the bank, and was fast gaining speed.

Little Gerda was so frightened that she began to cry, and no one was there to hear her except the sparrows. They could not carry her to land, but they flew along the shore twittering, "We are here! Here we are!" as if to comfort her. The boat drifted swiftly down the stream, and Gerda sat there quite still, in her stocking feet. Her little red shoes floated along behind, but they could not catch up with her because the boat was gathering headway. It was very pretty on both sides of the river, where the flowers were lovely, the trees were old, and the hillsides afforded pasture for cattle and sheep. But not one single person did Gerda see.

"Perhaps the river will take me to little Kay," she thought, and that made her feel more cheerful. She stood up and watched the lovely green banks for hour after hour.

Then she came to a large cherry orchard, in which there was a little house with strange red and blue windows. It had a thatched roof, and outside it stood two wooden soldiers, who presented arms to everyone who sailed past.

Gerda thought they were alive, and called out to them, but of course they did not answer her. She drifted quite close to them as the current drove the boat in toward the bank. Gerda called even louder, and an old, old woman came out of the house. She leaned on a crooked stick; she had on a big sun hat, and on it were painted the most glorious flowers.

"You poor little child!" the old woman exclaimed. "However did you get lost on this big swift river, and however did you drift so far into the great wide world?" The old woman waded right into the water, caught hold of the boat with her crooked stick, pulled it in to shore, and lifted little Gerda out of it.

Gerda was very glad to be on dry land again, but she felt a little afraid of this strange old woman, who said to her:

"Come and tell me who you are, and how you got here." Gerda told her all about it. The woman shook her head and said, "Hmm, hmm!" And when Gerda had told her everything and asked if she hadn't seen little Kay, the woman said he had not yet come by, but that he might be along any day now. And she told Gerda not to take it so to heart, but to taste her cherries and to look at her flowers. These were more beautiful than any picture book, and each one had a story to tell. Then she led Gerda by the hand into her little house, and the old woman locked the door.

The windows were placed high up on the walls, and through their red, blue, and yellow panes the sunlight streamed in a strange mixture of all the colors there are. But on the table were the most delicious cherries, and Gerda, who was no longer afraid, ate as many as she liked. While she was eating them, the old woman combed her hair with a golden comb. Gerda's pretty hair fell in shining yellow ringlets on either side of a friendly little face that was as round and blooming as a rose.

"I've so often wished for a dear little girl like you," the old woman told her. "Now you'll see how well the two of us will get along." While her hair was being combed, Gerda gradually forgot all about Kay, for the old woman was skilled in magic. But she was not a wicked witch. She only dabbled in magic to amuse herself, but she wanted very much to keep little Gerda. So she went out into her garden and pointed her crooked stick at all the rose bushes. In the full bloom of their beauty, all of them sank down into the black earth, without leaving a single trace behind. The old

woman was afraid that if Gerda saw them they would remind her so strongly of her own roses, and of little Kay, that
she would run away again.

Then Gerda was led into the flower garden. How fragrant
and lovely it was! Every known flower of every season was
there in full bloom. No picture book was ever so pretty and
gay. Gerda jumped for joy, and played in the garden until
the sun went down behind the tall cherry trees. Then she
was tucked into a beautiful bed, under a red silk coverlet
quilted with blue violets. There she slept, and there she
dreamed as gloriously as any queen on her wedding day.

The next morning she again went out into the warm sunshine to play with the flowers—and this she did for many a
day. Gerda knew every flower by heart, and, plentiful
though they were, she always felt that there was one missing, but which one she didn't quite know. One day she sat
looking at the old woman's sun hat, and the prettiest of all
the flowers painted on it was a rose. The old woman had
forgotten this rose on her hat when she made the real roses
disappear in the earth. But that's just the sort of thing that
happens when one doesn't stop to think.

"Why aren't there any roses here?" said Gerda. She
rushed out among the flower beds, and she looked and she
looked, but there wasn't a rose to be seen. Then she sat
down and cried. But her hot tears fell on the very spot
where a rose bush had sunk into the ground, and when her
warm tears moistened the earth the bush sprang up again,
as full of blossoms as when it disappeared. Gerda hugged it,
and kissed the roses. She remembered her own pretty roses,
and thought of little Kay.

"Oh how long I have been delayed," the little girl said. "I
should have been looking for Kay. Don't you know where
he is?" she asked the roses. "Do you think that he is dead
and gone?"

"He isn't dead," the roses told her. "We have been down
in the earth where the dead people are, but Kay is not
there."

"Thank you," said little Gerda, who went to all the other flowers, put her lips near them and asked, "Do you know where little Kay is?"

But every flower stood in the sun, and dreamed its own fairy tale, or its story. Though Gerda listened to many, many of them, not one of the flowers knew anything about Kay.

What did the tiger lily say?

"Do you hear the drum? *Boom, boom!* It has only two notes, always *boom, boom!* Hear the women wail. Hear the priests chant. The Hindoo woman in her long red robe stands on the funeral pyre. The flames rise around her and her dead husband, but the Hindoo woman is thinking of that living man in the crowd around them. She is thinking of him whose eyes are burning hotter than the flames—of him whose fiery glances have pierced her heart more deeply than these flames that soon will burn her body to ashes. Can the flame of the heart die in the flame of the funeral pyre?"

"I don't understand that at all," little Gerda said.

"That's my fairy tale," said the lily.

What did the trumpet flower say?

"An ancient castle rises high from a narrow path in the mountains. The thick ivy grows leaf upon leaf where it climbs to the balcony. There stands a beautiful maiden. She leans out over the balustrade to look down the path. No rose on its stem is as graceful as she, nor is any apple blossom in the breeze so light. Hear the rustle of her silken gown, sighing, 'Will he never come?' "

"Do you mean Kay?" little Gerda asked.

"I am talking about my own story, my own dream," the trumpet flower replied.

What did the little snowdrop say?

"Between the trees a board hangs by two ropes. It is a swing. Two pretty little girls, with frocks as white as snow, and long green ribbons fluttering from their hats, are swinging. Their brother, who is bigger than they are, stands behind them on the swing, with his arms around the ropes to hold himself. In one hand he has a little cup, and in the other a clay pipe. He is blowing soap bubbles, and as the swing flies the bubbles float off in all their changing colors. The last bubble is still clinging to the bowl of his pipe, and fluttering in the air as the swing sweeps to and fro. A little black dog, light as a bubble, is standing on his hind legs and trying to get up in the swing. But it does not stop. High and low the swing flies, until the dog loses his balance, barks, and loses his temper. They tease him, and the bubble bursts. A swinging board pictured in a bubble before it broke—that is my story."

"It may be a very pretty story, but you told it very sadly and you didn't mention Kay at all."

What did the hyacinths say?

"There were three sisters, quite transparent and very fair. One wore a red dress, the second wore a blue one, and the third went all in white. Hand in hand they danced in the clear moonlight, beside a calm lake. They were not elfin folk. They were human beings. The air was sweet, and the sisters disappeared into the forest. The fragrance of the air grew sweeter. Three coffins, in which lie the three sisters, glide out of the forest and across the lake. The fireflies hover about them like little flickering lights. Are the dancing sisters sleeping or are they dead? The fragrance of the flowers says they are dead, and the evening bell tolls for their funeral."

"You are making me very unhappy," little Gerda said. "Your fragrance is so strong that I cannot help thinking of those dead sisters. Oh, could little Kay really be dead? The roses have been down under the ground, and they say no."

"Ding, dong," tolled the hyacinth bells. "We do not toll for little Kay. We do not know him. We are simply singing our song—the only song we know."

And Gerda went on to the buttercup that shone among its glossy green leaves.

"You are like a bright little sun," said Gerda. "Tell me, do you know where I can find my playmate?"

And the buttercup shone brightly as it looked up at

Gerda. But what sort of song would a buttercup sing? It certainly wouldn't be about Kay.

"In a small courtyard, God's sun was shining brightly on the very first day of spring. Its beams glanced along the white wall of the house next door, and close by grew the first yellow flowers of spring shining like gold in the warm sunlight. An old grandmother was sitting outside in her chair. Her granddaughter, a poor but very pretty maidservant, had just come home for a little visit. She kissed her grandmother, and there was gold, a heart full of gold, in that kiss. Gold on her lips, gold in her dreams, and gold above in the morning beams. There, I've told you my little story," said the buttercup.

"Oh, my poor old Grandmother," said Gerda. "She will miss me so. She must be grieving for me as much as she did for little Kay. But I'll soon go home again, and I'll bring Kay with me. There's no use asking the flowers about him. They don't know anything except their own songs, and they haven't any news for me."

Then she tucked up her little skirts so that she could run away faster, but the narcissus tapped against her leg as she was jumping over it. So she stopped and leaned over the tall flower.

"Perhaps you have something to tell me," she said.

What did the narcissus say?

"I can see myself! I can see myself! Oh, how sweet is my own fragrance! Up in the narrow garret there is a little dancer, half dressed. First she stands on one leg. Then she stands on both, and kicks her heels at the whole world. She is an illusion of the stage. She pours water from a teapot over a piece of cloth she is holding—it is her bodice. Cleanliness is such a virtue! Her white dress hangs from a hook. It too has been washed in the teapot, and dried on the roof. She puts it on, and ties a saffron scarf around her neck to make the dress seem whiter. Point your toes! See how straight she balances on that single stem. I can see myself! I can see myself!"

"I'm not interested," said Gerda. "What a thing to tell me about!"

She ran to the end of the garden, and though the gate was fastened she worked the rusty latch till it gave way and the gate flew open. Little Gerda scampered out into the wide world in her bare feet. She looked back three times, but nobody came after her. At last she could run no farther, and she sat down to rest on a big stone, and when she looked up she saw that summer had gone by, and it was late in the fall. She could never have guessed it inside the beautiful garden where the sun was always shining, and the flowers of every season were always in full bloom.

"Gracious! how long I've dallied," Gerda said. "Fall is already here. I can't rest any longer."

She got up to run on, but how footsore and tired she was! And how cold and bleak everything around her looked! The long leaves of the willow tree had turned quite yellow, and damp puffs of mist dropped from them like drops of water. One leaf after another fell to the ground. Only the blackthorn still bore fruit, and its fruit was so sour that it set your teeth on edge.

Oh, how dreary and gray the wide world looked.

FOURTH STORY

The Prince and the Princess

The next time that Gerda was forced to rest, a big crow came hopping across the snow in front of her. For a long time he had been watching her and cocking his head to one side, and now he said, "Caw, caw! Good caw day! Good caw day!" He could not say it any better, but he felt kindly inclined toward the little girl, and asked her where she was going in the great wide world, all alone. Gerda understood him when he said "alone," and she knew its meaning all too well. She told the crow the whole story of her life, and asked if he hadn't seen Kay. The crow gravely nodded his head and cawed, "Maybe I have, maybe I have!"

"What! do you really think you have?" the little girl cried, and almost hugged the crow to death as she kissed him.

"Gently, gently!" said the crow. "I think that it may have

been little Kay that I saw, but if it was, then he has forgotten you for the Princess."

"Does he live with a Princess?" Gerda asked.

"Yes. Listen!" said the crow. "But it is so hard for me to speak your language. If you understand crow talk, I can tell you much more easily."

"I don't know that language," said Gerda. "My grandmother knows it, just as well as she knows baby talk, and I do wish I had learned it."

"No matter," said the crow. "I'll tell you as well as I can, though that won't be any too good." And he told her all that he knew.

"In the kingdom where we are now, there is a Princess who is uncommonly clever, and no wonder. She has read all the newspapers in the world and forgotten them again—that's how clever she is. Well, not long ago she was sitting on her throne. That's by no means as much fun as people suppose, so she fell to humming an old tune, and the refrain of it happened to run:

Why, oh, why, shouldn't I get married?

"'Why, that's an idea!' said she. And she made up her mind to marry as soon as she could find the sort of husband who could give a good answer when anyone spoke to him, instead of one of those fellows who merely stand around looking impressive, for that is so tiresome. She had the drums drubbed to call together all her ladies-in-waiting, and when they heard what she had in mind they were delighted.

"'Oh, we like that!' they said. 'We were just thinking the very same thing.'

"Believe me," said the crow, "every word I tell you is true. I have a tame ladylove who has the run of the palace, and I had the whole story straight from her." Of course his ladylove was also a crow, for birds of a feather will flock together.

"The newspapers immediately came out with a border of hearts and the initials of the Princess, and you could read an announcement that any presentable young man might go to the palace and talk with her. The one who spoke best, and who seemed most at home in the palace, would be chosen by the Princess as her husband.

"Yes, yes," said the crow, "believe me, that's as true as it is that here I sit. Men flocked to the palace, and there was much crowding and crushing, but on neither the first nor the second day was anyone chosen. Out in the street they were all glib talkers, but after they entered the palace gate where the guardsmen were stationed in their silver-braided uniforms, and after they climbed up the staircase lined with footmen in gold-embroidered livery, they arrived in the brilliantly lighted reception halls without a word to say. And when they stood in front of the Princess on her throne, the best they could do was to echo the last word of her remarks, and she didn't care to hear it repeated.

"It was just as if everyone in the throne room had his stomach filled with snuff and had fallen asleep; for as soon as they were back in the streets there was no stopping their talk.

"The line of candidates extended all the way from the town gates to the palace. I saw them myself," said the crow. "They got hungry and they got thirsty, but from the palace they got nothing—not even a glass of lukewarm water. To be sure, some of the clever candidates had brought sandwiches with them, but they did not share them with their neighbors. Each man thought, 'Just let him look hungry, then the Princess won't take him!'"

"But Kay, little Kay," Gerda interrupted, "when did he come? Was he among those people?"

"Give me time, give me time! We are just coming to him. On the third day a little person, with neither horse nor carriage, strode boldly up to the palace. His eyes sparkled the way yours do, and he had handsome long hair, but his clothes were poor."

"Oh, that was Kay!" Gerda said, and clapped her hands in glee. "Now I've found him."

"He had a little knapsack on his back," the crow told her.

"No, that must have been his sled," said Gerda. "He was carrying it when he went away."

"Maybe so," the crow said. "I didn't look at it carefully. But my tame ladylove told me that when he went through the palace gates and saw the guardsmen in silver, and on the staircase the footmen in gold, he wasn't at all taken aback. He nodded and he said to them:

"'It must be very tiresome to stand on the stairs. I'd rather go inside.'

"The halls were brilliantly lighted. Ministers of state and privy councilors were walking about barefooted, carrying golden trays in front of them. It was enough to make anyone feel solemn, and his boots creaked dreadfully, but he wasn't a bit afraid."

"That certainly must have been Kay," said Gerda. "I know he was wearing new boots. I heard them creaking in Grandmother's room."

"Oh, they creaked all right," said the crow. "But it was little enough he cared as he walked straight to the Princess, who was sitting on a pearl as big as a spinning wheel. All the ladies-in-waiting with their attendants and their attendants' attendants, and all the lords-in-waiting with their gentlemen and their gentlemen's men, each of whom had his page with him, were standing there, and the nearer they stood to the door the more arrogant they looked. The gentlemen's men's pages, who always wore slippers, were almost too arrogant to look as they stood at the threshold."

"That must have been terrible!" little Gerda exclaimed. "And yet Kay won the Princess?"

"If I weren't a crow, I would have married her myself, for all that I'm engaged to another. They say he spoke as well as I do when I speak my crow language. Or so my tame ladylove tells me. He was dashing and handsome, and he was not there to court the Princess but to hear her wisdom. This he liked, and she liked him."

"Of course it was Kay," said Gerda. "He was so clever

that he could do mental arithmetic even with fractions. Oh, please take me to the palace."

"That's easy enough to say," said the crow, "but how can we manage it? I'll talk it over with my tame ladylove, and she may be able to suggest something, but I must warn you that a little girl like you will never be admitted."

"Oh, yes I shall," said Gerda. "When Kay hears about me, he will come out to fetch me at once."

"Wait for me beside that stile," the crow said. He wagged his head and off he flew.

Darkness had set in when he got back.

"Caw, caw!" he said. "My ladylove sends you her best wishes, and here's a little loaf of bread for you. She found it in the kitchen, where they have all the bread they need, and you must be hungry. You simply can't get into the palace with those bare feet. The guardsmen in silver and the footmen in gold would never permit it. But don't you cry. We'll find a way. My ladylove knows of a little back staircase that leads up to the bedroom, and she knows where they keep the key to it."

Then they went into the garden and down the wide promenade where the leaves were falling one by one. When, one by one, the lights went out in the palace, the crow led little Gerda to the back door, which stood ajar.

Oh, how her heart did beat with fear and longing. It was just as if she were about to do something wrong, yet she only wanted to make sure that this really was little Kay. Yes, truly it must be Kay, she thought, as she recalled his sparkling eyes and his long hair. She remembered exactly how he looked when he used to smile at her as they sat under the roses at home. Wouldn't he be glad to see her! Wouldn't he be interested in hearing how far she had come to find him, and how sad they had all been when he didn't come home. She was so frightened, and yet so happy.

Now they were on the stairway. A little lamp was burning on a cupboard, and there stood the tame crow, cocking her head to look at Gerda, who made the curtsy that her grandmother had taught her.

"My fiancé has told me many charming things about you, dear young lady," she said. "Your biography, as one might say, is very touching. Kindly take the lamp and I shall lead the way. We shall keep straight ahead, where we aren't apt to run into anyone."

"It seems to me that someone is on the stairs behind us," said Gerda. Things brushed past, and from their shadows on the wall they seemed to be horses with spindly legs and waving manes. And there were shadows of huntsmen, ladies and gentlemen, on horseback.

"Those are only dreams," said the crow. "They come to take the thoughts of their royal masters off to the chase. That's just as well, for it will give you a good opportunity to see them while they sleep. But I trust that, when you rise to high position and power, you will show a grateful heart."

"Tut tut! You've no need to say that," said the forest crow.

Now they entered the first room. It was hung with rose-colored satin, embroidered with flowers. The dream shadows were flitting by so fast that Gerda could not see the lords and ladies. Hall after magnificent hall quite bewildered her, until at last they reached the royal bedroom.

The ceiling of it was like the top of a huge palm tree, with leaves of glass, costly glass. In the middle of the room two beds hung from a massive stem of gold. Each of them looked like a lily. One bed was white, and there lay the Princess. The other was red, and there Gerda hoped to find little Kay. She bent one of the scarlet petals and saw the nape of a little brown neck. Surely this must be Kay. She called his name aloud and held the lamp near him. The dreams on horseback pranced into the room again, as he awoke—and turned his head—and it was not little Kay at all.

The Prince only resembled Kay about the neck, but he was young and handsome. The Princess peeked out of her lily-white bed, and asked what had happened. Little Gerda cried and told them all about herself, and about all that the crows had done for her.

"Poor little thing," the Prince and the Princess said. They praised the crows, and said they weren't the least bit angry with them, but not to do it again. Furthermore, they should have a reward.

"Would you rather fly about without any responsibilities," said the Princess, "or would you care to be appointed court crows for life, with rights to all scraps from the kitchen?"

Both the crows bowed low and begged for the permanent office, for they thought of their future and said it was better to provide for their "old age," as they called it.

The Prince got up, and let Gerda have his bed. It was the utmost that he could do. She clasped her little hands and thought, "How nice the people and the birds are." She closed her eyes, fell peacefully asleep, and all the dreams came flying back again. They looked like angels, and they drew a little sled on which Kay sat. He nodded to her, but this was only in a dream, so it all disappeared when she woke up.

The next day she was dressed from her head to her heels in silk and in velvet too. They asked her to stay at the palace and have a nice time there, but instead she begged them to let her have a little carriage, a little horse, and a pair of little boots, so that she could drive out into the wide world to find Kay.

They gave her a pair of boots, and also a muff. They dressed her as nicely as could be and, when she was ready to go, there at the gate stood a brand new carriage of pure gold. On it the coat of arms of the Prince and Princess glistened like a star.

The coachman, the footman, and the postilions—for postilions there were—all wore golden crowns. The Prince and the Princess themselves helped her into the carriage, and wished her Godspeed. The forest crow, who was now a married man, accompanied her for the first three miles, and sat beside Gerda, for it upset him to ride backward. The other crow stood beside the gate and waved her wings. She did not accompany them because she was suffering from a headache, brought on by eating too much in her new position. Inside, the carriage was lined with sugared cookies, and the seats were filled with fruit and gingerbread.

"Fare you well, fare you well," called the Prince and Princess. Little Gerda cried and the crow cried too, for the first few miles. Then the crow said good-by, and that was the saddest leave-taking of all. He flew up into a tree and waved his big black wings as long as he could see the carriage, which flashed as brightly as the sun.

FIFTH STORY

THE LITTLE ROBBER GIRL

The carriage rolled on into a dark forest. Like a blazing torch, it shone in the eyes of some robbers. They could not bear it.

"That's gold! That's gold!" they cried. They sprang forward, seized the horses, killed the little postilions, the coachman, and the footman, and dragged little Gerda out of the carriage.

"How plump and how tender she looks, just as if she'd been fattened on nuts!" cried the old robber woman, who had a long bristly beard, and long eyebrows that hung down over her eyes. "She looks like a fat little lamb. What a dainty dish she will be!" As she said this she drew out her knife, a dreadful, flashing thing.

"Ouch!" the old woman howled. At just that moment her own little daughter had bitten her ear. This little girl, whom she carried on her back, was a wild and reckless creature. "You beastly brat!" her mother exclaimed, but it kept her from using that knife on Gerda.

"She shall play with me," said the little robber girl. "She must give me her muff and that pretty dress she wears, and sleep with me in my bed." And she again gave her mother such a bite that the woman hopped and whirled around in pain. All of the robbers laughed, and shouted:

"See how she dances with her brat."

"I want to ride in the carriage," the little robber girl said,

and ride she did, for she was too spoiled and headstrong for
words. She and Gerda climbed into the carriage and away
they drove over stumps and stones, into the depths of the
forest. The little robber girl was no taller than Gerda, but she
was stronger and much broader in the shoulders. Her skin
was brown and her eyes coal-black—almost sad in their expression. She put her arms around Gerda, and said:

"They shan't kill you unless I get angry with you. I think
you must be a Princess."

"No, I'm not," said little Gerda. And she told all about
what had happened to her, and how much she cared for
little Kay. The robber girl looked at her gravely, gave a little
nod of approval, and told her:

"Even if I should get angry with you, they shan't kill you,
because I'll do it myself!" Then she dried Gerda's eyes, and
stuck her own hands into Gerda's soft, warm muff.

The carriage stopped at last, in the courtyard of a robber's
castle. The walls of it were cracked from bottom to top.
Crows and ravens flew out of every loophole, and bulldogs
huge enough to devour a man jumped high in the air. But
they did not bark, for that was forbidden.

In the middle of the stone-paved, smoky old hall, a big
fire was burning. The smoke of it drifted up to the ceiling,
where it had to find its own way out. Soup was boiling in a
big caldron, and hares and rabbits were roasting on the spit.

"Tonight you shall sleep with me and all my little animals," the robber girl said. After they had something to eat
and drink, they went over to a corner that was strewn with
rugs and straw. On sticks and perches around the bedding
roosted nearly a hundred pigeons. They seemed to be
asleep, but they stirred just a little when the two little girls
came near them.

"They are all mine," said the little robber girl. She seized
the one that was nearest to her, held it by the legs and
shook it until it flapped its wings. "Kiss it," she cried, and
thrust the bird in Gerda's face. "Those two are the wild
rascals," she said, pointing high up the wall to a hole barred
with wooden sticks. "Rascals of the woods they are, and

they would fly away in a minute if they were not locked up."

"And here is my old sweetheart, Bae," she said, pulling at the horns of a reindeer that was tethered by a shiny copper ring around his neck. "We have to keep a sharp eye on him, or he would run away from us too. Every single night I tickle his neck with my knife blade, for he is afraid of that." From a hole in the wall she pulled a long knife, and rubbed it against the reindeer's neck. After the poor animal had kicked up its heels, the robber girl laughed and pulled Gerda down into the bed with her.

"Are you going to keep that knife in bed with you?" Gerda asked, and looked at it a little frightened.

"I always sleep with my knife," the little robber girl said. "You never can tell what may happen. But let's hear again what you told me before about little Kay, and about why you are wandering through the wide world."

Gerda told the story all over again, while the wild pigeons cooed in their cage overhead, and the tame pigeons slept. The little robber girl clasped one arm around Gerda's neck, gripped her knife in the other hand, fell asleep, and snored so that one could hear her. But Gerda could not close her eyes at all. She did not know whether she was to live or whether she was to die. The robbers sat around their fire, singing and drinking, and the old robber woman was turning somersaults. It was a terrible sight for a little girl to see.

Then the wood pigeons said, "Coo, coo. We have seen little Kay. A white hen was carrying his sled, and Kay sat in the Snow Queen's sleigh. They swooped low, over the trees where we lay in our nest. The Snow Queen blew upon us, and all the young pigeons died except us. Coo, coo."

"What is that you are saying up there?" cried Gerda. "Where was the Snow Queen going? Do you know anything about it?"

"She was probably bound for Lapland, where they always have snow and ice. Why don't you ask the reindeer who is tethered beside you?"

"Yes, there is ice and snow in that glorious land," the

reindeer told her. "You can prance about freely across those great, glittering fields. The Snow Queen has her summer tent there, but her stronghold is a castle up nearer the North Pole, on the island called Spitzbergen."

"Oh, Kay, little Kay," Gerda sighed.

"Lie still," said the robber girl, "or I'll stick my knife in your stomach."

In the morning, Gerda told her all that the wood pigeons had said. The little robber girl looked quite thoughtful. She nodded her head, and exclaimed, "Leave it to me! Leave it to me.

"Do you know where Lapland is?" she asked the reindeer.

"Who knows it better than I?" the reindeer said, and his eyes sparkled. "There I was born, there I was bred, and there I kicked my heels in freedom, across the fields of snow."

"Listen!" the robber girl said to Gerda. "As you see, all the men are away. Mother is still here, and here she'll stay, but before the morning is over she will drink out of that big bottle, and then she usually dozes off for a nap. As soon as that happens, I will do you a good turn."

She jumped out of bed, rushed over and threw her arms around her mother's neck, pulled at her beard bristles, and said, "Good morning, my dear nanny-goat." Her mother thumped her nose until it was red and blue, but all that was done out of pure love.

As soon as the mother had tipped up the bottle and dozed off to sleep, the little robber girl ran to the reindeer and said, "I have a good notion to keep you here, and tickle you with my sharp knife. You are so funny when I do, but never mind that. I'll untie your rope, and help you find your way outside, so that you can run back to Lapland. But you must put your best leg forward and carry this little girl to the Snow Queen's palace, where her playmate is. I suppose you heard what she told me, for she spoke so loud, and you were eavesdropping."

The reindeer was so happy that he bounded into the air. The robber girl hoisted little Gerda on his back, carefully tied her in place, and even gave her a little pillow to sit on. "I don't do things half way," she said. "Here, take back your fur boots, for it's going to be bitter cold. I'll keep your muff, because it's such a pretty one. But your fingers mustn't get cold. Here are my mother's big mittens, which will come right up to your elbows. Pull them on. Now your hands look just like my ugly mother's big paws."

And Gerda shed happy tears.

"I don't care to see you blubbering," said the little robber girl. "You ought to look pleased now. Here, take these two loaves of bread and this ham along, so that you won't starve."

When these provisions were tied on the back of the reindeer, the little robber girl opened the door and called in all the big dogs. Then she cut the tether with her knife and said to the reindeer, "Now run, but see that you take good care of the little girl."

Gerda waved her big mittens to the little robber girl, and said good-by. Then the reindeer bounded away, over stumps and stones, straight through the great forest, over swamps and across the plains, as fast as he could run. The wolves howled, the ravens shrieked, and *ker-shew, ker-shew!* the red streaks of light ripped through the heavens, with a noise that sounded like sneezing.

"Those are my old Northern Lights," said the reindeer. "See how they flash." And on he ran, faster than ever, by night and day. The loaves were eaten and the whole ham was eaten—and there they were in Lapland.

SIXTH STORY

The Lapp Woman and the Finn Woman

They stopped in front of the little hut, and a makeshift dwelling it was. The roof of it almost touched the ground, and the doorway was so low that the family had to lie on their stomachs to crawl in it or out of it. No one was at home except an old Lapp woman, who was cooking fish over a whale-oil lamp. The reindeer told her Gerda's whole story, but first he told his own, which he thought was much more important. Besides, Gerda was so cold that she couldn't say a thing.

"Oh, you poor creatures," the Lapp woman said, "you've still got such a long way to go. Why, you will have to travel hundreds of miles into the Finmark. For it's there that the Snow Queen is taking a country vacation, and burning her blue fireworks every evening. I'll jot down a message on a dried codfish, for I haven't any paper. I want you to take it to the Finn woman who lives up there. She will be able to tell you more about it than I can."

As soon as Gerda had thawed out, and had had something to eat and drink, the Lapp woman wrote a few words on a dried codfish, told Gerda to take good care of it, and tied her again on the back of the reindeer. Off he ran, and all night long the skies crackled and swished as the most beautiful Northern Lights flashed over their heads. At last they came to the Finmark, and knocked at the Finn woman's chimney, for she hadn't a sign of a door. It was so hot inside that the Finn woman went about almost naked. She was small and terribly dowdy, but she at once helped little Gerda off with her mittens and boots, and loosened her clothes. Otherwise the heat would have wilted her. Then the woman put a piece of ice on the reindeer's head, and read what was written on the codfish. She read it three times and when she knew it by heart, she put the fish into the kettle of soup, for they might as well eat it. She never wasted anything.

The reindeer told her his own story first, and then little Gerda's. The Finn woman winked a knowing eye, but she didn't say anything.

"You are such a wise woman," said the reindeer, "I know that you can tie all the winds of the world together with a bit of cotton thread. If the sailor unties one knot he gets a favorable wind. If he unties another he gets a stiff gale, while if he unties the third and fourth knots such a tempest rages that it flattens the trees in the forest. Won't you give this little girl something to drink that will make her as strong as twelve men, so that she may overpower the Snow Queen?"

"Twelve strong men," the Finn woman sniffed. "Much good that would be."

She went to the shelf, took down a big rolled-up skin, and unrolled it. On this skin strange characters were written, and the Finn woman read them until the sweat rolled down her forehead.

The reindeer again begged her to help Gerda, and little Gerda looked at her with such tearful, imploring eyes, that the woman began winking again. She took the reindeer aside in a corner, and while she was putting another piece of ice on his head she whispered to him:

"Little Kay is indeed with the Snow Queen, and everything there just suits him fine. He thinks it is the best place in all the world, but that's because he has a splinter of glass in his heart and a small piece of it in his eye. Unless these can be gotten out, he will never be human again, and the Snow Queen will hold him in her power."

"But can't you fix little Gerda something to drink which will give her more power than all those things?"

"No power that I could give her could be as great as that which she already has. Don't you see how men and beasts are compelled to serve her, and how far she has come in the wide world since she started out in her naked feet? We mustn't tell her about this power. Strength lies in her heart, because she is such a sweet, innocent child. If she herself cannot reach the Snow Queen and rid little Kay of those pieces of glass, then there's no help we can give her. The Snow Queen's garden lies about eight miles from here. You may carry the little girl there, and put her down by the big bush covered with red berries that grows in the snow. Then don't you stand there gossiping, but hurry to get back here."

The Finn woman lifted little Gerda onto the reindeer, and he galloped away as fast as he could.

"Oh!" cried Gerda, "I forgot my boots and I forgot my mittens." She soon felt the need of them in that knife-like cold, but the reindeer did not dare to stop. He galloped on until they came to the big bush that was covered with red berries. Here he set Gerda down and kissed her on the mouth, while big shining tears ran down his face. Then he ran back as fast as he could. Little Gerda stood there without boots and without mittens, right in the middle of icy Finmark.

She ran as fast as ever she could. A whole regiment of snowflakes swirled toward her, but they did not fall from the sky, for there was not a cloud up there, and the Northern Lights were ablaze.

The flakes skirmished along the ground, and the nearer they came the larger they grew. Gerda remembered how large and strange they had appeared when she looked at them under the magnifying glass. But here they were much more monstrous and terrifying. They were alive. They were the Snow Queen's advance guard, and their shapes were most strange. Some looked like ugly, overgrown porcupines. Some were like a knot of snakes that stuck out their heads in every direction, and others were like fat little bears with every hair a-bristle. All of them were glistening white, for all were living snowflakes.

It was so cold that, as little Gerda said the Lord's Prayer, she could see her breath freezing in front of her mouth, like a cloud of smoke. It grew thicker and thicker, and took the shape of little angels that grew bigger and bigger the moment they touched the ground. All of them had helmets on their heads and they carried shields and lances in their hands. Rank upon rank, they increased, and when Gerda had finished her prayer she was surrounded by a legion of angels. They struck the dread snowflakes with their lances and shivered them into a thousand pieces. Little Gerda walked on, unmolested and cheerful. The angels rubbed her hands and feet to make them warmer, and she trotted briskly along to the Snow Queen's palace.

But now let us see how little Kay was getting on. Little Gerda was furthest from his mind, and he hadn't the slightest idea that she was just outside the palace.

SEVENTH STORY

What Happened in the Snow Queen's Palace, and What Came of It

The walls of the palace were driven snow. The windows and doors were the knife-edged wind. There were more than a hundred halls, shaped as the snow had drifted, and the largest of these extended for many a mile. All were lighted by the flare of the Northern Lights. All of the halls were so immense and so empty, so brilliant and so glacial! There was never a touch of gaiety in them; never so much as a little dance for the polar bears, at which the storm blast could have served for music, and the polar bears could have waddled about on their hind legs to show off their best manners. There was never a little party with such games as blind-bear's buff or hide the paw-kerchief for the cubs, nor even a little afternoon coffee over which the white fox vixens could gossip. Empty, vast, and frigid were the Snow Queen's halls. The Northern Lights flared with such regularity that you could time exactly when they would be at the highest and lowest. In the middle of the vast, empty hall of snow was a frozen lake. It was cracked into a thousand pieces, but each piece was shaped so exactly like the others that it seemed a work of wonderful craftsmanship. The Snow Queen sat in the exact center of it when she was at home, and she spoke of this as sitting on her "Mirror of Reason." She said this mirror was the only one of its kind, and the best thing in all the world.

Little Kay was blue, yes, almost black, with the cold. But he did not feel it, because the Snow Queen had kissed away his icy tremblings, and his heart itself had almost turned to ice.

He was shifting some sharp, flat pieces of ice to and fro, trying to fit them into every possible pattern, for he wanted to make something with them. It was like the Chinese puzzle game that we play at home, juggling little flat pieces of wood about into special designs. Kay was cleverly arranging his pieces in the game of ice-cold reason. To him the patterns were highly remarkable and of the utmost importance, for the chip of glass in his eye made him see them that way. He arranged his pieces to spell out many words; but he could never find the way to make the one word he was so eager to form. The word was "Eternity." The Snow Queen had said to him, "If you can puzzle that out you shall be your own master, and I'll give you the whole world and a new pair of skates." But he could not puzzle it out.

"Now I am going to make a flying trip to the warm countries," the Snow Queen told him. "I want to go and take a look into the black caldrons." She meant the volcanos of Etna and Vesuvius. "I must whiten them up a bit. They need it, and it will be such a relief after all those yellow lemons and purple grapes."

And away she flew. Kay sat all alone in that endless, empty, frigid hall, and puzzled over the pieces of ice until he almost cracked his skull. He sat so stiff and still that one might have thought he was frozen to death.

All of a sudden, little Gerda walked up to the palace through the great gate which was a knife-edged wind. But Gerda said her evening prayer. The wind was lulled to rest, and the little girl came on into the vast, cold, empty hall. Then she saw Kay. She recognized him at once, and ran to throw her arms around him. She held him close and cried, "Kay! dearest little Kay! I've found you at last!"

But he sat still, and stiff, and cold. Gerda shed hot tears, and when they fell upon him they went straight to his heart. They melted the lump of ice and burned away the splinter of glass in it. He looked up at her, and she sang:

> Where roses bloom so sweetly in the vale,
> There shall you find the Christ Child, without fail.

Kay burst into tears. He cried so freely that the little piece of glass in his eye was washed right out. "Gerda!" He knew her, and cried out in his happiness, "My sweet little Gerda, where have you been so long? And where have I been?" He looked around him and said, "How cold it is here! How enormous and empty!" He held fast to Gerda, who laughed until happy tears rolled down her cheeks. Their bliss was so heavenly that even the bits of glass danced about them and shared in their happiness. When the pieces grew tired, they dropped into a pattern which made the very word that the Snow Queen had told Kay he must find before he became his own master and received the whole world and a new pair of skates.

Gerda kissed his cheeks, and they turned pink again. She kissed his eyes, and they sparkled like hers. She kissed his hands and feet, and he became strong and well. The Snow Queen might come home now whenever she pleased, for there stood the order for Kay's release, written in letters of shining ice.

Hand in hand, Kay and Gerda strolled out of that enormous palace. They talked about Grandmother and about the roses on their roof. Wherever they went, the wind died down and the sun shone out. When they came to the bush that was covered with red berries, the reindeer was waiting to meet them. He had brought along a young reindeer mate who had warm milk for the children to drink, and who kissed them on the mouth. Then these reindeer carried Gerda and Kay first to the Finn woman. They warmed themselves in her hot room, and when she had given them directions for their journey home they rode on to the Lapp woman. She had made them new clothes, and she was ready to take them along in her sleigh.

Side by side, the reindeer ran with them to the limits of the North country, where the first green buds were to be seen. Here they said good-by to the two reindeer and to the Lapp woman. "Farewell," they all said.

Now the first little birds began to chirp, and there were green buds all around them in the forest. Through the woods came riding a young girl on a magnificent horse that Gerda recognized, for it had once been harnessed to the golden carriage. The girl wore a bright red cap on her head, and a pair of pistols in her belt. She was the little robber girl, who had grown tired of staying at home, and who was setting out on a journey to the North country. If she didn't like it there, why, the world was wide, and there were many

other places where she could go. She recognized Gerda at
once, and Gerda knew her too. It was a happy meeting.

"You're a fine one for gadding about," she told little Kay.
"I'd just like to know whether you deserve to have someone
running to the end of the earth for your sake."

But Gerda patted her cheek and asked her about the
Prince and the Princess.

"They are traveling in foreign lands," the girl told her.

"And the crow?"

"Oh, the crow is dead," she answered. "His tame ladylove is now a widow, and she wears a bit of black wool
wrapped around her leg. She takes great pity on herself, but
that's all stuff and nonsense. Now you tell me what has
happened to you and how you caught up with Kay."

Gerda and Kay told her their story.

"*Snip snap snurre, basse lurre,*" said the robber girl. "So
everything came out all right." She shook them by the hand,
and promised that if ever she passed through their town she
would come to see them. And then she rode away.

Kay and Gerda held each other by the hand. And as they
walked along they had wonderful spring weather. The land
was green and strewn with flowers, church bells rang, and
they saw the high steeples of a big town. It was the one
where they used to live. They walked straight to Grandmother's house, and up the stairs, and into the room, where
everything was just as it was when they left it. And the
clock said *tick-tock*, and its hands were telling the time. But
the moment they came in the door they noticed one change.
They were grown-up now.

The roses on the roof looked in at the open window, and
their two little stools were still out there. Kay and Gerda sat
down on them, and held each other by the hand. Both of
them had forgotten the icy, empty splendor of the Snow
Queen's palace as completely as if it were some bad dream.
Grandmother sat in God's good sunshine, reading to them
from her Bible:

"Except ye become as little children, ye shall not enter
into the Kingdom of Heaven."

Kay and Gerda looked into each other's eyes, and at last they understood the meaning of their old hymn:

> Where roses bloom so sweetly in the vale,
> There shall you find the Christ Child, without fail.

And they sat there, grown-up, but children still—children at heart. And it was summer, warm, glorious summer.

Notes

PREFACE

1. The summaries I consulted were Erik Dal, "Research on Hans Christian Andersen," *Orbis Litterarum* 17 (1962), 166–83; Elias Bredsdorff, "A Critical Guide to the Literature on Hans Christian Andersen," *Scandinavica* 6 (1967), 108–25.
2. English-language biographies include Signe Toksvig, *The Life of Hans Christian Andersen* (New York: Harcourt, Brace, 1934); Rumer Godden, *Hans Christian Andersen* (New York: Alfred A. Knopf, 1955); Reginald Spink, *Hans Christian Andersen and His World* (New York: G. P. Putnam's Sons, 1972); Elias Bredsdorff, *Hans Christian Andersen* (New York: Charles Scribner's Sons, 1975); Bo Grønbech, *Hans Christian Andersen* (Boston: Twayne Publishers, 1980). The two translations from Danish are Hans Christian Andersen, *The True Story of My Life,* trans. Mary Howitt (New York: American-Scandinavian Foundation, 1926) (hereafter cited in the text as *TS*); and *The Fairy Tale of My Life* (New York: Paddington Press, 1975), reprint of the 1868 edition (hereafter cited in the text as *FT*).

CHAPTER 1

1. The version of *The Snow Queen* I have used throughout is contained in *The Complete Andersen,* trans. Jean Hersholt (New York: Heritage Press, 1942).
2. Spink, *Hans Christian Andersen and His World,* 66, 5.
3. No less an authority than T. S. Eliot is reported to have deplored the fact that Andersen's fairy tales are usually read when we are children, so that their value is missed then and ignored later (Miron Grindea, "The Triumphant Ugly Duckling," *Adam International Review* 22, nos. 248–49 [1955]: 3).
4. Spink, *Hans Christian Andersen and His World,* 70.
5. See, for instance, Robert Graves, *The White Goddess* (New York: Vintage Books, 1958), which in its entirety makes this point.

CHAPTER 2

1. Right away we run into a problem of translation, or translations. The original text reads merely "et griin," which translates "a grin" or, in context, perhaps "a smirk." Then where did the "carnal" come from? There have been many Andersen translators, and what most of them did to him was deplored by Elias Bredsdorff in an article entitled "How a Genius is Murdered," *The Norseman*, ed. H. K. Lehmkuhl (London, 1949), 166–69, and again more recently in his Andersen biography (*Hans Christian Andersen*, 333–37). Even in German, to which Danish translates most easily, such mayhem seems to occur (Leif Ludwig Albertsen, "Die Deutschen und ihr Märchendichter Andersen. Bemerkungen zur Übersetzungsproblematik an Hand der 'Prinzessin auf der Erbse,' " *Anderseniana*, ed. H. Topsøe-Jensen [Odense: H. C. Andersens Hus], 1970–73, pp. 71–87). But the translation I used, by Jean Hersholt, is praised by Bredsdorff as among the best! ("H. C. Andersen in Britain," *Adam International Review* 22, nos. 248–49 [1955]: 22). Then why did Hersholt take the seemingly unwarranted liberty of inserting a word not to be found in the original—and why do I maintain it? Well, Hersholt no doubt thought long and hard before deciding on a suitable opposite to "a good, pious thought" and concluded that a simple grin just was not a sufficiently specific contrast. A clarifying slant into the sinful was indicated. It remains to be determined—on the basis of what is to follow—whether Hersholt's version, and our use of it, are justified.

2. Other translations, slightly bowdlerized, read here "demon" instead of "devil." I was gratified to find in the original: "Det var en ond Trold! Det var en of de Allervörste, det var 'Djævelen'!" ("That was a wicked Troll! That was one of the worst of all, that was 'The Devil'!") It had to be The Devil, not only for stylistic reasons, because a demon is not much different from and not much of a crescendo over a goblin or a troll, but mainly because a demon is merely evil whereas The Devil Himself is Evil Itself. Therefore he is the only suitably dramatic and powerful counterplayer to the forces of heaven. The whole story would lose its metaphysical proportions if The Devil did not have a hand in it. Demons cause mischief, but only The Devil deals in sin. We are told right off that this tale, like *Faust*, will only apparently be about men and women (or children) but in fact will be about the great struggle between Good and Evil, between The Devil and God.

3. Cf. Wolfgang Lederer, *The Fear of Women* (New York: Grune and Stratton, 1968), 17, 125.

4. See, for instance, Joseph Campbell, *The Masks of God, Oriental Mythology* (New York: Viking Press, 1962), 13ff.

5. See, for instance, Martin A. Larson, *The Religion of the Occident* (New York: Philosophical Library, 1959), 520–38.

6. See Gershom Scholem, *Von der mystischen Gestalt der Gottheit* (Zurich: Rhein Verlag, 1962); also, by the same author, *Major Trends in Jewish Mysticism* (New York: Schocken Books, 1961 [1941]), Sixth Lecture, 205–43.

7. Paul Evdokimov, *Les Ages de la vie spirituelle* (Paris: Desclee de Brouwer, 1964), 73. This and all subsequent French and German passages have been translated by the author.

8. See, for instance, Milton's *Paradise Lost*, bk. 1, verses 33–48.

CHAPTER 3

1. Eight years before writing *The Snow Queen*, he had already described a similar "hanging garden" in his novel *Only a Fiddler* (Boston: Houghton Mifflin, 1908), 9.

2. Spink, *Hans Christian Andersen and His World*, 6.

3. Svend Larsen, "The Life of Hans Christian Andersen," in *Hans Christian Andersen*, ed. Svend Dahl (Copenhagen: Committee for Danish Cultural Activities Abroad, 1955), 16.

4. Bredsdorff, *Hans Christian Andersen*, 15.

5. Spink, *Hans Christian Andersen and His World*, 7.

6. Ibid., 8.

7. "The one-room dwelling was approximately seven by twelve feet, with an alcove and a very tiny kitchen in the rear. The back yard was also small, having cobblestones instead of grass, and one gooseberry bush" (Mary Ann Rubeck, "Annotations Documenting and Interpreting the Reflection of Hans Christian Andersen's Life in His Fairy Tales" [Ph.D. diss., State University of New York at Buffalo, 1981], 67).

8. "That sight" perhaps found expression many years later in some of his paper cutouts. There is one, white on black, showing what is apparently a naked, hairless woman standing grotesquely on spread, half-bent legs; her arms are held out sideways and her index fingers are pointing to her bald head. Sticking out from her chest on each side are two—or possibly three—clearly nippled elongated breasts (a total of four or six), which hang down, depleted, almost to her thighs. The cutout, dating from 1859, is entitled "Fertility Goddess"! Another, in bright red paper, has an even more hideous face with buck teeth and oversized jug-handle ears. Her posture is the same, and she clearly shows two similarly slack breasts sticking out to either side (a total of four) from what seems to be her chest and abdomen. This cutout, dated February 1869, is entitled "Afrodite." (Kjeld Heltoft, *H. C. Andersens Billedkunst* [Denmark: Gyldendal, 1969], 109, 132.) Only in an asylum was he likely

to have seen old crones whose uncovered shapes could have resembled such horrors.

9. She no doubt became the model for "Naomi, the child of the Jew's daughter," in *Only a Fiddler:* "She had then little yellow laced boots on, and these had made an inextinguishable impression on [Christian]" (11).

10. Bredsdorff, *Hans Christian Andersen*, 20.

11. This is an embellishment, invented by or for the benefit of Hans Christian. His father did admire Napoleon, but he enlisted as a musketeer, after having been offered a—for him—considerable sum of money to take the place of a farmer who was keen to get out of the army (Bredsdorff, *Hans Christian Andersen*, 21).

12. *The Complete Andersen*, vi.

13. Larsen, "The Life of Hans Christian Andersen," 16.

14. Bredsdorff, *Hans Christian Andersen*, 23, 24.

15. Andersen's father apparently died of tuberculosis. (Hans Brix, "Hans Christian Andersen," *The American-Scandinavian Review* 10 [1922]: 730–38, 731.)

16. See his story *She Was Good for Nothing* (also found in *The Complete Andersen*).

17. Spink, *Hans Christian Andersen and His World*, 18.

18. For an essay on his lifelong preoccupation with death, see Ib Ostenfeld, "H. C. Andersens anfægtelser og deres tilbageslag i eventyrene," *Anderseniana*, 1974–77, pp. 305–28.

19. Apparently ten rix dollars could have been expected, with utmost frugality, to last him about a month.

20. P. M. Pickard, *I Could a Tale Unfold* (London: Tavistock Publications, 1959), reflecting the profound concern and uneasiness any modern reader would experience at this point, engages in the clever conceit of having the fourteen-year-old Hans Christian examined by a typical 1959 child-guidance team consisting of a social worker, a psychologist, and a psychiatrist. They debate whether to "take him on" in therapy with the goal of "curing" him. They feel that "such an original personality might well be helped towards contributing something quite novel to art—though it would be impossible at present to have any idea of the direction in which this novelty might lie." They suggest that it might after all be best to return him to nineteenth-century Copenhagen, with its renowned classical tradition and patronage of the impoverished arts (69–82).

Less amusing but more professional (that is, full of jargon and diagnostic terms) is the study by child psychiatrist Professor M. Tramer, "Geistige Reifungsprobleme (III): Die Entwicklung Hans Christian Andersens (1805–1875)," *Zeitschrift für Kinderpsychiatrie* 23 (1956): 33–47. He scrutinizes Andersen's youth in the light of his entire life, in retrospect. But since he bases himself almost entirely on Andersen's autobiography, both his facts and many of his conclusions are questionable. Even so, he offers three valuable insights: (a) a finding of infantilism in a fragile psyche does not yet signify a definitive fate; (b) the to-be-elicited developmental strengths determine what the prognosis is to be; and (c) even with difficult inner conditions, the prognosis may be favorable.

CHAPTER 4

1. François Flahault, who subjects *The Snow Queen* to a fascinating structural analysis operating primarily with the opposing principles of disjunction and conjunction (for example, Winter = Kay = Disjunction, Summer = Gerda = Conjunction) and with the means of mediation and the mediators between the disjunctions, notes in *L'Extrême Existence* (Paris: François Maspero, 1972): "The splinter of mirror which injures Kay is, in effect, an 'anti-love' (disjunctive) . . . the piece of glass penetrates his heart like an arrow of Amor (Cupid)—but with the opposite effect" (100).

2. I disagree strongly with Robinson V. Ureaka, "Adult Symbolism in the Literary Fairy Tales of the Late Nineteenth Century" (Ph.D. diss., University of Nebraska, 1971), who claims that "when a piece of the shattered mirror entered Kay's eye, he became evil" (185). Difficult, yes; evil, not at all.

3. Anna Freud, *The Ego and Its Mechanisms of Defense* (New York: International Universities Press, 1946), 172–80.

4. *The Complete Andersen, Longer Stories,* 384.

5. In *Only a Fiddler,* a novel he published in 1837, eight years before *The Snow Queen,* Andersen includes this episode: " 'There stands a maiden for you on your window,' said the servant girl . . . and pointed at the frozen window-pane. The hostess had shaken her head thoughtfully, for exactly such a maiden, seven years before, had stood upon the window at which her husband sat shoe-making. 'Dost thou see, mother,' he had said, 'the handsome maiden there? She beckons me!' and two months after he lay in his grave. That must have been the cold death-maiden who was come for him" (252).

6. Andersen was a terrible hypochondriac, always concerned about the slightest indisposition. That he saw at least some, if not all, of his ills as inflicted upon him by relatives of the Ice Maiden is evidenced by the following account he wrote, at twenty-one, of a trip by coach: "The carriage rolled rapidly, but an ice-cold little Elf rushed along even faster and blew so cold at me that I caught cold" (*Der Dichter und die Welt* [letters], trans. E. von Hollander [Weimar: Gustav Kiepenheuer Verlag, 1917], 11). The anxiety must have pursued him, on each such occasion, that any little ice-cold Elf could turn out to be the Snow Queen herself.

7. In *The Nightcap of the "Pebersvend,"* he writes that the children of Eisenach in Germany sometimes called Tannhäuser's Lady Venus, who lives in a mountain nearby, "Lady Holle"; the "Hell" in this instance is one of vice, not of death—if indeed Andersen is not guilty of some confusion.

CHAPTER 5

1. When Karen first wears her red shoes to church, she is told it is "naughty" to do so. What is "naughty" in a child becomes "sin" in the adult.

2. Concerning the confirmation rite and the symbolism of red, Andersen offers these further contributions: In *The Bell* (1845) he writes that confirmation day "was a tremendously important day in their lives, for on this day they were leaving childhood behind and becoming grown-up persons. Their *infant souls* would take wing into the *bodies of adults*" (emphasis mine). In other words, they are to remain children at heart (in their souls), even though they now have adult bodies. And in *A View from Vartou's Window* (1847), he writes: "Soon enough will come that solemn confirmation time, when the candidates walk together hand in hand, and you among them, in a white dress which your mother, with much time and labor, has fashioned from her own confirmation dress of long years ago. *You will get a red shawl too;* it is far too big for you, but at least everyone can see how large it is, much too large" (emphasis mine). Alluded to here is apparently a local custom according to which little girls could wear a red shawl—*after* the confirmation, I presume, for surely it would be out of place *during* the rite. The red shawl would then be the symbol of the "adult body," of the new— at least hypothetically, conditionally—permissible sexuality. But Andersen hastens to add that this red shawl is still much too big, and that the girl will have to wait 'til she grows into it! And in his novel *O.T.* (New York: Hurd and Houghton, 1870) he writes: "When a girl is confirmed, all manner of fancies awake! . . . She experiences a kind of inclination for the heart of man; but this may not be acknowledged, except for two friends: to the clergyman and the physician" (213).

3. Heinrich Zimmer, *The King and the Corpse*, Bollingen Series 11 (Princeton, N.J.: Princeton University Press, 1948–57).

4. Karen did get rid of her first pair of red shoes, the ones made by "Old Mother Shoemaker"; at the orders of the "Old Lady," these shoes are burned, and Karen is given "proper" clothes and "an education." We will hear a lot more about shoes and shoemakers, but here, to my knowledge, is the only time we encounter "Old Mother Shoemaker" and her ability to make shoes

out of "old scraps of red cloth"—in other words, out of what happens to be available, what happens to exist. "Old Mother Shoemaker," particularly in contrast to the "Old Lady," is simply Old Mother Nature, who creates not just the shoes but the child and provides her with her natural instincts. The energetic "Old Lady," on the other hand, stands for what is "proper" (good manners and Christian morality) and for education. The first pair of red shoes can be removed through education because the girl had never deliberately chosen them; they just, as it were, came with her from birth. The second pair of red shoes, on the other hand, were willingly, or willfully and rebelliously, chosen; so she refuses to give them up, until finally they won't come off. This time only cutting off a part of herself, of her personality—a major and dramatic act of sacrifice and expiation—will free her of their compulsion.

CHAPTER 6

1. For a further exposition of this theme, see Wolfgang Lederer, "Chaos, Order and Psychotherapy," in *Is It Moral to Modify Man?* ed. Claude A. Frazier (Springfield, Ill.: Charles C Thomas, 1973), 23–48.

2. William Michelsen points out that, to a considerable degree, Andersen himself had no other story but his own to tell—at least up to the story of the Snow Queen ("Symbol og Ide I 'Snedronningen,'" *Anderseniana* 8 [1940]: 35–56, 47). We think it is true also of the Snow Queen story and of many of the stories he wrote later on.

3. And we may add: While they read their pulp stories, they no doubt comb their hair as the Old Woman combed Gerda's hair—though few could afford a golden comb. The obsessive grooming problems of adolescent girls and their preoccupation with their cleanliness, weight, pimples, and hairstyling are means of concentrating on their own bodies in a safe and neutral manner, relegating sexuality to the dim realm of "later."

4. It is, of course, quite possible, and happens not infrequently, that a girl intellectualizes defensively, or a boy enters a flower stage. A whole estranged generation has been referred to as "flower children." But, on the whole, and somehow more appropriately, boys at that age intellectualize and become scientists, and girls become flowers.

5. What I call a "moratorium," Eigil Nyborg considers a "regression" (*Den Indre Linie I H. C. Andersens Éventyr* [Denmark: Gyldendal, 1962], 143, 146–147). I prefer my term because growth and ripening do continue during such a phase.

CHAPTER 7

1. Carlos Castañeda, *Journey to Ixtlán* (New York: Simon and Schuster, 1972).

2. A. Heidel, *The Gilgamesh Epic and Old Testament Parallels* (Chicago: University of Chicago Press, 1946), 20–29.

3. Graves, *The White Goddess*, 80.

4. H. R. Ellis Davidson, *Gods and Myths of Northern Europe* (Baltimore: Penguin Books, 1964), 146–47; see also Graves, *White Goddess*, 57.

5. This type has, of course, been noted and labeled by the mythographers. In Stith Thompson, *Motif Index of Folk Literature* (Bloomington: Indiana University Press, 1955) it comes under the heading of "Suitor Tests" (type H 310); Antti Aarne and Stith Thompson's *The Types of the Folk Tale* (Helsinki: Academia Scientiarum Fennica, 1964) would give it number 851A (princess sets riddles for suitors). I prefer my "riddle princess" as both more specific and shorter. That the theme of problem-or-puzzle solving is important because universal has been demonstrated by Jan de Vries, who wrote a 438-page paper on it, citing 631 references from 41 ethnic groups all over the world ("Das Märchen von Klugen Rätsellösern," *Folklore Fellows Communications* [Helsinki] 73 [1928]: 438).

6. Sigmund Freud, *Das Motiv der Kästchenwahl*, vol. 10 of *Ges. Werke*, ed. Anna Freud (London: Imago Publishing, 1948), 37.

7. *Grimm's Fairy Tales* (New York: Pantheon, 1944), 240.

8. *The Complete Andersen*, editor's notes, xvi. He also wrote a spoof on the riddle princess in the story *Clumsy Hans* (1855).

9. Ibid., Fairytales, 49–50.

10. Lederer, *The Fear of Women*, 165–66 and fig. 28.

11. An example of one of these virgin princesses is Good Queen Maeve of Ireland. Ibid., 102.

CHAPTER 8

1. See Lederer, "The Sow and the Farrow," in *The Fear of Women*, 61ff.

2. Ibid., 150, 154, 204.

3. See ibid., "Broomsticks and Acts of Faith," 192–211.

4. Cf. Joseph Campbell, *The Masks of God: Primitive Mythology* (New York: Viking Press, 1959), 331.

5. Flahault aptly calls her "un garçon manqué" (*L'Extrême Existence*, 130).

CHAPTER 9

1. *The Complete Andersen*, editor's notes, xvii.

CHAPTER 10

1. Flahault points out how closely the palace of the Snow Queen resembles the world as seen by a schizophrenic (quoting from a case history recorded in *Le Journal d'une schizophrène* by M. A. Sechehaye): "For me insanity was like a country—opposed to reality—bathed in an implacable light . . . it was an immensity without boundaries, unlimited, flat, a mineral world, moonlike, cold as the expanses of the North Pole. In all that vastness, everything is fixed, immovable, stiff, crystallized." And Kay's behavior (his catatonia) conforms no less to the schizophrenic syndrome: "He has lost his affects. . . . And so the mirror of ice continues the work of the glass splinter." Flahault quotes another patient, this one written up by L. Binswanger in *Le Cas Suzanne Urban:* "An evil spirit accompanies me and poisons all my joy. All that is beautiful, simple, is changed into a grimace. He makes a caricature out of life" (Flahault, *L'Extrême Existence,* 110–13). These parallels and resemblances are striking but, I believe, do not relate to any knowledge of insanity Andersen may have had—from childhood observation or from books—or any intent on his part to convey the inner world of the insane. Kay is not crazy, he is just held fast in his moratorium. But a term that bridges both concepts is alienation. Kay is alienated from the world of the emotions, but not in the sense in which, years ago, a psychiatrist would have been called an "alienist."

2. "One could imagine Hell as a cage made of mirrors: in it one can see only one's own face infinitely multiplied" (Evdokimov, *Les Ages de la vie spirituelle,* 73).

3. Cf. Erich Neumann, *The Origins and History of Consciousness,* Bollingen Series 42 (New York: Pantheon Books, 1954 [1949]), 50ff., 298.

4.   Dies ist der Jugend edelster Beruf!
    Die Welt, sie war nicht, eh ich sie erschuf.

    (This is the noblest task of youth!
    The world was not ere I created it.)
                        Goethe, *Faust,* pt. II, act 2

5. Actually, Hersholt's translation here reads "bits of *glass,*" which confuses, accidentally or on purpose, the mirror of the Snow Queen with the mirror of the Devil.

6. Recall that the lovers in *The Ice Maiden* are similarly frustrated: the young man falls victim to the demon and drowns in the icy lake *on the eve of his marriage*! Similarly, in *The Marsh King's Daughter* princess Helga vanishes from her own wedding feast (obviously before the wedding night) to ascend to "the bright Kingdom of Heaven" (*The Complete Andersen,* Fairy Tales, 296).

7. Simon Grabowski, "The Refrigerated Heart," *Scandinavica* 10 (1971): 43–58, is similarly dissatisfied: "Kay never obtains any fundamental insight into himself and the potential integrative resources of his own psyche . . . he comes to stand before us as a truly 'weak' man, a man who can never derive basic, vital strength from the treasure-caves of his own psyche, but must depend on the tangible outside assistance of a 'strong' woman . . . this reflects the over-awed, paralytic attitude towards women so characteristic of Andersen in his own personal life." Grabowski contrasts this to Novalis's "Märchen von Hyazinth und Rosenbluete" in *Die Lehrlinge zu Sais*, which, up to a point, has a strikingly similar setting and shares the position, typical of German romanticism, that "thought" is to be equated with "sickness." But in his tale it is the boy, Hyazinth, who has to undertake the journey himself and who, in his stage-by-stage quest for "the mother of things, the veiled maiden" comes full circle from the globality of childhood (when Rosenbluete is his "sister" and playmate) and through a period of differentiation to eventual integration, an acceptance of Rosenbluete as the sought-for salvation from intellectuality, as the agent of "integration of his sex-drive into a larger psychic entity." The conclusion of "Hyazinth und Rosenbluete" is drastically different from that of *The Snow Queen:* ". . . and he stood before the heavenly maiden, he lifted the delicate, the iridescent veil, and Rosenbluetchen sank into his arms . . . they lived for many many years among their parents and friends, and innumerable grandchildren . . . for in those days people could have as many children as they pleased" (*Novalis* [Reinbeck bei Hamburg: Rohwolt, 1963], 19–23). Both redemption and immortality are here clearly sexual. Novalis wrote his tale around the year 1800—before Andersen was born. Andersen is likely to have read it, and to have been influenced by it. But he did not understand it, or understood it only in his own way.

Nyborg also regrets "the unreleasing end" of the tale, which only returns to the status quo: "The transformation which should have been a basis for synthesis has not taken place" (*Den Indre Linie I H. C. Andersens Eventyr*, 154).

And Kierkegaard, who wrote an entire book to criticize Andersen's novel *The Improvisatore*, was aware that it was mostly sexuality that was omitted, and teasingly said that Andersen was like one of the flowers "where he and she are sitting on the same stem, which is not fit for production of novels, where a deeper unity is demanded and where a stronger cleavage is therefore also required" (Martin Lotz, "The Object World of Hans Christian Andersen," *Scandinavian Psychoanalytic Review* 6 [1983]: 3–19, 12).

CHAPTER 11

1. All his life Andersen considered this his "fateful date," though he later changed it to 6 September to conform with a printing error in his autobiography. It was also on that day that he was recommended for a study grant by the Royal Theatre. He memorialized the date every year until his death, though eventually in an increasingly despondent mood (Niels Birger Wamberg, "H. C. Andersen og hans skæbnedato," *Anderseniana*, 1970–73, pp. 188–204).

2. "He thought of going all the way back to Funen by boat in the hope that the ship would sink and he would be drowned" (Bredsdorff, *Hans Christian Andersen*, 31). His predicament was in truth quite serious, and later on he formulated it like this: "When the sculptor commences modelling the clay, we do not yet understand the work of art which he will create. . . . How much more difficult is it then to discover in the child the worth and fate of the man! We here see the poor boy . . . the instinct within him, and the influence without, show, like the magnetic needle, only two opposite directions. He must either become a distinguished artist or a miserable, confused being." And he feared both alternatives: "A rare artist must he become, or a miserable bungler—a sparrow-hawk with yellow wings, which for his superiority is pecked to death by its companions" (*Only a Fiddler*, 40, 41).

3. *TS*, 47. With reference to this episode, Helge Topsøe-Jensen and Paul V. Rubow, "Hans Christian Andersen the Writer," *American-Scandinavian Review* 18 (1930): 205–12, comment that, despite Andersen's constant appeals to God he was "in his religious action and reaction like a savage . . . what he actually did was to use *magic* . . . whether he had learned it of the witches or invented it himself" (210–11).

4. Andersen was so absorbed in his theatrical activities that he found no time to study or even to make little excursions out of town. But he did learn somewhat how to conduct himself with poise and a certain elegance, and acquired a sense of language and music that later stood him in good stead (Povl Ingerslev-Jensen, "Statist Andersen," *Anderseniana*, 1970–73, pp. 137–87). The roles he was permitted to play have been reconstructed through a survey of the costumes of the time, preserved at the Royal Theatre (Frederick J. Marker, "H. C. Andersen as a Royal Theatre Actor," *Anderseniana*, 1966–69, pp. 278–84).

5. Bredsdorff, *Hans Christian Andersen*, 39–40.

6. Ibid., 44.

7. Julius Clausen, "Young Hans Christian Andersen," *American-Scandinavian Review* 43 (1955): 47–52, 51.

8. Meisling had grounds for criticism. Andersen, while adept at mathematics, was surprisingly poor in Latin and spelling, and these shortcomings he feared would eventually keep him out of the University. A recent study suggests that the problem was not cultural or characterological but neurological. Andersen, it is claimed, must have been constitutionally dyslexic, with auditory and visual defects—a complicated word-blindness and dysgrammaticism with clumsy sentence construction. If this diagnosis is correct, it could offer an additional reason for Andersen's "oral" style of writing (Axel Rosendal, "Årsagerne til H. C. Andersen stavevanskeligheder," *Anderseniana*, 1974–77, pp. 160–84). Regardless of the validity of this contention, it is certainly true that Meisling traumatized Andersen deeply. Nightmares about him troubled the writer all his life, and only close to his death did he have a dream in which something like a reconciliation with Meisling takes place (Bredsdorff, *Hans Christian Andersen*, 67–68).

9. Bredsdorff, *Hans Christian Andersen*, 70.

10. *Journey on Foot to Amager; Love on Saint Nicolas' Tower.*

11. Spink, *Hans Christian Andersen and His World*, 33–34.

12. Andersen, *Der Dichter und die Welt*, 44–45.

13. Ibid., 47.

14. Bredsdorff, *Hans Christian Andersen*, 76–77.

15. Otto, the hero of *O.T.*, writes: "Was I not once convinced that I loved Sophie, and that I never could bear it if she were lost to me? and yet it needed only the conviction 'She loves thee not,' and my strong feeling was dead. Sophie even seems to me less beautiful; I see faults where I formerly could only discover amiabilities! Now, she is to me almost wholly a stranger" (253).

16. He never overcame his distrust, but knew himself well enough to see it and to deplore it. Thus he writes in his diary in 1850: "I felt I was bound to him. His friendship was a greening palm against which I rested my head. Then along came a certain woman and I said to her: 'My faith is in him!' 'Your faith!' she repeated, smiling. Oh, in that smile there was devouring death. It breathed over my tree, which seemed to bend; I grew dizzy. Oh, what a deadly poison filled the air in that instant,—I grieve that he could change toward me, could be the first of us to feel less warmly! And yet in that instant I too felt the same change. I distrust him. I can be shaken in my faith merely by a mocking smile" (Carl Lorain Withers, "The Private Notebook of H. C. Andersen," *The Forum* 78 [1927]: 417–29, 421).

17. Heinrich Harries, "H. C. Andersen und Heinrich Zeise," *Anderseniana*, 1962–65, pp. 233–95, 236. Oddly enough, one of these poems, "Der Soldat," beginning with "Es geht mit gedämpfter Trommeln Klang" (Adalbert von Chamisso, *Chamissos*

Werke [Leipzig und Wien: Meyers Klassiker Ausgaben, 1907], vol. 1, 134), became a typically death-loving marching song of the German army (Lederer, *The Fear of Women*, 262–65). The popular tune is not by Schumann—who also set this same poem to music—but by a man named Friedrich Silcher, who composed it in 1837 (Gerhard Pallman and Ernst Lothar von Knorr, *Soldaten Kameraden* [Hamburg: Hanseatische Verlagsanstalt, 1942]). It is also odd in other ways. Among the poems translated by Chamisso, it is the only military one. The others deal in more typically Andersenian fashion with a little girl expecting a brother to be born out of a fountain ("Die kleine Liese am Brunnen"); a young man watching smiling blue eyes through ice-flowers on a windowpane ("Märzveilchen"—the last line reading "God help him when the ice-flowers melt!"); a mother daydreaming happily about the future of her baby boy who, according to the ravens, is some day to be hanged as a robber ("Muttertraum"); a fiddler who has to play at his beloved's wedding ("Der Spielmann"); and a rejected lover who, having to live in the same house with his now-married beloved, longs for death ("Der Müllergesell"). "Der Soldat" ("The Soldier") is, for all I know, the only poem Andersen wrote in that vein, the only time he ever wrote anything about a real soldier—and one could well wonder: whatever got into him? He claims in his autobiography (*FT*, 5) that the poem was inspired by his witnessing the execution of the Spanish soldier in 1808. But was it? Is the execution the main thing, or is it a love poem? I am offering a rough translation, so that the reader may judge:

> The muffled drums mark our pace
> How long yet the road, how far the place
> Oh, were it but over and he were at rest
> My heart is breaking in my chest.

> I've loved just him as long as I live
> Him alone, who now his life must give.
> To martial music we reach the square
> I too, I too am commanded there.

> Now for the last time does he sight
> God's world bathed in joyful light
> Now they are binding tight his eyes
> God take you up into paradise!

> The nine of us took aim at last
> Eight bullets simply whistled past
> Their aim by grief and pain was marr'd
> But I, I shot him through the heart.

18. F. J. Billeskov Jansen, "Quelques extraits du Journal Parisien," *Adam International Review* 22, nos. 248–49 (1955): 38.

19. Grindea, "The Triumphant Ugly Duckling," 3.

20. Bredsdorff, *Hans Christian Andersen*, 149.

21. Julius Clausen, "H. C. Andersen Abroad and At Home," *American-Scandinavian Review* 18 (1930): 228–34, 229.

22. Bredsdorff, *Hans Christian Andersen*, 150, 286–88.

23. *FT*, 215, and Peter Ostwald, *Schumann* (Boston: Northeastern University Press, 1985), 163–64.

24. Miron Grindea, Editorial Comment, *Adam International Review* 22, no. 248–49 (1955): 2.

25. Bredsdorff, "H. C. Andersen in Britain," 22.

26. Bredsdorff, *Hans Christian Andersen*, 194–95.

27. Ibid., 234.

28. He did give an answer, of sorts, toward the end of his life when, at sixty-five, he published the long story—or short novel—*Lucky Peer*, a deeply cynical and pessimistic work. There a wise mentor, an Edvard Collin figure, whom Andersen, perhaps in acknowledgment of the loving care he was then receiving from the Melchior family, makes a Jew, tells the spectacularly successful singer and composer Peer: "How young you are, dear friend, that it can please you to be with these people! In a way they are good enough, but they look down on us plain citizens. For some of them it is only a matter of vanity, an amusement, and for others a sort of sign of exclusive culture, when they receive into their circles artists and the lions of the day. These belong in the salon much as the flowers in a vase; they decorate and then they are thrown away" (*The Complete Andersen*, Longer Stories, 373). Lucky Peer, incidentally, is "lucky" not just in his career, but above all because he drops dead at the height of it, being thus spared the many years of decline that Andersen suffered—and from having to ask for the hand of the now willing aristocratic young lady he loved. "Lucky Peer! More fortunate than millions!" (384).

29. In 1837 he wrote to Henriette Hanck: "My name is gradually beginning to shine, and that is the only thing for which I live. I covet honour and glory in the same way the miser covets gold; both are probably empty, but one has to have something to strive for in this world, otherwise one would collapse and rot" (Bredsdorff, *Hans Christian Andersen*, 134). The famous Danish critic, Georg Brandes, wrote in 1869—and Andersen, then sixty-four, must have been smarting when he read it—that "the criticism that can with justice be made of Andersen's 'Story of my Life' is not so much that the author is throughout occupied with his own private affairs (for that is quite natural in such a work); it is that his personality is scarcely ever occupied with anything greater than itself, is never absorbed in an idea, is never entirely free from the

ego. The revolution of 1848 in this book affects us as though we heard someone sneeze; we are astonished to be reminded by the sound that there is a world outside of the author" (*Creative Spirits of the Nineteenth Century* [New York: Thomas Y. Crowell, 1923], 40).

30. Brandes, who knew Andersen personally, wrote of him:

> A great man he did become. A man never. It never occurred to him for one second of his life that he might for once, in a good cause, attack the mighty . . . only one fundamental trait, one untiring, all-consuming, all absorbing ambition never faltered nor failed for one moment of his long life . . . to become famous, to be honored and considered, fêted and paid homage to! . . . He writes with amazing frankness: "Only in being admired by all can my soul find happiness; the most unimportant person who does not do so has power to make me feel despondent!" He trembled before every breath of wind that might rend a leaf from his laurel tree.
>
>   ("Hans Christian Andersen,"
>   *Contemporary Review* 87 [1905]: 640–56, 640–41)

31. There was another, "unserious"—meaning halfhearted—infatuation. Andersen met the Countess Mathilde Barck, seventeen years of age, in Scania in 1839, and felt himself "leaning towards" her. He alludes to her in his *Picture Book Without Pictures:* "A poet whispered a name which he begged the wind not to betray—a count's coronet sparkles above it, and therefore he did not say it aloud." A correspondence ensued, but by 25 January 1844, he wrote to a friend: "I think you have heard me mention Countess Barck . . . one of the most beautiful girls I have seen. Some years ago she made a strong impression on me. I almost think I could have fallen in love with her, but it did not happen, a poor poet and a countess—I went away!" (Elias Bredsdorff, "H. C. Andersen og Mathilda Barck," *Anderseniana*, 1974–77, pp. 137–57).

32. Spink, *Hans Christian Andersen and His World*, 74.

33. A detailed account of Andersen's relatonship with Dickens ("A Friendship and its Dissolution") is given by Elias Bredsdorff "Hans Andersen and Charles Dickens," *Anglistica*, vol. 7 (Copenhagen: Rosenkilde and Bagger, 1956).

34. Quoted from Spink, *Hans Christian Andersen and His World*, 92.

35. Ibid., 94. The italics are Dickens's; but we cannot fail to notice once again the importance of *boots* (or shoes) in Andersen's scheme of things.

36. He was sixty-two years old before he could be persuaded to buy himself his first bed. He wrote: "Now I am going to have a house, even a bed, my own *bed;* it terrifies me! I am being weighed down by furniture, bed and rocking chair, not to mention books

and paintings. . . . I have had to invest one hundred rix dollars in a bed, and it is going to be my death-bed, for if it does not last that long, then it isn't worth the money. I wish I were only twenty, then I'd take my inkpot on my back, two shirts and a pair of socks, put a quill at my side and go into the wide world" (Bredsdorff, *Hans Christian Andersen*, 251).

37. Andersen, *Der Dichter und die Welt*, 70.

Chapter 12

1. Hans Christian Andersen, *Poems*, trans. Murray Brown (Berkeley, Calif.: Elsinore Press, 1972), 86.

2. Waldemar Westergaard, ed., *The Andersen-Scudder Letters* (Berkeley: University of California Press, 1949), xxiii.

3. *A Poet's Bazaar* (1842), about a journey to Turkey; *In Sweden* (1851); *In Spain* (1863).

4. Paul V. Rubow, "Et vintereventyr," in *Reminiscenser* (Copenhagen: Ejnar Munksgaard, 1940), points out to what degree all of Andersen's tales are permeated by motifs common in folktales. But whenever it could be done without stunting the story he eliminated from them the more cruel and violent features (Sara P. Rodes, "The Wild Swans," *Anderseniana*, 1951–54, pp. 352–67, 353).

5. Spink, *Hans Christian Andersen and His World*, 53.

6. Bredsdorff, *Hans Christian Andersen*, 123–24.

7. Bettina Hürlimann, *Three Centuries of Children's Books in Europe* (London: Oxford University Press, 1967), xii.

8. Ureaka, "Adult Symbolism in the Literary Fairy Tales of the Late Nineteenth Century," 18–35.

9. Martin Lotz, "The Object World of Hans Christian Andersen," *Scandinavian Psychoanalytic Review* 6 (1983): 3–19, suggests what may have been driving Andersen to write his stories: "He found his own way of identifying with his father by telling fairy tales to children. This was an activity that would remind him of some of the few moments where he had seen his father happy" (13). He was, in other words, wearing his father's shoes.

10. Grønbech, *Hans Christian Andersen*, 91–92.

11. For a Kleinian interpretation of this story, see Stephen Wilson, "Hans Andersen's *Nightingale*. A Paradigm for the Development of Transference Love," *International Review of Psychoanalysis* 7 (1980): 483–86.

12. W. H. Auden speaks of "the namby-pamby Christianity of some of his heroes" ("Some Notes on Andersen," *Adam International Review* 22, nos. 248–49 [1955]: 12).

13. Ordinarily Andersen rewrote and polished his stories a good deal, and the final product might be quite different from the

first draft (Grønbech, *Hans Christian Andersen,* 133); but of *The Snow Queen* he wrote: "It has been sheer joy for me to put on paper my most recent fairy tale, 'The Snow Queen'; it permeated my mind in such a way that it came out dancing over the paper!" (Bredsdorff, *Hans Christian Andersen,* 177). Indeed he had begun writing *The Snow Queen* on 5 December 1844, and it was published in book form on 21 December! (ibid., 353–54)—a speed, not just of writing but of printing and publishing, unheard of in our electronic age.

CHAPTER 13

1. Brun and Brun have similarly attempted to discern a pattern of personality development in Andersen's story *Thumbelina.* Gudrun Brun and George C. Brun, "A Psychological Treatise on Hans Andersen's Fairy Tale *Thumbelina,*" *Acta Psychiatrica et Neurologica* 21 (1946): 141–49.

2. *The Dryad* (1868), *The Complete Andersen,* Longer Stories, 165.

3. *The Great Sea Serpent,* ibid., Shorter Tales, 361.

4. *Anne Lisbeth,* ibid., Longer Stories, 29.

5. Andersen, *Poems,* 23.

6. William Mishler discusses the same theme at the hand of Andersen's story of *The Steadfast Tin Soldier* who, "with his bayonet and missing leg [is] both erect and castrated. . . . The soldier's love and his steadfastness are . . . linked by way of an absence, a blanking out of erotic desire . . . he forbids himself the dancer with the very breath with which he appropriates her . . . seeing [her] will keep her at a distance. . . . [There is] a conjunction of erotic love and death . . . [and] steadfastness is another name for fear" ("H. C. Andersen's *Tin Soldier* in a Freudian Perspective," *Scandinavian Studies* 50 [1978]: 389–95).

The one-legged tin soldier, who knows himself to be both different and defective, falls in love with the dancer because he believes her also to have only one leg, and so to be a kindred spirit. The story has a curious sequel. Another great storyteller, Thomas Mann, used to refer to himself in intimate communications as a "steadfast tin soldier" (Letter of 6 April 1944, *Briefe,* 1937–47, ed. Erika Mann [Frankfurt: S. Fischer Verlag, 1963], 359). Mann's lightest but also most moving novel, *Royal Highness,* tells of a prince who is lonesome because he is a prince and because he has only one (good) arm. The prince falls in love with a millionaire's daughter, whom he perceives as being crippled in her own way and thus—with regard to both uniqueness and impairment—similar to himself. The steadfastness, for Thomas Mann, has a heightened meaning, not just as a quality admirable in itself but as an "in-spite-of," as manifesting the "heroism of weakness," which to him is the only true heroism (Thomas

Mann, *Über mich Selbst* [On Myself], in *Gesammelte Werke in Einzel-bänden*, Frankfurter Ausgabe, ed. Peter de Mendelssohn [Frankfurt: S. Fischer Verlag, 1983], 72). Indeed, many of his characters suffer some impairment they function "in spite of." The core of Mann's credo was to be "steadfast"—to "stand fast"—to hold oneself "prop-erly" and "as if it were nothing" ("Haltung bewahren"—an expres-sion of posture which like the French "tenue" refers equally to the body and to the spirit). To a somewhat lesser extent this was—as a matter of necessity more than of conviction—true also for Hans Christian Andersen. He too can be seen and admired as a "hero of weakness," a man who functions despite—and achieves because of—his defect.

7. Alfred C. Kinsey, in *Sexual Behavior of the Human Male* (Phila-delphia: W. B. Saunders, 1948), has this to say:

> Not only do . . . earlier developing boys have four years' head start, and not only do they have higher rates of activity in those initial years, but they continue to have higher rates throughout the subse-quent age periods. . . . there is still a discernible difference in the age group 31 to 35, which is 20 to 25 years after the time of onset of adolescence!
>
> (307)

> Moreover, it is possible that the patterns which are established by the earliest sexual activity, meaning patterns of higher frequency for younger-maturing boys, and patterns of lower frequency for older-maturing boys, are the patterns by which the individual's subsequent life is ordered. . . . It can be suggested that the frequency of sexual activity may, to some degree, be dependent upon a general metabolic level which the individual maintains through much of life.
>
> (309)

> At [the age of 50] 100% of the early adolescent males are still sexually active, and their frequencies are still 20% higher than the frequencies of the later-maturing males. . . . On the other hand, some of the males (not many) who were late adolescents and who have had five years less of sexual activity, are beginning to drop completely out of the picture; and the rates of this group are definitely lower in this older age group.
>
> (319–23)

> Those individuals who become adolescent late . . . more often delay the start of their sexual activities and have the minimum frequencies of activity, both in their early years and throughout the remainder of their lives. If any of these individuals have deliberately chosen low frequencies in order to conserve their energies for later use, they appear never to have found the sufficient justification for such use at any later time. It is probable that most of these low rating individuals never were capable of any higher rates and never could have in-

creased their rates to match those of the more active segments of the population.

(325)

There is some reason for thinking that . . . early-adolescent males are more often the more alert, energetic, vivacious, spontaneous, physically active, socially extrovert and/or aggressive individuals in the population. Actually, 53% of these early-adolescent boys are so described on their histories, while only 33% of the late-adolescent boys received such personality ratings. Conversely, 54% of the males who were late-adolescent were described as slow, quiet, mild in manner, without force, reserved, timid, taciturn, introvert, and/or socially inept, while only 41% of the early-adolescent boys fell under such headings.

(325–26)

There is evidence that the late-maturing males have more limited sexual capacities which would be badly strained if, through any circumstance, they tried to raise their rates to the levels maintained by the sexually more capable persons.

(326)

CHAPTER 14

1. Spink, *Hans Christian Andersen and His World,* 16.
2. Ibid., 62.
3. The river washes away her wooden shoes, as it had washed away Gerda's red ones. But there is a difference: Gerda had discarded her red shoes intentionally. She had thrown them into the river as a sacrifice and the river had *accepted* them. In the case of the washerwoman, the River of Life *deprives* her of the last and most essential necessity; here her worn-out shoes and their disappearance stand for her failing and finally vanishing will to live.
4. On the importance of fathers, see Wolfgang Lederer, *Dragons, Delinquents and Destiny,* Psychological Issues Monograph no. 15 (New York: International Universities Press, 1964).
5. Hans Christian Andersen, *The Improvisatore,* 2 vols. (London: Richard Bentley, 1845), 1, 149.
6. It is perhaps pertinent, in this context, to point out, as Brandes has done, that

almost all the animals which appear in Andersen's nursery stories are tame animals, domestic animals. . . . The wild nightingale . . . is a tame and loyal bird. Take even the swan, that noble, royal bird . . . how does it end? Alas, as a domestic animal. This is one of the points where it becomes difficult to pardon the great author. . . . How could you, we feel tempted to exclaim, have the heart to permit the swan to end thus! Let him die if needs must be! That would be tragic and great. Let him spread his wings and impetuously soar through the air, rejoicing in his beauty and his strength! . . . That is free and delightful. Anything would be better than this conclusion: "Into the garden came little children, who threw bread and corn into the water. And they ran to their father and mother, and bread and cake were thrown into the water; and they all said: 'The new one is the most beautiful of all! so young and handsome!' and the old swans bowed their heads before him." Let them bow, but let us not forget that there is something which is worth more than the recognition of all the old swans and geese and ducks, worth more than receiving bread-crumbs and cake as a garden bird,—the power of silently gliding over the waters, and free flight!

> (Georg Brandes, *Creative Spirits of the Nineteenth Century* [New York: Thomas Y. Crowell, 1923], 24)

Andersen never wanted to be free, always relied on "bread-crumbs and cakes" thrown him by his assorted protectors.

CHAPTER 15

1. Andersen, *Der Dichter und die Welt*, 48.
2. *The Comet*, in *The Complete Andersen*, Shorter Stories, 394.
3. Andersen, *Poems*, 86.
4. Andersen, *Der Dichter und die Welt*, 8. On subsequent visits—in 1825, 1829, 1830, and 1832—he stayed at the house of Colonel Høegh-Guldberg and barely visited his mother; he found her to be increasingly alcoholic and arranged to have his "support" for her—tiny sums of money—doled out to her by the Colonel (Bredsdorff, *Hans Christian Andersen*, 50, 81).
5. As suggested by the story *She Was Good for Nothing*.
6. Andersen, *Der Dichter und die Welt*, 30.
7. Ibid., 32.
8. Spink, *Hans Christian Andersen and His World*, 39.
9. Grønbech comments: "Today's reader cannot fail to notice with a certain distaste how the three main characters [in Andersen's novel *O.T.*] try to put as much distance as possible between themselves and their poverty-stricken families. They wish to forget their origins and establish themselves in the world of the bourgeoisie and the aristocracy" (*Hans Christian Andersen*, 69).
10. Andersen, *Der Dichter und die Welt*, 102. In the novel *O.T.*, the protagonist and Andersen-figure Otto "never before had felt, never before reflected, what it was to stand alone in the world, to be lovingly bound to no one with the band of consanguinity" (83). He feels that way after the death of his grandfather.
11. Westergaard, *The Andersen-Scudder Letters*, 96, 98.
12. See *A Story from the Sand Dunes*, *The Old Church Bell*; *Little*

Tuck, She Was Good for Nothing; The Story of a Mother, The Comet; and the poem *The Dying Child.*

13. See *Lucky Peer.*

14. Andersen told the story of a woman who "deserted" her little son, in that she had him raised by other people (as his own half-sister had been "put out" to be raised), in *Anne Lisbeth.* She is punished with madness and death!

15. *The Merry Night of Halloween* in Andersen, *Poems,* 6.

16. Hanged men show up not only in his poetry but also in his drawings and cutouts, sometimes in multiples and sometimes without obvious connection to the composition as a whole (Heltoft, *H. C. Andersens Billedkunst,* 27, 39, 117).

CHAPTER 16

1. Spink, *Hans Christian Andersen and His World,* 6.

2. This episode is replicated in the life of Christian, the young "hero" of *Only a Fiddler* (105–6).

3. Spink, *Hans Christian Andersen and His World,* 7. On 8 February 1842, he wrote in his almanac, "When I came home I found a letter from my mother's daughter [!]; I experienced that which I have described in O.T. Feverish. A terrible night, sensuous thoughts and despair mockingly filled my mind" (Bredsdorff, *Hans Christian Andersen,* 154).

4. In *Only a Fiddler,* he writes, "Naomi had seen, it is true, glorious works in marble in Vienna, Lucca, and Bologna, but she did not understand how to value them—she could not discover the beautiful in these works of art. It was not until she was in Florence that the mist fell from her eyes" (271–72).

5. Bredsdorff, *Hans Christian Andersen,* 107.

6. Ibid., 156.

7. Ibid., 94.

8. Ibid., 282–83.

9. Having reached the conclusion that Karen represented the feared half-sister, I was then informed by Professor Børger Madsen of the University of California at Berkeley that the half-sister's name *was* Karen.

10. *The Complete Andersen,* Shorter Tales, 438.

11. Lederer, *The Fear of Women,* ch. 5: "Frau Welt, or The Perfume of Decay," 35–43.

12. In Andersen's story *Lucky Peer* the young hero, in a fever, has the following nightmare: He finds himself inside a castle, "feels anguish, a strange fear, as never before. There was no exit to be found, but from the floor way up to the roof, and from all the walls, there smiled at him lovely young girls. . . . He wanted to

speak to them, but his tongue found no words; his speech was completely gone; not a sound came from his lips. Then he threw himself upon the earth, more miserable than he had ever been. One of the elfin maidens approached him; surely she meant well, for she had taken the shape he would most like to see; she looked like the pharmacist's daughter; he was almost ready to believe that it was she, but soon he saw that *she was hollow in back* and had only a beautiful front—open in the back, with nothing at all inside." She tells him he must stay with her forever, "or the walls will squeeze you until the blood flows from your brow!" And the walls trembled, and the air became like that of a baking oven. He found his voice. "O Lord, O Lord, have You forsaken me?" he cried from the depth of his soul (*The Complete Andersen*, Longer Stories, 349).

In *Only a Fiddler* (185) Andersen states that "according to the Danish popular belief the elves are hollow behind like a baking-trough"—a slightly more benign version than his.

13. Lederer, *The Fear of Women*, 41. In 1850, when Andersen was forty-five years old and presumably in full possession of his virility, he wrote a related and equally slimy fantasy of his own into his private notebook: "In the woods there are many mushrooms of all colors, some quite vermilion. A few of these were covered with warts like cream pastry dotted with almonds. Some mushrooms were green as grass, and still others were white and jelly-like. We can easily imagine all these mushrooms changed at midnight to pretty women, alluring and caressing. And now they are seen by day; the pitch-black and sickening ones are dying bacchanalian spirits" (Carl Lorain Withers, "The Private Note-Book of Hans Christian Andersen," *The Forum* 78 [1927]: 417–29).

14. *The Complete Andersen*, Longer Stories, 108.

15. See Lederer, *The Fear of Women*, ch. 5, "Frau Welt, or The Perfume of Decay," and ch. 19, "Envy and Loathing—The Patriarchal Revolt."

16. Cf. his poem *The Dying Child:* "Your salt tears burn upon my face . . ."

17. Spink, *Hans Christian Andersen and His World*, 44.

18. *The Complete Andersen*, Introduction, xiv.

19. Ibid.

CHAPTER 17

1. *The Complete Andersen*, Longer Stories, 201.

2. Ibid., 1.

3. Obviously, a cobbler cannot *earn* himself rich; he is bound to remain poor and helpless unless assisted by "Lady Luck"—the old gypsy woman. There is no trace here of manly assertiveness.

4. *The Complete Andersen,* editor's notes, xxviii.

5. Ibid., Longer Stories, 62.

6. Ibid., editor's notes, xxxiii.

7. Ibid., Longer Stories, 102.

8. Ibid., Shorter Tales, 293.

9. Ibid., Longer Stories, 316.

10. It is noteworthy that the loss of the girl "he cared more for . . . than anyone else in the world" reminded him of the death of his *father*—not of his *mother!*

11. Westgaard, *The Andersen-Scudder Letters,* 144.

12. *The Complete Andersen,* Fairy Tales, 92.

13. In all fairness it should be said that, at least in the days of Riborg Voigt, money would have posed a shocking problem indeed, in the sense that to support her Andersen would have had to capitalize on his University degree and enter some sort of government employ. He would have had to become an official and, perhaps, would not have found time or energy to be a poet. Such at least may have been his reasoning and his conscious fear. Seeing the matter as a choice between domesticity and creativity he would, without hesitation, have chosen the latter. For a brilliant treatment of the life-and-death struggle between creativity and domesticity, see G. B. Shaw's *Man and Superman.*

14. *The Complete Andersen,* Shorter Tales, 252.

15. Andersen, *Der Dichter und die Welt,* 143–44.

16. Kai Friis Möller, "The Poet and the Fair Sex," *American-Scandinavian Review* 18 (1930): 220–27, 220.

17. Bredsdorff, *Hans Christian Andersen,* 283.

18. *The Complete Andersen,* Shorter Stories, 424.

19. *The Complete Hans Christian Andersen* (New York: Avenel Books, 1981), 663–68; Paoul Høybye, "Om H. C. Andersens udkast," *Anderseniana,* 1970–73, pp. 376–88.

20. Andersen, *Die Dichter und die Welt,* 69.

21. Ibid., 41.

CHAPTER 18

1. Andersen, *Der Dichter und die Welt,* 32.

2. A little later, in his novel *The Improvisatore,* he has a different reaction to the cross-dressing of others. It is carnival in Rome: "Carriages drove past; almost all the drivers were dressed as ladies, but it looked to me horrible; those black whiskers under womens' caps; the vigorous movements, all were painted to me in frightful colours, nay, were detestable, as it seemed to me" (vol. 1, 215). (Was it that the female impersonators were full-grown men with whiskers, not "innocent" youths, that upset him?)

Two years later, in *Only a Fiddler*, he plays with transvestism in a quasi-Shakespearean manner: "One man, a Dane—a boy certainly not above eighteen . . . he had delicate, flexible limbs . . . and upon the fresh lip curled the mustache. He was called Mr. Christian . . . he rested his arm on Ladislaf's shoulder. . . . The Danish boy pressed a kiss upon Ladislaf's lips. 'I am thine,' said he, 'only thine.' And Ladislaf answered, smiling, 'Mine! thou wast mine upon the sea.' " It is not immediately obvious, and we are told only several paragraphs later, that "Christian" is in fact the lovely, half-Jewish girl Naomi, disguised as a man. This device continues through several chapters and has the expectable complications (217ff.).

3. Andersen, *Die Dichter und die Welt*, 33–34.

4. Ibid., 38.

5. Ibid., 40.

6. Hans Brix writes, "Young men whom he sought as companions were repelled by his over-sensitiveness and the uncontrollability of his moods. The age of sensibility was passed. The ideals of the time required the cold, reserved elegance of a man of the world. Andersen expressed himself with the suddenness of an April shower, and his childishness was boundless" ("Hans Christian Andersen," 734).

7. Andersen, *Der Dichter und die Welt*, 45.

8. Ibid., 52–53.

9. Such a "crossing-over" from boyhood friend to heterosexual love is suggested in two famous novels. In Thomas Mann's *The Magic Mountain*, the hero, Hans Castorp, is drawn to the slovenly but sensuous Slavic beauty Madame Chauchat because of her resemblance to his boyhood friend, Przibislav Hippe; an incident involving a borrowed pencil marks the highpoint of each relationship and underlines their emotional equivalence, if not identity. In Hermann Hesse's *Der Steppenwolf*, the hero is, in similar manner, attracted to a girl who reminds him of a boyhood friend; the friend's name was Hermann, and the hero learns with delight that the girl's name is Hermine. She is a prostitute who takes his sexual "redemption" in hand, leaving the physical aspects to another woman but herself appearing to the hero alternately dressed as a girl or as a young man! Thus both Hans Castorp and the Steppenwolf were "led" to heterosexual love, as over a bridge, from the starting point of a homosexual boyhood infatuation.

10. Möller, "The Poet and the Fair Sex," 221.

11. Bredsdorff, *Hans Christian Andersen*, 137.

12. Andersen, *Der Dichter und die Welt*, 113.

13. Ibid., 119.

14. Albert Hansen, "H. C. Andersen: Beweis seiner Homosexualität," *Jahrbuch für sexuelle Zwischenstufen* 3 (1901): 202–30.

15. Hjalmar Helweg, *H. C. Andersen. En psykiatrisk Studie* (Copenhagen: H. Hagerup, 1927), reprinted 1954, and "H. C. Andersen und die Behauptung seiner Homosexualität," *Zeitschrift für die gesamte Neurologie und Psychiatrie* 118 (1929): 777–88.

16. Bredsdorff, *Hans Christian Andersen*, 233.

17. Spink, *Hans Christian Andersen and His World*, 104.

18. Bredsdorff, *Hans Christian Andersen*, 57.

19. Ibid., 69, 70.

20. Ibid., 75, 83, 16.

21. Ibid., 84.

22. Ibid., 85.

23. Ibid., 87.

24. Ibid., 88.

25. Ibid., 92.

26. Wilhelm von Rosen, "Venskabets mysterier," *Anderseniana*, 1978–81, pp. 167–214, 210.

27. Bredsdorff, *Hans Christian Andersen*, 91.

28. Von Rosen, "Venskabets mysterier," 211.

29. Ibid., 212.

30. Ibid., 213.

31. On the other hand, Edvard was sometimes—no doubt quite unintentionally—a tease. When Andersen left on his longest journey in the fall of 1840, "Edvard C. was the last person of whom I took leave, he pressed a kiss on my mouth. Oh, it was as if my heart was going to burst!" Andersen wrote in his diary (Bredsdorff, *Hans Christian Andersen*, 145). He must have been thoroughly bewildered by these occasional outbursts of affection in the otherwise so frigid Edvard, and this may explain why he continued to woo him. As to the 'Du'—he achieved it, as it were, once removed. At the end of a journey in 1861, on which Edvard's son Jonas had accompanied him, he writes in his diary: "In the evening I carried out what I had decided to do all the time: I suggested to him [Jonas] that he should say 'Du' to me; he was surprised but in a firm voice said *yes!* and thanked me. Later on, after I had gone to bed, he came in to me before lying down, took my hand, once more repeating a deeply felt 'Thank you!' so that tears came into my eyes; he pressed a kiss on my forehead and I felt very happy" (ibid., 239).

32. Bredsdorff, *Hans Christian Andersen*, 150.

33. Ibid., 160, 179, 180.

34. Ibid., 181.

35. Ibid., 265–66.

36. Edvard Collin, *Andersen og det Collinske Huus* (Copenhagen, 1882).

37. Bredsdorff, *Hans Christian Andersen*, 276, 304.

38. Von Rosen, "Venskabets mysterier," 210–14.

39. Bredsdorff, *Hans Christian Andersen*, 167, 169, 170. In those days, writes Bredsdorff, Andersen "in a sense was at one and the same time in love with both Jenny Lind and with the hereditary grand duke, well knowing that he could never attach himself fully to either of them" (175).

40. Ibid., 230. There is a great deal of kissing going on in Andersen's autobiography—not with women, of course; that would have been altogether improper; but men supposedly embrace and kiss him all the time. We have however one little episode on record that throws some doubt on the question of who kisses whom. In 1866 he visited Robert Lytton, son of Bulwer Lytton, in Lisbon, and says of the occasion: "Lytton read aloud [two of my stories], kissed my hand. He did the same in the hall at my departure, embraced me and kissed me." Lytton wrote of the same meeting: "Andersen, the Danish poet (the 'ugly duckling') has been here, and quite in his element . . . I read aloud after dinner . . . one of his little stories: and he was so well pleased with my doing this, that he jumped up and kissed me, as Mrs. Disraeli would say, 'all over.' He is a perfect faun, half child, half God" (Bredsdorff, *Hans Christian Andersen*, 250). So perhaps his other rapturous reports of affections received should be taken *cum grano salis?*

41. Brandes, "Hans Christian Andersen," 650.

42. On the other hand, Brandes also notes that Andersen rarely introduces the child into his nursery stories as taking part in the action and conversation (*Creative Spirits of the Nineteenth Century*, 24). In this regard *The Snow Queen* is once again outstanding and exceptional.

43. Phyllis Greenacre, "Hans Christian Andersen and Children," *Psychoanalytic Study of the Child* 38 (1983): 617–35.

44. Ibid.

45. In view of Andersen's fine understanding of and rapport with children, and his frequent contact with them, the question imposes itself: did he not ever wish to have children of his own? There is, to my knowledge, no direct evidence that he ever had such yearnings. He wanted to be a child with children, not a parent. But there is a curious circumstance that perhaps betrays his guilt at having "wasted his semen." As an old man he three times records very similar dreams in his diary. On 9 May 1865: "Tonight a terrible dream about a dead child that I carried." On 1 June 1868: "Dreamt hideously about a child who rested on my chest and became a wet piece of cloth." On 29 August 1874: "This disgusting dream I often dream: about a child that withers at my chest and turns into a wet piece of cloth" (Nyborg, *Den Indre Linie I H. C. Andersens Eventyr*, 133). What starts as a (potential) child and ends

as a wet piece of cloth would plausibly be the product of masturbation. Much earlier, in *Only a Fiddler*, his guilt is spelled out. A man relates:

> There is in Norway the story of a girl who had a horror of becoming a mother, and therefore, the evening before her marriage, went to the water-mill where the witch dwelt, to ask for some remedy which should prevent this. The witch gave her twelve seeds, which she was to fling into the mill-pond. This she did . . . but at each seed which she flung into the water there was heard a slight sigh: it was a child's heart which broke each time. She became a wife, but remained childless; in old age remorse seized her. Her hand was unstained with blood, and yet she was a murderess, and endured agony of mind as an infanticide . . . a murderess of a whole race! Such a murderer am I! such a murderer shall I be! for I cherish within me a horror of becoming the husband of any woman.
>
> (69)

Clearly, Andersen's only sexual outlet, the sin of Onan, made him feel that he was a murderer.

46. Spink, *Hans Christian Andersen and His World*, 108.

47. One of his drawings (see Frontispiece) shows an elongated, Andersen-like character trying desperately to emerge from a large bottle in which he is enclosed. He braces his feet and one hand against the insides of the bottle, while the fingers of the other hand, in spite of the absurdly elongated arm, barely manage to touch the base of the cork, or stopper. Clearly, the man cannot get out. An impassive female angel hovers above and to one side— quite out of reach and quite unhelpful (Heltoft, *H. C. Andersens Billedkunst*).

CHAPTER 19

1. Andersen, *Der Dichter und die Welt*, 69.

2. Alexander Heidel, *The Gilgamesh Epic and Old Testament Parallels* (Chicago: University of Chicago Press, 1946), 21–22, 28–29. Translation of Latin passages, and some minor modifications, by the author.

3. Mme Leprince de Beaumont, *The Fairy Tale Book* (New York: Simon & Schuster, 1958).

4. Even Goethe's Faust is redeemed from the musty isolation of his scholastic study, not by Mephisto—who merely removes him physically into the great world—but by the physical love of Gretchen: only through her intervention and, as it turns out, self-sacrifice, does Faust truly come to life. The final redemption of his soul is also the work of a woman, the *Mater Gloriosa*, Goethe's term for the Virgin Mary. That the Virgin, as *redemptrix*, far outdistances her son in

popularity can be proven by any glimpse at the inside of a Catholic or Orthodox church. To the Protestant Andersen, this iconography, psychologically congenial, was doctrinally taboo. On the theme of the "forever redeeming female," see also Lederer, *The Fear of Women*, ch. 30, "The Loneliness of Outer Space."

5. Zimmer, *The King and the Corpse*, 90–95.

6. Ibid., 177n.

7. In Andersen's *The Wild Swans* (*The Complete Andersen*, Fairy Tales, 131), Elisa, the pure little princess, has to save her eleven older brothers from their bewitchment into swans by her silent, industrious, sacrificial love. She almost loses her life in the process, but she succeeds, except with the youngest brother. The shirt of nettle fibers, by means of which she exorcizes the others, is in his case not quite finished. One sleeve is lacking, so he retains one swan's wing instead of an arm, and remains a not-quite-human creature—like Andersen.

CHAPTER 20

1. *The Complete Andersen*, Shorter Tales, 437.

2. See Andersen, *Der Dichter und die Welt*, 31.

3. *The Complete Andersen*, Introduction, xii; also Spink, *Hans Christian Andersen and His World*, 31. The episode is retold in *Only a Fiddler* (149–50).

4. Bredsdorff, *Hans Christian Andersen*, 56.

5. Möller, "The Poet and the Fair Sex," 220.

6. Bredsdorff, *Hans Christian Andersen*, 67.

7. Personal communication, Professor Børger Madsen, Department of Scandinavian Studies, University of California at Berkeley. Based on Andersen's diaries, which have not been translated into English and were thus not available to me.

8. Ibid.

9. Martin Lotz suggests that in the boy's mind—and by that he is referring to the unconscious part of the mind—he may have, in addition, entertained intense guilt feeling over having "defeated his father as a rival, and sent him away, with his disease and final death as a result" ("The Object World of Hans Christian Andersen," 6). Such guilt would have become unbearable in the close physical proximity of the maternal bed.

10. On a visit to Odense in 1832, where he found his mother in the last stages of alcoholism, he wrote to Edvard Collin: "I feel in bad spirits here, all the memories of my childhood, every spot has a dark influence on me" (Bredsdorff, *Hans Christian Andersen*, 82). It was not just her repugnant condition at that time, but also repugnant memories, that oppressed him.

11. Andersen himself was well aware that he had to be saved *from* mother, that he could never expect to be saved *by* her. Recall the statement in the story of *The Girl Who Trod on the Loaf:* "A mother's tears of grief for her erring child always reach it, but they do not redeem; they only burn, and make the pain greater." The ambivalence inherent in this sentence needs perhaps to be made explicit. Mother sheds tears for her erring child because he is erring far away, in the big world, to be away from her. Her tears burn and make the pain greater. This is the pain of guilt for having to leave her, for having to err in the wide world to stay away from her. It is also the pain of having to resist the love for and the dependency on the mother; the guilt is also of feeling, besides the love, such aversion and horror.

12. This fictional scene may again be an echo of Mrs. Meisling's seduction attempt at Elsinore (Bredsdorff, *Hans Christian Andersen,* 119).

13. *The Improvisatore,* vol. 2, 231.

14. Bredsdorff, *Hans Christian Andersen,* 281.

15. *Only a Fiddler,* 71, 136.

16. Nyborg, *Den Indre Linie I H. C. Andersens Eventyr,* 128.

17. Brandes, "Hans Christian Andersen," 645–46.

18. Hans Brix wrote of him: "Present happiness was experienced only at a few, rare moments soon followed by the deepest depression" ("Hans Christian Andersen," 731).

19. Michelsen, "Symbol og Ide I 'Snedronningen,' " 37.

20. "Is it not all one how high we may be placed in life," he writes in *Only a Fiddler,* "if we are only firmly placed?" (41). But he had disavowed his lowly origins, and was not firmly placed anywhere.

21. Johan E. de Mylius, "Lykkedrøm og Kunstnerkald," *Anderseniana,* 1970–73, pp. 30–59.

22. Von Rosen, "Venskabets mysterier," 213.

23. Andersen's play *The Mulatto,* with which he had some success, deals with "the clash between despised coloreds and arrogant whites: the action centers on an inferior person who, after many hardships, is found to have full value" (Grønbech, *Hans Christian Andersen,* 72). In other words: another wish-fulfilling autobiography.

24. Bredsdorff, *Hans Christian Andersen,* 179.

25. Ibid., 179–80.

26. Ib Ostenfeld writes: "The constant anxiety in Andersen's mind is the reason for his many travels. It was an escape so as not to have to face life" ("H. C. Andersens anfægtelser og deres tilbageslag i eventyrene," *Anderseniana,* 1974–77, pp. 305–28, 324).

27. "My poor stork never returned again! Has he, perhaps, died from sorrow for the loss of his wife and young ones? or is he,

perhaps, still on his travels in order that he may forget them? God forgive me! but I really believe one may forget every loss on a journey" (*Only a Fiddler*, 45). In his stories, too, such as in *Under the Willow Tree* or *A Story from the Sand Dunes*, men travel to forget.

CHAPTER 21

1. Spink, *Hans Christian Andersen and His World*, 44. Erik Dal endorses to this effect a doctoral dissertation by Hans Brix, who asserts that "the little mermaid's unrequited love for the prince represents the author's love for Louise Collin" (Introduction to *The Little Mermaid by Hans Christian Andersen*, trans. David Hohnen [Copenhagen: Høst & Søn, 1959], 10). We have already seen that a good case can be made for interpreting her predicament as representing Andersen's relationship to Edvard Collin. And for a totally different approach, according to which the story of the Little Mermaid is an "extraordinarily intense dream-exposition of the metamorphosis of girl . . . from child to woman . . . an eloquent expression of some general features of human adolescence," see Dorothy Dinnerstein, "*The Little Mermaid* and the Situation of the Girl," *Contemporary Psychoanalysis* 3 (1967): 104–12.

2. We are reminded of the story of *The Princess and the Frog*, but there it is properly the physical love of the princess that redeems the cold, wet, aquatic frog and turns him into a beautiful prince.

3. Christine E. Fell comments: "When she had a language she was unaware; when aware, she could not talk." Her loss of a tongue condemns her to a state of utter loneliness, since she is unable to tell the prince what she needs or what she has given up for him ("Symbolic and Satiric Aspects of Hans Christian Andersen's Fairy Tales," *Leeds Studies in English* 1 [1967]: 83–91).

4. One who, in his childhood, gained "indelible impressions" from Andersen's fairy tales was Thomas Mann ("Lebensabriss," in *Über mich selbst*, 110). And Maren Dunsby points to the special significance of *The Little Mermaid* for Mann's novel *Doktor Faustus* (". . . ob sie nun mit dem Fisch-schwanz kam, oder mit Beinen," *Anderseniana*, 1978–81, pp. 61–75). The hero of that novel, Adrian Leverkuehn, is, like Andersen, essentially asexual. He has only two brief sexual encounters in his life: once with a prostitute, once with a man. His chronicler reports:

> He talked to me of the little mermaid in Andersen's fairytale, which he dearly loved and admired, especially the truly superb description of the revolting realm of the sea witch . . . whither the child, in her longing, had dared to go, in order to obtain human legs in place of her fishtail and so that, through the love of the black-eyed prince . . . she may perhaps . . . obtain an immortal soul. He played with the

comparison between the knife-like pains, which the silent beauty had to suffer at every step with her walking-tools, and those he himself continuously had to put up with. He called her his sister in sorrow and engaged in a kind of intimate and humorously realistic critique of her actions, her stubbornness, her sentimental infatuation with the two-legged human world. "It started with her cult of the marble statue at the bottom of the sea," he said, "with the boy, evidently by Thorwaldsen, in whom she delights to an impermissible degree. Her grandmother should have taken the thing away . . . and then the hysterical overestimation of the world above and the 'immortal soul.' . . . A proper nymph would have seduced that knucklehead of a prince, who does not appreciate her and who right in front of her marries another—would have seduced him on the marble steps of his castle, would then have pulled him into the water and affectionately drowned him, instead of letting her fate depend on his stupidity. Probably he would have loved her with her native fishtail much more passionately than with those painful human legs."

> (Thomas Mann, *Doktor Faustus,* in
> *Gesammelte Werke,* ed. Mendelssohn
> [Frankfurt: S. Fischer Verlag, 1980],
> 461–62)

We already know that one meaning of immortality is progeny. When the Little Mermaid obtains two legs that she can spread, that are split (have a cleft in between), she has become a sexual woman; by contrast, the single tail is phallic. Seen in this light, the passage just quoted obtains a deeper meaning. Later on Adrian soliloquizes: "He [the devil] led her to my bed to be my concubine, so that I started to make love to her and loved her more and more, whether she came with a fishtail or with legs. More often she may have come with the tail, because the knife-like pain she suffered in her legs exceeded her pleasure, and I was quite taken by the sweet transition of her delicate body into the scaly tail. But my delight was greater, after all, in her pure, human form, and so I, for my part, had greater joy when she came to me with legs" (669). Perhaps Andersen, in his most daring moments, had similar bisexual fantasies.

CHAPTER 22

1. My introduction of Jungian terminology at this point is neither doctrinal nor partisan, but a matter of convenience: the terms just seem useful and, I believe, self-explanatory in this context. For a more comprehensive Jungian interpretation of Andersen's tales, see Nyborg, *Den Indre Linie I H. C. Andersens Eventyr,* which however, to my knowledge, has never been translated from the Danish.

2. Cf. Lederer, *The Fear of Women*, ch. 30.

3. C. G. Jung, *Collected Works* (New York: Bollingen Foundation, 1956), vol. 5, 292–93.

4. A beautiful example of this process comes from no less an exponent of the logos than Bertrand Russell, who says of himself: "I have found . . . that if I have to write upon some rather difficult topic the best plan is to think about it with very great intensity . . . for a few hours or days, and at the end of that time give orders, so to speak, that the work is to proceed underground. After some months, I return consciously to the topic and find that the work has been done" (*The Conquest of Happiness* [London: Unwin Books, 1971 (1930)], 49–50).

5. To the Charybdis, the sucking whirlpool of loneliness and depression, is opposed that other deadly danger, the many-headed monstrous Scylla of intense and frightening involvement that could well have torn a man like Andersen to pieces. Herman Melville, having chosen to brave the latter and trying desperately to write his stories amid the din of New York and the confusion of his own household, longed for "the calm, the coolness, the silent grass-growing mood in which a man *ought* to compose" and dreamt of the lost paradise of bachelorhood where "easy-hearted men had no wives and children to give them anxious thoughts" (Raymond Weaver, *The Shorter Novels of Herman Melville* [Greenwich, Conn.: Fawcett, 1928], 18–19). Andersen, by virtue of some instinctive knowledge of what his system could or could not stand, avoided both matrimony and—New York. He had many invitations to the New World, often dreamt of going there, but always postponed the journey. He said that he feared the rigors of the crossing. America herself, young and brash and noisy, no doubt frightened him even more.

6. Helen's son by Faust, Euphorion, is poetry impersonated! J. W. Goethe, *Faust*, pt. 2.

7. See Robert Graves, *The Greek Myths* (Baltimore: Penguin Books, 1955), ch. 24.

8. Jung, *Collected Works*, vol. 9, 2, p. 10. Actually, for Andersen the shadow did not *always* appear as a girl. In one story—*The Shadow*, published in 1847—some aspects of Andersen's "shadow" appear in the form of his shadow! It is the story of a learned but poor writer, obviously Andersen himself, whose shadow separates from him and commences an existence of its own. By virtue of its ability to climb walls and look in at windows, the shadow learns the secrets of important people and, through blackmail, becomes rich. Dressed as a man and therefore accepted as a man, he now hires his former master, the writer, to act as *his* shadow. They travel together to a watering place where the shadow meets a

princess. The writer, no longer able to bear the humiliating treatment accorded him by his erstwhile shadow, finally rebels. The shadow has him arrested; as the wedding between shadow and princess is celebrated, the rebellious shadow's-shadow, the writer, is executed.

In this story, the shadow does, indeed, exhibit qualities Andersen had repressed in himself and that he now presents as criminal: the ruthless determination to win both wealth and the princess, to succeed both materially and sexually. In addition, Andersen conveys what he must have painfully felt, particularly after the failure of the *affair* Jenny Lind—that is, the sensation that his own unattached and unrelated existence had the insubstantial quality of a shadow.

9. Jung, *Collected Works*, vol. 5, 112.

10. Examples of Andersen trying to get even with his critics include the stories *Something* (1858), *Ole the Tavern Keeper* (1859), and *What One Can Invent* (1869).

11. Andersen, *Poems*, 32.

Index

Compositor: Huron Valley Graphics
Text: 10 / 12 Palatino
Display: Palatino
Printer: Maple-Vail Book Mfg. Group
Binder: Maple-Vail Book Mfg. Group